More Praise for *From Smart to Wise*

"With examples from today's best leaders, Kaipa and Radjou have created a practical guide for accelerating your own wise leadership development, a true competitive advantage in today's rapidly changing world. We can all benefit from the self-reflection that *From Smart to Wise* encourages. By defining our unique 'noble purpose,' we can bring about meaningful change and progress in our companies, communities, and society."

—**Indra K. Nooyi**, chairman and CEO, PepsiCo, Inc.

"Developing wisdom can turn a long and arduous trip into a compelling, sustainable, and inspiring leadership journey. Read this fascinating book and let it teach you the tools you'll need to go from smart to wise!"

—**Marshall Goldsmith**, *New York Times* best-selling author, *MOJO* and *What Got You Here Won't Get You There*

"*From Smart to Wise* is a practical and powerful book that reminds us of the ultimate destination of our leadership journeys: wisdom earned through experience and shared in service of others. Even better, Prasad Kaipa and Navi Radjou offer a step-by-step road map for getting there, complete with real-world examples sure to inspire and challenge us along the way."

—**John R. Ryan**, president and CEO, Center for Creative Leadership

"This extraordinary book takes the intangible concept of wisdom and brings it to life, giving it context and ways for us to practice wise leadership in our daily lives. Kaipa and Radjou show us how to connect with other leaders in today's interdependent world to cocreate a field of wise leadership. You must read *From Smart to Wise*. It is a journey worth taking."

—**Cynthia Cherrey**, president, the International Leadership Association; vice president, Princeton University

"Getting from smart to wise is the most important leadership challenge of the twenty-first century. Prasad Kaipa and Navi Radjou offer a guidebook to this transformation, one that any leader will find of great use."

—**Daniel Goleman**, author, *Emotional Intelligence*

"*From Smart to Wise* is a good example of what it talks about. It is wise, clear, and grounded in real experience. It reminds us that our humanity is the key to success in business, and also that a purpose greater than profit is needed to create a world that is fulfilling as well as productive."

—**Peter Block**, author, *Stewardship* and *Abundant Community*

"*From Smart to Wise* is a very timely and unique book. Kaipa and Radjou offer us a pathway to evolve from behaving smartly to acting and leading wisely, extending benefits of wise leadership not only to ourselves and our companies but also to our societies."

—**Jeff Smith**, CEO and cofounder, LUNAR Design

"*From Smart to Wise* is the book managers from all walks of life and in all institutions ought to read. Kaipa and Radjou credibly and convincingly make the point that smartness is no longer sufficient to be sustainably successful today and provide those interested in becoming wise leaders with a useful road map."

—**Dr. Klaus M. Leisinger**, chairman, Novartis Foundation for Sustainable Development

"Ordinary organizations become extraordinary organizations when some wise leaders embrace the collective good and invite others to do the same. *From Smart to Wise* is a magnificent book about how to become a person of wisdom and influence."

—**Robert E. Quinn**, professor, Ross School of Business, University of Michigan; author, *Deep Change*

"Kaipa and Radjou have spent most of their lives bringing the wisdom traditions to bear on the art of business. *From Smart to Wise* offers depth, context, and timeless tools to lift the mechanical into the noble, marrying the practical and the compassionate—a rare, effective, uplifting companion."

—**Mark Nepo**, best-selling author, *Seven Thousand Ways to Listen* and *The Book of Awakening*

"*From Smart to Wise* is a game changer! Read it to find how to apply practical wisdom in your business. Use the framework in this book to create your own wise leadership road map—and you too can become a highly effective leader like Warren Buffett, Ratan Tata, and Alan Mulally."

—**Professor Theodore R. Malloch**, Yale University; director, The Academy of Business in Society; and author, *Doing Virtuous Business*

From SMART *to* WISE

From SMART *to* WISE

ACTING AND LEADING WITH WISDOM

Prasad Kaipa

Navi Radjou

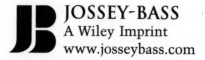

JOSSEY-BASS
A Wiley Imprint
www.josseybass.com

Published by Jossey-Bass

A Wiley Imprint

One Montgomery Street, Suite 1200, San Francisco, CA 94104-4594—www.josseybass.com

Jossey-Bass books and products are available through most bookstores. To contact Jossey-Bass directly call our Customer Care Department within the U.S. at 800-956-7739, outside the U.S. at 317-572-3986, or fax 317-572-4002.

Wiley publishes in a variety of print and electronic formats and by print-on-demand. Some material included with standard print versions of this book may not be included in e-books or in print-on-demand. If this book refers to media such as a CD or DVD that is not included in the version you purchased, you may download this material at http://booksupport.wiley.com. For more information about Wiley products, visit www.wiley.com.

Library of congress cataloging-in-publication data

Kaipa, Prasad, date.
  From smart to wise : acting and leading with wisdom / Prasad Kaipa, Navi Radjou. – First edition.
      pages cm
  Includes bibliographical references and index.
  ISBN 978-1-118-29620-2 (cloth); 978-1-118-33185-9 (ebk); 978-1-118-33407-2 (ebk); 978-1-118-33518-5 (ebk)
  1. Leadership. 2. Wisdom. I. Radjou, Navi. II. Title.
  HD57.7.K345 2013
  658.4'092–dc23

                          2012048513

Printed in the United States of America

FIRST EDITION

HB Printing   10 9 8 7 6 5 4 3 2 1

Maatru devo bhava (Respect Mother—as your personal God)

Pitru devo bhava (Respect Father—as your personal God)

Aachaarya devo bhava (Respect Teacher—as your personal God)

—Taittriya Upanishad

• • •

We dedicate this book to our parents and teachers

CONTENTS

PREFACE

If its first twelve years are any indication, the twenty-first century risks going down in history as the century of scandals. A series of increasingly high-profile financial scandals—Enron, subprime mortgages, the LIBOR rate rigging—coupled with bailouts have knocked corporations off their high pedestal. Business leaders now grace the covers of leading magazines for all the wrong reasons—among them, Bob Diamond, Barclays Bank's former CEO implicated in the LIBOR scandal, and Rajat Gupta, McKinsey & Company's former managing director convicted of insider trading.

Diamond and Gupta are smart leaders known for their sharp intellect, and their organizations benefited greatly from their smartness. What got these leaders into trouble is not their lack of intelligence but their lapses in judgment. In a 2009 *McKinsey Quarterly* survey of 2,207 executives, only 28 percent responded that the quality of strategic decisions in their companies was generally good, 12 percent thought good decisions were altogether infrequent, and the rest (60 percent) thought that there were as many bad decisions as good. Smartness is like a wild horse: riding it can be exhilarating for a while until you are thrown from it. To tame and harness smartness for the long run, you need wisdom— the stuff that gives you ethical clarity and a sense of purpose. When wisdom provides the moral compass, smartness can become even more potent. Clearly, the need of the hour is for smart leaders who can act and lead with wisdom. Many business leaders who attended World Business Economic sessions in 2010 and 2011 have called for business reformation and renewal by rethinking values. Many corporate leaders intuitively appreciate the value of wisdom. Yet with a few notable exceptions, like Warren Buffett, Bill Gates, Bill George, John Mackey, Narayana Murthy, Ratan Tata, and Oprah Winfrey, they don't know how to operationalize it in a business context. Some leaders view wisdom as a noble concept but difficult to put in practice in the business world. Others hear about wisdom in a religious context when they go to church on Sunday but are at a loss on how to apply this spiritual wisdom at work on Monday morning.

Wisdom is both timeless and timely. Yet few attempts have been made to date in the West to articulate wisdom in the language of business, let alone provide corporate leaders with. practical tools to systematically apply wisdom in their day-to-day work. This book frames wisdom in a modern context that makes it accessible and practical for smart, busy leaders like you, so that you can learn to act and lead as a wise leader. By reading this book, you will gain new perspectives, learn new capabilities, and develop new practices that will help you become a wise leader no matter what role you play in your organization.

We have been studying the concept of wise leadership—the practice of wisdom in a leadership context—since 1989. Both of us share the motivation to help leaders discover the genius that lies dormant within the wider ecosystem of employees, customers, and partners and to tap into that collective intelligence to bring value to their organizations as well as the larger society.

In our multiple lines of work as management consultants, advisors, business researchers, and teachers, we have worked with over seventy companies around the world and with hundreds of top executives in different parts of the world. This book is the result of our cumulative experiences, insights, study, and observations.

The germ of this book came from our own desire to discover our full potential. We both consider ourselves smart, but we have not always been wise when it really mattered. We came to realize that our own smartness created invisible boundaries to what we could accomplish and where we could go with our lives and our profession. As part of this process, we realized that by breaking down boundaries, we could change our lives. In that sense, this book reflects our own experiences and personal journeys. By sharing our learning with you, we hope to ignite your leadership genius.

Prasad: I grew up in two worlds. One was the world of science, competition, and academic smartness and the other the world of wisdom and contemplation. Like many other Indian children from traditional families in the 1970s, I went to a Sanskrit teacher to study Hindu scriptures in the mornings while attending regular school during the rest of the day. I got my doctorate in physics at the Indian Institute of Technology in Chennai, India. For a long time, the path of smartness and the path of wisdom did not intersect in my actions or my consciousness. While working as a physicist at the University of Utah, I moved gradually into the world of technology and tool making and ended up at Apple. As a research fellow at Apple University, I had the opportunity to interview several Nobel laureates, high achievers, psychologists, and spiritual leaders while researching how people learn, lead, think, communicate, create, and collaborate. I became interested in the relationship between ordinary and extraordinary changes in thinking, between individual learning and team learning, and began thinking about how to synthesize ancient wisdom (e.g., from classical Hindu texts like the *Upanishads*) with contemporary ways of thinking. Through such personal explorations, interviews with extraordinary leaders, and experimentation with corporate clients as an educator and a facilitator, I gained insight into the concept of practical wisdom and its application in the field of leadership and innovation.

Since 1990, my research and consulting focus has been on cross-cultural leadership and innovation, and it has led me to understand more about smart and wise leadership. I have had the opportunity to work closely, as a coach and an advisor, with over one hundred CEOs, executive team members, and board members from the United States, Europe, and Asia over the past twenty-three years. Those experiences helped to hone my understanding of the importance of values and a noble purpose and shaped my thinking further around wise leadership. This book draws on these lessons.

Navi: I grew up in India in a bicultural (French and Indian) environment and was the first child in my family to go to college. I set high standards for myself, which led me to the United States to study for an M.B.A. Then it dawned on me that there is more to life than becoming a smart management consultant who would make organizations run smarter and help them compete and win in the marketplace at all costs. I decided to dedicate my career to helping smart corporate executives evolve into wise leaders who are open to learning from others and willing to serve a higher purpose. Over thirteen years, in various capacities—first as an industry analyst, then as an academic researcher, and now as an independent strategy advisor—I have helped hundreds of business leaders worldwide cultivate an open, collaborative, and global mind-set that they can use to act and lead wisely in today's interconnected world. My purpose is to leverage my multicultural background, interdisciplinary educational training, and extensive consulting experience to create practical new business frameworks that integrate Western and Eastern perspectives on innovation and leadership. This book and my first one—*Jugaad Innovation: Think Frugal, Be Flexible, Generate Breakthrough Growth*—are aimed at helping people leverage the ingenuity and wisdom that we all possess so we can transcend our differences and forge a wise global community.

• • •

In this book, we distill practical wisdom into six capabilities that twenty-first-century business leaders can use to cultivate wise leadership. Here you will learn how to evolve from a smart leader to a wise leader by discovering your noble purpose, acting authentically and appropriately, learning when to lead and when to let others lead, deciding with discernment, knowing when to hold on and when to let go, and cultivating enlightened self-interest. Through the practice of these six capabilities, you will gain practical wisdom, using values and ethics to guide your smartness towards serving a noble purpose. Warren Buffett, CEO of Berkshire Hathaway; Ratan Tata, former chairman of Tata Group; Oprah Winfrey, CEO of OWN and Harpo Productions; and Narayana Murthy, cofounder of Infosys, are some of today's leaders who have found ways to apply practical wisdom in their businesses and made their companies highly successful. You can too—and in the dynamic, complex, globalized business context of today, cultivating this kind of practical wisdom is both a smart move and a wise one.

November 2012

Prasad Kaipa
Campbell, California

Navi Radjou
Palo Alto, California

CHAPTER ONE

WISE LEADERS WANTED

We'll start with a truism: in business, you need to be smart. In fact, smartness—whether it's called cleverness, practical intelligence, or savvy—is the operating currency of twenty-first-century organizational culture. The leaders the world admires are tremendously smart, whether they're in business—like Bill Gates of Microsoft, Indra Nooyi of PepsiCo, Tim Cook of Apple, and Ursula Burns of Xerox—or in politics—like U.S. presidents Obama and Clinton and former U.S. secretary of state Condoleezza Rice.

What all very smart leaders have in common is an ability to impress us with their intellectual prowess and ability to succeed at very high levels. They see patterns in seemingly random information. They take decisive action while others are still trying to understand or appreciate the situation. They seize opportunities that many regard as too risky and show an ability to make strategic choices that confer them a competitive edge. Some are big picture thinkers; some excel at executing strategies and others at innovating breakthrough products.

All this considered, it seems desirable to be a smart leader, and it is. When we exercise our smarts, we not only experience success; we also feel strong and capable, operating at the top of our game. We want more of this good thing. If we are in the

1

position of leading an organization, we want to leverage our smartness to succeed and help others succeed.

But these are complex and uncertain times, and many leaders are discovering that smartness alone is insufficient to achieve both success and a sense of accomplishment and fulfillment. Smartness and more smartness is increasingly failing to bring meaningful growth and prosperity to organizations and their leaders. In our experience, wise leadership succeeds where smart leadership cannot.

Thus, this book is not about moving you from smart leadership to *smarter* leadership, but about setting a trajectory toward *wise* leadership—an expanded capacity to act and lead wisely (without losing your smartness). It's about what potentiates your wise leadership and what it is that wise leaders do differently. At its core it is an exploration of practical wisdom—how reflective actions, thoughtful application of smartness, and the deployment of enlightened self-interest allow you to become successful in a sustainable way while making a difference to others along the way. And it contains a road map and personalized tools for you to make the journey.

THE PITFALLS OF SMART LEADERSHIP

Smart leaders are an eclectic bunch that includes brilliant strategists and functional experts as well as superefficient tacticians and gifted managers of people. They may be start-up entrepreneurs or high up in the ranks of large, global corporations. They can be quite diverse when it comes to their perspectives, actions, and motivations.

For the purposes of this book, we'll divide smart leaders into two broad categories according to their primary area of strength, which we refer to as functional smart and business smart. To generalize, functional smart leaders excel in one field or function, such as R&D or operations, and tend to dig deep to establish their expertise in the domain that they have chosen. Effective execution is their forte. They tend to be cautious in risk taking, think carefully before they act, and when they act, they tend to stick to what they know best. Whereas functional smart leaders go deep, business smart leaders go broad. They tend to be big picture thinkers who are risk takers at heart. They are prone to taking action quickly and generally have a competitive temperament. (You might not identify yourself strongly with either category at first, but as you read further, keep looking for patterns of behaviors that match yours.)

We'll discuss these differences more in depth later in this chapter, and we'll also examine a quality nearly every smart leader we've met or studied has in common: a powerful and ever-increasing tendency to play to their own strengths. As they succeed and move up, smart leaders tend to become increasingly attached to their particular type of smartness and show themselves less able to exhibit or appreciate the other type of smartness. This makes sense: most people build their skills and expertise on their existing strengths and temperaments; success breeds success. But this consolidation can exact costs—personal, professional, and organizational—that the otherwise very smart leader doesn't see coming.

We'll talk about this peculiar kind of blindness shortly, but first we turn to an example of an exception to the rule: a leader whose actions over time have shown an evolution from a highly consolidated style of smartness into wisdom.

Bill Gates is an exemplar of the kind of smart leader we call "business smart." Gates was only twenty years old when he cofounded Microsoft with Paul Allen. Despite his unassuming appearance and apparent shyness, Gates, a Harvard dropout, was a determined and ambitious businessman who used every opportunity to outsmart the competition with great strategic moves that helped Microsoft reach a market capitalization of over $616 billion in December 1999.[1]

That supremacy took a blow in May 1998 when the U.S. Department of Justice filed suit against Microsoft, accusing the company of abusing its alleged monopoly power on Intel-based personal computers in its handling of operating system and Web browser sales. A number of European countries followed with similar lawsuits. All of a sudden, a company and a business leader who were riding high faced a formidable threat.

Gates appeared by video at Microsoft's antitrust trial, a decision that was widely interpreted as a snub to the Department of Justice. Under questioning, he appeared combative and defensive. He told the media that the lead government attorney was "out to destroy Microsoft." When the deposition was read in court, Gates's condescending attitude toward his accusers and the legal system in general stood out. According to CNN, that testimony helped turn public opinion against Microsoft and Gates. Microsoft settled the case in 2001, but in the aftermath of the lawsuit, Microsoft lost its momentum in the marketplace. Its market capitalization dropped from $616 billion in 1999 to about $260 billion in 2012.

While Microsoft was contending with scaling back its operations, Gates made a major course correction in his life journey. In early 2000, while awaiting the court decision, he stepped down as Microsoft's chief executive to focus on his passion for software, becoming the company's chief software architect and chairman of the board. Being a great strategist, Gates probably realized that it would be better to have a different CEO representing Microsoft to the outside world. In the same year, he and his wife established the Bill & Melinda Gates Foundation; by 2008, Gates had completed his transition to foundation and philanthropic activities (he remains the nonexecutive chairman of Microsoft).

As cochair of the Gates Foundation, Gates has awarded billions of dollars in grants to various charitable organizations and scientific research programs. While some people initially accused Gates of using his charitable activities to sugarcoat his image, his foundation is respected and appreciated for its compassionate and highly effective approaches to combating global problems ranging from infectious diseases to lack of education. Gates, the successful but polarizing figure for his ultracompetitive strategy, has become a more righteous and moral figure in the eyes of many people.

From what we can understand through observation and a study of his career, Gates's actions in his business and personal life suggest that he evolved from a smart leader to a wise one. He moved beyond his corporate role at Microsoft and explored how he could use his wealth, smarts, and leadership skills to contribute to the common good. We see this as a reflection of how Gates shifted his perspective and broadened his approach beyond building a business empire to solving big problems facing the global community.

We have never discussed this book with Gates, and our view of him as a leader who broadened his approach from smartness to wisdom is based on inference. But our analysis of his actions suggests that Gates managed to transcend his particular style of smartness (in which he had remained fixed for a long time) by shifting his perspective, an ability that this book is designed to foster.

THE FUNCTIONAL SMART LEADER AND THE BUSINESS SMART LEADER

We all tend to have a perspective on life that is relatively narrow, shaped by our predispositions, assumptions, and experiences. Psychologists call this phenomenon our perceptual filter—think of it as a pair of tinted glasses—and describe the ways it conditions how we organize and interpret the meaning of everything we experience in our environment.[2] The longer you wear your perceptual filter without challenging it or finding a vantage point outside it, the more you tend to get attached to your limited perspective. Worse, you end up seeing only what you want to see and rarely observe anything that is outside your zone of interest. You develop a well-worn autopilot mode and, unknowingly, a tunnel vision: you see only a limited portion of the whole spectrum of smart leadership possibilities and positive human endeavor.

Generally business smart leaders, many of them known for their intensity and risk taking, tend to perceive the world through a set of filters that for ease of identification we'll call "red." Business smart leaders thus tend to operate in what we designate the red zone at one end of a metaphorical spectrum of leadership style and skill, where the emphasis is on characteristics like drive, vision, and risk taking. At the other end of our metaphorical spectrum are functional smart leaders. Intensely focused on and competent in their particular area of technical or business expertise, they tend to wear what we call a blue set of filters, which make them see the world in terms of their own narrow focus. Hence, they are at ease while operating within a blue zone, where the emphasis is on qualities like groundedness, execution excellence, and deep expertise. What is highly visible and exciting to leaders operating in the red zone is often practically invisible or unappealing to those operating in the blue zone, and vice versa. Both kinds of smart leaders see what they are conditioned to see, in both cases narrowing their experience of a wider spectrum of reality.

It's not just senior leaders—or people in the business field alone—who wear these filters. We all wear them—whether we are a teacher, an architect, a husband, a mother, and whether we work in a nonprofit, government, or business. These filters do color our perspective and shape our motivation, decisions, and actions.

To actually see the world as it is, not as we are used to seeing it, we first need to become aware of and then set aside our perceptual filters. It means stepping out of the zone that we know so well and in which we feel capable and comfortable. When we appreciate and embrace the objective world as it is—in its full range of colors, so to speak—and bridge the gap between our subjective reality and the rest of the world, we become capable of wisdom.

Wearing these red or blue glasses all the time hurts us in another way: it prevents us from incorporating certain qualities like prudence, judgment, humility, ethics, and the common good, vitally important when we widen our focus to include the whole spectrum of leadership potential. Many smart leaders have an intellectual understanding of—and an intuitive appreciation for—such qualities, but since they can't discern them in relation to their leadership privileges and duties, they don't incorporate them into their role. A leader who removes her filters and experiences the full spectrum becomes highly aware of the gaps between her intentions and actual behaviors—so much so that that values and ethics, which may have been less tangible before, become the cornerstone of her leadership approach.

Gates, for instance, was known for his intensely competitive personality while running Microsoft: you could say that his filters were truly red. Yet after going through the antitrust trial, Gates realized that he was seeing the world differently from the American public, Department of Justice, or judges, and that understanding led to reflection and introspection, which helped him find a larger purpose: using his smartness for the betterment of humanity. By creating the Bill & Melinda Gates Foundation and taking an active role in it, Gates gradually became aware of his red filters and was able to consciously remove them to gain a larger perspective on how exactly he could best contribute to the world. In the process, he evolved from a smart leader to a wise leader; he didn't lose or change his essential business smarts, but he became able to deploy his gifts mindfully across a wide range of situations.

Gates's Microsoft career represents the typical trajectory of business smart leaders who perceive the world through red filters and tend to operate in the red zone. Tim Cook, who became CEO of Apple in 2011, was for most of his career the epitome of the other type of smartness: the functional smart leader who generally operates in the blue zone. A closer look at Cook's contribution to Apple will show why it's vital for functional smart leaders to drop their blue filters and step out of the blue zone to grow personally and professionally.

In the 1980s, Apple was not known for its operational efficiency, and the situation was not very different in early 1998, when
Jobs interviewed Cook for a position to head up Apple's supply
chain operations. As a functional smart leader, Cook was driven
to bring higher efficiency and bottom-line productivity to Apple.
He knew how to squeeze every last bit of fat out of operations.
While Jobs, renowned for his business smartness, was in the media
spotlight and creating great demand for Apple products, Cook
operated behind the scenes to manufacture and distribute those
products efficiently. Since he became CEO, however, it appears
that Cook has begun to remove his blue filters and broaden his
perspective. He seems to have realized that he would never be
able to match Jobs's larger-than-life personality, yet he had to
serve the interests of Apple effectively at this critical juncture.
That apparent change in perspective enabled Cook to step up and
take on roles that Jobs had traditionally assumed. In this way,
Cook is stepping out of his autopilot zone—the blue zone—and
is learning to act as a wise leader.

As he starts to lead with practical wisdom, Cook is now spending more time discussing strategy with investors, reaching out to
developers, and focusing on top-line growth. In his first year as
CEO, Apple's stock increased in value by 76 percent, and Apple
became the most valuable company in the world. He provided
great dividends to shareholders, supported philanthropic activities by matching employee contributions, and defended Apple's
innovation lead by winning a patent infringement case against
rival Samsung.[3]

Cook does not seem to be trying to emulate the agenda or
style laid down by Jobs, whom he greatly admired. In other words,
he *didn't trade his blue filters for Jobs's red filters*. In moving beyond
the functional smart style more often than not, Cook wisely didn't
switch to the style that Steve Jobs, a strong-willed and mercurial
business smart leader, had operated from. In fact, many of Cook's
recent decisions are contrary to what Jobs would have done, such
as paying dividends and improving working conditions at Apple

factories in China. We regard Cook's actions as more balanced and wiser than many of those Jobs took. He has broadened his perspective with practical wisdom and is evolving into a wise leader.

Gates and Cook alike consciously and gradually detached themselves from their particular type of smartness and discovered a larger sense of purpose. By changing their perspective, they gained wisdom, which provides an ethical compass. You don't have to be Gates or Cook to become aware of your filters and remove them and use wisdom as a compass to guide your leadership behavior. You can begin your journey from smart to wise leadership right now.

EVOLVING FROM SMART TO WISE

Smartness is another word for *intelligence*, which means many things in both popular understanding and scholarly circles.[4] Our use of it here is closest to a definition from Robert Sternberg, a renowned contemporary scholar in the area of human intelligence who described "successful intelligence" as "one's ability to attain one's goals in life, given one's sociocultural context, by adapting to, shaping, and selecting environments, through a balance of analytical, creative, and practical skills."[5] This is aligned with our own definition of *smart leadership* as a capacity that goes beyond simply being a smart or intelligent person to being a person who applies his or her smartness through action for moving forward for primarily personal growth and success.

It's this quality—intelligence applied through action in the service of personal growth and success—that we divide into two main styles: business smartness and functional smartness, or in our shorthand, the red zone and the blue zone. Each represents significantly different intelligences, energies, and capabilities. Each of us is born without filters, but with innate tendencies and external conditioning, we tend to put on the red or blue filters that gradually color our perspective, and we soon forget that we have those filters on. This skewed perspective influences where we focus our own developmental efforts, and typically we end up cultivating exclusively either a blue or a red perspective.

As we grow older, we tend to lean on our particular area of strength, honing our capabilities in that area. As we do so, we become attached to that kind of intelligence, and without much conscious thought, we can get stuck there. Our strength becomes a winning formula, and we grow dependent on it, which eventually makes us weak and vulnerable in other areas. The type of smartness—functional or business—that we gravitate toward shapes our worldview and defines our personality. We can develop such an attachment to our kind of smartness that we see only negative aspects of the other kind of smartness without recognizing—or being willing to accept—the limitations of our own kind of smartness. Yet our two definitions of smartness—functional and business—are actually complementary.

Functional smartness is grounded in issues that are concrete, tangible, and tactical, and when this becomes well developed, it leads to operational and execution smartness. Functional smartness also allows us to focus on developing strength in the domain that we are inherently good at—say, marketing or finance—without getting distracted by anything outside that domain. Functional smart leaders, at least those we have studied, are generally comfortable with details. They take on work with careful focus, and whatever they accept as work, they execute it effectively and deliver predictable, high-quality, and reliable results. Many of them are effective managers and maintain a healthy bottom line by pursuing operational efficiencies. Using a sports metaphor, functional smart leaders tend to play defense, protecting their turf against the competition. Not surprisingly, they are often risk averse, preferring to place safe bets when considering investing in new projects because their motivation stems from a basic need to be safe and secure. Being a functional smart leader offers many advantages and benefits because such a leader tends to be prudent and efficient. Over time, these leaders grow in their ability to apply their practical intelligence to bring success to themselves and their organization.

Business smart leaders, in contrast, are often driven by the desire to do bigger and better things and are not easily intimidated by risks. They tend to have a visionary perspective and are strategic in their approach as they focus on entrepreneurial growth opportunities more than bottom-line profitability.

Business smart leaders relish high-stakes games and sometimes have a winner-take-all mentality. They can be dynamic, proactive, and even aggressive in search of growth, as Bill Gates was during his tenure as Microsoft's CEO. As a general rule, business smart leaders focus on creating new markets while at the same time seeking to dominate existing markets by grabbing market share from competitors.

Former GE CEO Jack Welch is a business smart leader who was famously nicknamed "Neutron Jack" during the 1980s for his extremely competitive mind-set.[6] When this tendency is unchecked, leaders on the edge risk becoming obsessive, quick tempered, and dissatisfied with the status quo. Some of these competitive leaders can also become moody, intense, and restless in pursuit of goals and success. To a small group of smart leaders, values and ethics usually play a secondary role to winning. If they can keep their business smart temperament in check, however, these leaders can balance self-interest with the greater good and use their intensity and strong focus on growth to deliver sustainable value not only to their organization but also to society.

Regardless of the kind of smartness we tend to act and lead out of, when we take the time to reflect, we realize the limitations of business smartness and functional smartness. Wise leaders transcend both kinds of smartness; they see the world as a kaleidoscope with all its many varied colors and then act out of that fuller perception. Wise leadership is not about giving up our smartness, but transcending it and gaining a broader perspective on life.

That perspective enables us to rein in our smartness and harness it to serve a larger purpose in an ethical and appropriate manner.

Wisdom is grounded in ethics, shared values, and serving a larger purpose. Thus, we define *wise leadership* as leveraging smartness for the greater good by balancing action with reflection and introspection, gateways to humility and ethical clarity. In contrast, smart leadership draws on all of our skills and strengths in the service of personal gain. Wisdom itself grounds us, helping us to shift from using our smartness for our own benefit—and often with a zero-sum mind-set—to using it for creating new value for a higher purpose.

The journey from smart to wise is about becoming able to see the strictly rational and logical way of focusing on what is tangible and personally beneficial as well as the authentic way of including intangibles, such as shared values and ethics, and the greater good. Attention to those intangibles allows us to avoid attachment to either kind of smartness. Ignoring them leaves us stuck with one kind of smartness or the other, unable to discover and claim wise leadership, which transcends and yet encompasses both kinds of smartness.[7] Hence, the journey to wise leadership consists in gaining an appreciation for values and ethics, simultaneously transcending one's smartness while also including it as a tool to serve a larger purpose.

The foundation for wise leadership is context sensitivity: discerning what kind of smartness is appropriate for a particular situation. Such context sensitivity is a key asset for leaders in a dynamically changing global business environment because it balances out conditioned responses and broadens a leader's field of awareness, helping him or her gain a larger perspective. As leaders advance in their careers, they tend not to increase their context sensitivity and broaden their perspective, but to surround themselves with others who share their worldview. This solidifies their position and makes it even more difficult to step out of their zone. As a result, both business smart and functional smart leaders struggle to adapt their success formulas—or let go of old ones and adopt new ones—even when the external context changes. For example, functional smart leaders at the now defunct Borders had perfected a bricks-and-mortar book distribution model that was successful during the pre-Internet era, but they failed to adapt its business model for a digital economy dominated by online commerce platforms like Amazon.com.

WHAT IS WISDOM?

Wisdom is traditionally associated with spirituality and religion and with abstract concepts such as truth, knowledge, beauty, and the right path. The path of pure wisdom might lead one to become a philosopher, a guru, or a monk—someone who practices or contemplates wisdom in a state detached from the world. In this view, wisdom is the gift of sages and spiritual leaders.[8] This picture is woefully incomplete. In fact, *wisdom is our birthright.* We all are born with the seeds of wisdom, but we sometimes don't cultivate or nurture those seeds to let them flourish, focusing instead on tending to our smartness—the acquisition and use of new knowledge for primarily personal benefit. In the organizational context, wise leaders are people (not just business leaders or politicians) who step up to take action in the service of others. This kind of wisdom is more pragmatic in nature, regardless of its roots, which is why we call it practical wisdom and leadership that embodies these principles, wise leadership.

Calling practical wisdom the master virtue, Aristotle described it as "figuring out the right way to do the right thing in a particular circumstance, with a particular person at a particular time."[9] The Bhagavad Gita, valued as a book of practical wisdom for Hindus, carries the key message that wise leaders understand how to balance the extremes and act from a state of equanimity.[10] In this book we focus on developing wise leadership in the business context. This kind of practical wisdom can have spiritual or non-spiritual roots or both, depending on the individual leader. What matters is that wise leadership is grounded in action and gives ethical clarity and higher purpose to smart leadership.

THE SIX LEADERSHIP CAPABILITIES

Wise leadership consists of applying and integrating smartness wisely for mutual, instead of just personal, benefit. Introspection, reflection, and care for the common good are essential practices that provide balance to smart leaders and help them bring authenticity and ethical clarity to their actions and lasting success to their endeavors. In other words, wisdom amplifies and elevates leaders' smartness, enabling them to operate at a higher plane.

In essence, wise leadership involves knowing the limits of smartness. It contextualizes your smartness and helps you act with role clarity, humility, and intuition to be effective in your organization. It does not necessitate turning away from spiritual wisdom, but rather using it actively and tempering it with smartness and enlightened self-interest so that it is both practical and pragmatic.

Our research and experience have shown us that most smart leaders rely on the same leadership capabilities throughout their careers.[11] Based on our research and wisdom texts from cultures around the world, we have identified six areas of capability that all leaders exhibit:

- *Perspective:* What influences and shapes a leader's worldview
- *Action orientation:* How a leader is driven to act—or not act
- *Role clarity:* How a leader chooses a role and how closely she identifies with it
- *Decision logic:* What framework a leader uses to decide
- *Fortitude:* How a leader determines when to hold and when to fold
- *Motivation:* What inspires and drives a leader's actions and decisions

Different leaders exercise these capabilities differently, depending on the kind of smartness they usually exhibit. For simplicity and in keeping with the image of smartness as being a set of filters that capture only a subset of the visible spectrum, we will speak of functional smart leadership as falling within the blue area at one end of the spectrum and business smart leadership as being within the red area at the other end of the spectrum. Wise leadership encompasses—and embodies—the full spectrum:

- *Perspective.* In terms of perspective, functional smart leaders who tend to operate in the blue zone are execution oriented, whereas business smart leaders who usually act and lead from the red zone are strategic, big picture thinkers.
- *Action orientation.* In the blue zone, leaders are risk averse and tend to act with great caution, as opposed to leaders in the red zone, who are proactive and opportunistic in their action orientation.
- *Role clarity.* Blue zone leaders operate within functional boundaries and tend to follow instructions, often letting others lead when risks are high. A red zone leader, by comparison, seeks to lead from the front as much as possible in order to control the outcome.
- *Decision logic.* Blue zone leaders make decisions aimed at short-term results and improving the bottom line, whereas a red zone leader is more likely to make vision-driven long-term decisions that affect revenue growth.
- *Fortitude.* Blue zone leaders can flip between being too stubborn and giving up too easily. A red zone leader perseveres as long as the outcome is aligned with his self-interest.
- *Motivation.* Leaders in the blue zone are motivated by basic safety and security needs and seek tangible benefits like job stability. A red zone leader more likely finds motivation in intangible success factors like title, recognition, and legacy.

Once smart leaders begin to evolve into wise leaders, they begin to exercise the same six capabilities very differently. To begin, their *perspective* shifts: rather than being execution oriented or thinking purely in strategic terms, they start focusing on a higher purpose as they gain a holistic perspective. As a result, they become fully engaged in what they do as a process but remain emotionally detached from the outcome so that they can maintain a balanced perspective and operate with equanimity. They demonstrate authenticity in their *actions* and ensure these actions are appropriate to different contexts. They gain greater *role clarity*—that is, they know when to take ownership of a situation and lead from the front and when to let others lead and give them credit for doing so. In addition, their *decision logic* becomes more refined: with greater discernment, they start making intuitive decisions that are ethically sound and yet eminently pragmatic. Moreover, they learn to demonstrate flexible *fortitude*—true courage under fire—discerning when to hold on to their decisions and when to fold. Finally, their *motivation* shifts as they act increasingly out of enlightened self-interest instead of being driven only by selfish interests.

In our research, we have found only a few leaders who are wise most of the time across all six capabilities. They are the exception. More often, we have encountered leaders who demonstrate some of the wise leadership capabilities but only infrequently. Growing as a wise leader takes practice, self-discipline, and a willingness to act consistently with your own purpose, values, and the context.

BECOMING A WISE LEADER

To become a wise leader, you don't need to cultivate new skills or competencies. Rather, you must learn to act and lead wisely using the six capabilities you already have: perspective, action orientation, role clarity, decision logic, fortitude, and motivation. The six following chapters focus on exactly what that means and how to do that.

Chapter 2 is about shifting your perspective and connecting to your noble purpose—or your North Star, as we call it. Wise leaders foster a holistic perspective that integrates diverse, distinct, and even polarizing worldviews. They use this perspective to evaluate the short- and long-term implications of their decisions, and to cultivate an integral mind-set—that is, the ability to see the whole picture rather than its individual components—that enables them to perceive the connectedness of events.

Chapter 3 is about being aware of your action orientation and acting authentically and appropriately for the greater good. Wise leaders intuitively know how to identify the right actions to take, examine the deeper implications, and take the appropriate next step based on the context and aligned with their North Star.

In chapter 4, we discuss gaining role clarity, which entails the ability to lead from any position. Wise leaders develop clarity about being a servant leader—serving their leadership role with humility and dedication—and appreciate the role of others in their success. Their roles do not define—or confine—their authentic self. They are willing and able to assume any role they deem appropriate with humility, enthusiasm, and equanimity and are therefore great team players.

The ability to decide with discernment and clarify your unique decision logic is the subject of chapter 5. Wise leaders make decisions that are both ethical (based on the values that they believe in) and pragmatic. They use discernment and objectivity in decision making; they are conscious of but not influenced by their biases and impulses in making important decisions. They explore all aspects of a complex situation before acting with a combination of logic, instinct, intuition, and emotion.

Chapter 6 examines the concept of flexible fortitude: knowing when to hold and when to fold. For the most part, wise leaders are resolute and resilient, but they also know when to relent and even pull the plug if a deteriorating situation can't be salvaged and threatens wider damage. They are open to learning new things and stretching their capabilities to do the best job possible, especially during crises.

Chapter 7 deals with discovery of the drivers of your motivation: wise leaders act out of their own volition instead of extrinsic motivation. They are driven by the desire to serve a noble purpose and contribute to the broader community knowing that by doing so, they can reap rewards for themselves as well as for their organization and even society at large. We call the wise leader's intrinsic motivation "enlightened self-interest."

Chapter 8 is about cocreating a field of wise leadership and tying the capabilities together with the concept of wisdom logic, the means by which you make the journey toward wise leadership your own. You cannot become wise just by reading a book or blindly following a structured process. We suggest ways for you to develop your own wisdom logic and bring practical wisdom to your team, organization, industry, community, and even nation on your journey to wise leadership.

THE PATH TO WISE LEADERSHIP

Smart leaders start their journey to wise leadership by diligently reflecting on the best practices of other wise leaders and practicing them appropriately in their own lives. Eventually, though, you need to embark on a more personal journey toward wise leadership. Each leader's path is unique and depends on where each finds herself in terms of the red zone or the blue zone to begin with—and how committed she is to that way of operating in and seeing the world. This is the foundation for developing wisdom logic—a personalized pathway to wise leadership (we elaborate on the concept of wisdom logic in chapter 8).

Many of the wise leaders we studied developed their wise leadership skills as a reaction or response to a certain event. We don't think Gates woke up one morning and said, "I want to become a wise leader." We suspect that he was forced to consider the ways his red zone leadership style wasn't working for him and for Microsoft and broadened his perspective to the point where he changed from being a red zone leader and embraced more of the attributes of wise leadership. For Tim Cook at Apple, we believe that Steve Jobs's advancing illness facilitated his evolution from the blue zone leadership to wise leadership.

We have developed a four-step approach you can use to start your journey toward your wise leadership: identify the primary zone you currently operate from, assess where you are on your path, create a road map, and find tools and feedback systems to help you stay on course to wise leadership.

Identify the Zone

You can kick-start your journey to wise leadership by first becoming aware of your tendency to operate most often in one of the two primary leadership zones: blue for functional smart and red for business smart.

While reading this chapter, you might have had some inkling of which zone—blue or red—you are comfortable operating in most of the time, although you might desire to act and lead from the other zone. Identify stories and actions that remind you of your own behavior. Highlight relevant sections in the book, and make notes so that you can quickly refer back to those sections when necessary. Once you read the first seven chapters, look back on your notes and highlight sections to identify patterns that belong to the blue zone or the red zone.

Assess Where You Are on the Path

Use the self-assessment here to identify how frequently you demonstrate wise leader capabilities through your behavior (you can also visit fromsmarttowise.com to take a more detailed self-assessment). When you look at the self-assessment results, you may discover—and be pleasantly surprised—that you are already acting as a wise leader in some capabilities. Celebrate your newly gained self-awareness, and if you like, you can ask your colleagues to use the assessment to evaluate you and share the results with you. Ask them to give concrete examples from the recent past that make them support their assessment if you want to identify the behaviors you want to change.

FROM SMART TO WISE LEADERSHIP SELF-ASSESSMENT

Directions: Using the following scoring scale, select how frequently you engage in each of the behaviors described below by circling your choice from 1 to 5. Then add your circled ratings for each item to obtain your overall wise leadership score.

 To take the assessment online and receive your automated results, scan the QR code on your mobile device or go to http://www.josseybassbusiness.com/2012/12/assess-kaipa-2.html.

Scoring Scale
1   Rarely
2   Occasionally
3   Sometimes
4   Frequently
5   Almost always

1. I pay attention to the broader business context as I make decisions about my projects.   1   2   3   4   5

2. I maintain my objectivity even when I am very enthusiastic about a project.   1   2   3   4   5

3. When I am asked to share my role or authority with others, I do it without taking it personally.   1   2   3   4   5

4. When performing a routine project, I take a big picture view to learn as much as I can from it.   1   2   3   4   5

5. My ethical compass directs my actions at work.   1   2   3   4   5

6. I stay focused on a project until completion regardless of whether I will benefit.   1   2   3   4   5

7. While taking critical actions, I stop to   1   2   3   4   5
   reflect on whether they align with my
   values and ethics.

8. When selecting my next project, I   1   2   3   4   5
   consciously disregard the potential for
   personal gain.

9. When faced with a tough decision, I   1   2   3   4   5
   explore all aspects of the issue holisti-
   cally with a long-term view.

10. My will is strong enough to control my   1   2   3   4   5
    emotions and impulses that get in the
    way.

11. I acknowledge that my happiness   1   2   3   4   5
    largely depends on the choice I make
    to be happy or unhappy.

12. I pay extra attention to ideas that   1   2   3   4   5
    expand my worldview and give me a
    broader perspective.

13. I pay attention to the project mission   1   2   3   4   5
    (the why) as much as to goals and
    strategy (the what and how).

14. When exploring new avenues, I am a   1   2   3   4   5
    thoughtful risk taker.

15. When faced with a task I don't enjoy, I   1   2   3   4   5
    regard it as a commitment to others to
    do the best job I can.

16. I make decisions that serve a larger   1   2   3   4   5
    purpose than just my own.

17. I bring equal focus and enthusiasm to   1   2   3   4   5
    concrete and conceptual projects.

18. I prioritize my actions based on the   1   2   3   4   5
    contribution I can make to others and
    a larger mission.

My Wise Leadership Score: _____

What Your Scores Mean

69–90	Congratulations, your scores—if you were truly honest with yourself—indicate you have successfully cultivated practical wisdom in your leadership capabilities and are well along on the path to wise leadership. Look at your Six Capabilities of Wise Leadership subscores below to help determine which areas to focus on in your continued evolution from smart to wise.
54–68	You have begun the transformation from smart leader to wise leader. Look at your Six Capabilities of Wise Leadership subscores below and focus special attention on your lowest-scored capabilities to continue to grow and cultivate wise leadership.
18–53	You have not yet transformed your smart leadership qualities to wise leader qualities. Remember, you have to demonstrate your practical wisdom more frequently for you to build your wise leader muscle.

To obtain your Six Capabilities of Wise Leadership subscores, transfer and add your ratings for the items indicated for each subscore below.

Perspective

#1	___
#12	___
#13	___
My perspective subscore	___

Action Orientation

#2	___
#7	___
#14	___
My action orientation subscore	___

Role Clarity

#3	___
#8	___
#15	___
My role clarity subscore	___

Decision Logic

#5	____
#9	____
#16	____
My decision logic subscore	____

Fortitude

#6	____
#10	____
#17	____
My fortitude subscore	____

Motivation

#4	____
#11	____
#18	____
My motivation subscore	____

What Your Subscores Mean

13–15	This capability is a strength for you. Build your wise leadership further by developing synergy among your capabilities.
10–12	You have begun to build this capability of wise leadership very well. Continue to cultivate it and exercise it more frequently until it becomes a reliable strength for you.
3–9	You have not yet developed your capability in this area and may be stuck in the red or blue zone. Read and apply the ideas and strategies in *From Smart to Wise* on this wise leadership capability to begin to make it a strength for you.

Gaining awareness of how you currently exercise wise leadership capabilities is the first step in the right direction. We recommend that everyone on your team get a copy of this book and spend one hour a week to discuss the insights and action steps from each chapter to help each other move along the path of wise leadership.

Keeping your own assessment results close by, continue to deepen that self-awareness by reading chapters 2 through 7, where you will learn about other wise leaders and the unique way in which they exercise the six leadership capabilities. In each of those chapters, we give details on how leaders tend to exercise a particular capability—say, perspective or motivation—when they operate in the blue or red zone and compare and contrast that with how wise leaders use that same capability. Each chapter gives examples of wise leaders and their best practices, as well as some tools and advice. Pick one tool or piece of advice from each chapter and practice what you have learned at least once a day. Also, discuss each chapter's key findings with your team members, say once a week. Creating a book club or a dialogue group on wise leadership around you will give you more motivation to practice what you learn in this book.

We believe that wisdom—and wise leadership—is our birthright. We can all journey toward it if we become aware of where we currently are operating from and progressively take our colored filters off and see—and interact with—the world in its full spectrum.

Create a Road Map Toward Wise Leadership

Once you have read this book completely and identified your wise leader score and action steps to increase that score, create a road map to move yourself toward your North Star, which represents your noble purpose (in chapter 2 we offer a tool that can help you discover and connect with your North Star). This road map is your developmental path: it will help you prioritize your efforts in cultivating wise leadership while you are moving toward your North Star.

Once you have the road map in hand, you can initiate your journey by focusing on any of the six capabilities. Pick the capability that you are most interested in working on, and reread the chapter that addresses that capability. Then discuss with your team (it could be a work team or family team or a circle of friends) your action plan to exercise that capability in a wise manner. Be open to suggestions from others, and get to work on it. When you are ready, you can identify another capability that you are interested in—or just go to the next one in order—and continue this cycle. Sometimes you might find that while you are working on improving how you act and lead in one capability, you are simultaneously getting better in another—which is not surprising, since the six wise leadership capabilities are integrated and interdependent.

In our experience, leaders who operate primarily in the business smart mode can make the biggest progress to understand wise leadership if they begin to pay more attention to motivation first—in other words, if they can act out of enlightened self-interest more often. Then they may need to pay special attention to perspective, action orientation, and role clarity. You might have to downplay your enthusiasm for quick and intense action, especially if you tend to operate in the red zone. If you primarily operate in the blue zone, you might want to increase your activity level and pay special attention to decision logic, fortitude, and motivation. Again, use your team to support your transformation into a wise leader—while you are also supporting their journey.

Stay the Course

Once you have prioritized one or more developmental areas and started acting on them, you are on the road to wise leadership. Be aware, however, that this journey is not a straight line but more like the movement of a clock—steady and continuous movements to both sides, with the real movement taking place on the clock face. Indeed, we have identified wise leadership as the diligent effort of shifting away from a particular zone you generally operate from. Expect to have lapses and sometimes get stuck in your traditional zone (after all, it is your comfort zone): it is important to demonstrate resilience and be kind to yourself. Be conscious of trying to unstick yourself and resume your journey—or, more appropriately, of removing the filters you are accustomed to and taking a fresh look at what is in front of you.

All journeys can be difficult: nobody likes changing entrenched habits, and the unknown is often associated with anxiety, leading many people to conclude that it's not worthwhile to leave safety behind and explore untraveled territory. So how can you determine whether you are breaking old habits and progressing on this journey?

Our book website, fromsmarttowise.com, provides more detailed assessment and feedback for you. We will continue to add more tools, graphs, and examples to help you on your wise leader journey. We hope our website will also serve as a social networking platform for aspiring wise leaders like yourself to share your discoveries and the best practices you learned along your journey to wise leadership.

Even after you have broadened your perspective to include the attributes of wise leadership, your primary strengths in the red or the blue zones won't be gone. In fact, when you are stressed or feel very confident (even arrogant), you might easily revert to autopilot mode and operate more from your primary strengths. Wise leadership is a dynamic state of consciousness, and it takes significant discipline and practice for you to operate consistently in that state. It requires being aware of where you are at any moment and paying close attention to the context you are in. Once you take action that you intuitively feel confident about, take time to reflect on what you did, the results it produced, and how it was appropriate to the context outside and within you. Such attention, reflection, and introspection are the basic tools you will use to integrate wise leadership. Use these tools in partnership with your study team. The more consistently you use them, the more adept you are likely to be and the more confident you will feel in operating from a place of wise leadership.

This book does not offer any magic bullet for becoming a wise leader. There is no such thing. It will, however, provide a framework for you to learn about yourself and guide your personal transformation as well as that of your organization. It is an iterative, interconnected process. We hope you will experience a radical broadening in perspective, which is at the heart of sustainable change. Then, by applying the new insights and lessons from the book, you will grow into a wise leader. Above all, we hope this book will inspire your own spirit of inquiry, just as conceiving of it and writing it did for us, and encourage you to embark on this rewarding path.

CHAPTER TWO

SHIFT YOUR PERSPECTIVE
Connect to Your Noble Purpose

Perspective, the first of the six leadership capabilities we identify, is also known as worldview, mental model, or mind-set. We place it first because it underpins all the others and is thus the most critical of all six capabilities. When a person's perspective shifts and broadens, profound change and growth become possible. Just ask Raj.

About six years ago, Raj came to us for help. After a hardscrabble childhood in India, he worked hard and graduated from top engineering and management schools in India and immigrated to the United States, where he found greater success. He emerged as a business leader who was talented at seeing entrepreneurial opportunities and driven to success. He started a software company that went public within five years, with him as CEO. It was the American dream come true. For many people in their early forties, that might have been the pinnacle of success. But for Raj, it was the start of a long period of soul searching and questioning that eventually led him to shift his perspective and, in the process, evolve from a smart leader to a wise leader.

After taking his company public, Raj stepped back from daily operations and hired a CEO from outside to run his company. Unfortunately, the new CEO had a command-and-control management style that clashed with the company's entrepreneurial culture; this, in combination with the dot-com bust, led to a crisis in the business. The new CEO eventually left, prompting Raj to reassume the CEO role. A naturally intense type A personality, Raj channeled all his high energy into his job. He worked long hours and made enormous progress with the team and key customers. He not only saved the company from crashing but brought it back to growth and profitability. Now the company had to be refocused as a broad-based and high-volume services company instead of being a specialized and high-value services provider. It was a difficult journey, and eventually the struggle and stress began to take its toll on Raj. That's when he turned to us for executive coaching.

We felt that Raj needed to find the root of his dissatisfaction and discover what he really wanted to achieve in his life. So we engaged him with exercises like visualization, projecting into the future and imagining where he was at that stage of life. Raj realized that his identity was too closely associated with his work and that he was behaving as if nothing else mattered to him. He visualized himself becoming a rich and successful person in the future but without the closeness of his family and friends and good health.

Raj felt shaken by the large mismatch between his own tacit expectations of wanting to have a happy family and his actual work practices. That emotional experience was a jolt that shifted his perspective and allowed him to arrive at a number of critical conclusions about his life and work and where he was headed. His family, health, and happiness had taken a secondary role for a long time, but he had not reflected much on this because he was unable to see himself separate from his work. Instead of being just one of the roles in his life, work had overtaken all other roles in Raj's life—even though the job that Raj was doing at that time was not particularly energizing to him.

Using our framework, Raj realized that he was operating mostly in the red zone, and to bring balance to his life, he had to shift and broaden his perspective. That meant taking off his red-tinted glasses and seeing the world without filters. After a period of introspection, Raj recognized that he valued his roles as husband, father, friend, and son as much as he did his role as chief executive of his company. His working identity, which he valued the most when he was wearing his red filter, was only a small part of his larger self and life. He came to see that the company could survive without him, but he behaved as if he could not survive without the company, a new perspective that brought him more clarity.

Exercises on managing his energy helped Raj clarify his priorities. He rediscovered activities—like cycling—that energized him and identified those that depleted his energy, such as listening to complaints and problems. With this new clarity about what was important and of value in his life, Raj found a CEO for his company whose energy, passion, and vision aligned well with that of the company. Raj resigned from the board. With that change in place, he refocused his attention on his family for the next three years before he started another company. When we saw Raj recently, he told us that those three years were the best years in his life because he had had the time to do things that were important and fulfilling, like spending time with his school-age children and elderly parents. It also allowed his wife to fulfill her dream and start her own company.

The broader perspective that Raj had gained stayed with him through the years. At one point he returned to India so that his children could experience what he had while growing up. As he turned fifty, he told us that the past decade had been extraordinary due to this change in perspective. He has taken on social entrepreneurship projects in the area of education, bringing his business smart leadership skills into the field to serve the greater good. His health has markedly improved, his wife's business is flourishing, and his children are back in the United States getting advanced degrees. Raj has achieved an enviable level of contentment.

Raj is like many other entrepreneurs and business smart leaders who operate in the red zone and have a tendency to be consumed by their passion for work and business success. Desh Deshpande, a successful serial entrepreneur in the technology sector and an innovation advisor to the White House under President Obama, notes that many business leaders, especially business smart leaders, place too much importance on success without recognizing that it is just a milestone along a life journey, not the end point. If we focus solely on success, he reckons, then we prioritize only tangible and measurable results like money and power and our position in society, and we ignore all the important intangibles like family, children, and personal growth.[1]

Leaders operating primarily in the blue zone, that is, functional smart leaders, have a different set of problems. They tend to be more sensitive about meeting short-term goals and ignore the big picture perspective to achieve those goals. In other words, they tend to get comfortable within the limited function that they boxed themselves into and usually are less inclined to think about, let alone explore, their full potential or long-term opportunities. They generally don't want to take big risks considering the complexity and volatility in the world.

Many functional smart leaders tend to have a narrow, though deep, view of life that they need to broaden; business smart leaders tend to have a big picture view, but one that often is primarily focused on personal success. In both cases, these smart leaders wear colored glasses constantly and need to remove them in order to shift and broaden their perspective, the fundamental first step on the path to becoming wise leaders. Without this shift, their ability to act and lead effectively as leaders can be severely hampered because they would continue to act in accordance with their limited view rather than using a broader perspective to take actions that are appropriate and context sensitive (we discuss how leaders can improve their action orientation in chapter 3). First, however, we must become aware of our current perspective before we can shift it to help us become wise leaders.

WHAT IS "PERSPECTIVE"?

Also known as worldview, mental model, or mind-set, our perspective of the world is based on the sum total of our knowledge and experiences. It defines us, shaping our thoughts and actions because it represents the way we see ourselves and situations, how we judge the relative importance of things, and how we establish a meaningful relationship with everything around us.

Cultivating a wise perspective is the first step toward developing wise leadership capacity. In our research, we found that a shift in perspective tends to occur in two ways: either it is triggered involuntarily by extreme external circumstances like a crisis (desperation), or it is induced voluntarily by a conscious effort to change oneself for the better through high aspiration. Raj's perspective shift came about through the latter: he reached out for help because he intuitively felt a need to change his life. But often we find that a perspective shift takes the former course: it is imposed on people after a life-changing event of some kind. That's exactly what happened to Viktor Frankl.

Frankl was born and raised in Vienna and became an accomplished psychiatrist and neurologist. During World War II, Frankl, who was Jewish, spent three years in a Nazi concentration camp, where he experienced an epiphany about the way we can find or create meaning in our lives regardless of how harsh our circumstances are. Frankl realized that although the Nazis could incarcerate him and torture his body, they could not control his mind and spirit. He believed that he retained the freedom to give meaning to his life even in the face of deprivation, suffering, and humiliation. The moment Frankl recognized that his mind and spirit were free and his identity was not restricted to his body and what he did, he reframed his self-perception. His perspective suddenly shifted from a helpless victim to an empowered individual. Frankl then helped other prisoners shift their own perspective, and based on these experiences, he established a new school of psychotherapy, called logotherapy, after his liberation from the camp.[2]

Ultimately, meaning motivates human beings more than power, Frankl postulated. Discovering meaning happens by creating a work or doing a deed, experiencing something (in Frankl's case, great and unavoidable suffering), or encountering someone.[3] These may sound like easy or everyday tasks, but we tend to get sidetracked along the way to finding meaning, and we suffer some more. Frankl's work, based on the concept that striving to find meaning in one's life should be a primary motivation and driving force, has broad implications beyond psychotherapy. Shifting perspective, as Frankl did, allows us to see patterns that we have never been aware of before. It can lead to our awareness of existential meaning and not just intellectual understanding in our lives and help us deal with difficult situations.

For our purposes, shifting perspective means becoming sensitive to the context around us and being able to see the world without any filters. It allows us to broaden our worldview and empathize with people who think and act radically different from us. A perspective shift could yield different insights and actions for different leaders depending on the kind of colored glasses— red or blue—they are used to wearing.

THE LIMITS OF A SMART PERSPECTIVE

The majority of leaders we studied and consulted with operate from a business smart or functional smart perspective. For these leaders, gaining a wiser perspective is a two-step process: acknowledging their smart perspective (and its limitations) and then broadening their perspective to overcome those limitations. Most leaders won't be motivated to shift their perspective until they realize why remaining primarily in either the blue or the red zone is detrimental to their long-term personal and professional success. Consequently, we first examine in more detail how the perspective of blue zone leaders differs from that of leaders who tend to operate in the red zone.

Leaders who usually operate in the blue zone tend to have a great execution perspective—they focus on what can be done in the short term—which shapes entirely how they decide, act, and interact with others. Although this short-term perspective is their great asset—enabling them to fix problems that are concrete and immediate—it can also be their weakness. For instance, although leaders in the blue zone are open to others' ideas, they tend to be selective and embrace only ideas that reinforce their own perspective. As a result, they may struggle to adopt and execute on innovative ideas that require them to stretch themselves beyond their comfort zone. Similarly, given their difficulty dealing with abstract concepts and long-term visions, these leaders may fail to perceive subtle signals that indicate a major shift in the external context and require them to radically revamp their execution plans.

Leaders operating in the red zone are, in contrast, visionaries who can see the big picture, formulate a long-term vision for their organization, and get others to line up behind that vision. Being entrepreneurial, they can quickly identify emerging trends and patterns and capitalize on new ideas. They spot opportunities for new businesses and products and swiftly act on them. However, their perspective can get clouded since they tend to focus on their uniqueness and tend to listen to advice that reinforces their perspective and ignore other critical input. As a result, sometimes they lose perspective and miss important opportunities because they are driven by a personal agenda that could override the broader interests of the organization. Subroto Bagchi, cofounder and chairman of Mindtree, an information technology consulting company, told us about an ambitious young finance executive in his organization who was in a hurry to become the company's chief financial officer. Although the smart young man had all the right qualifications, he did not have the emotional maturity or discernment to be an effective CFO. Bagchi offered to mentor the young man and help him develop a wise perspective. But the young man could not wait and left

Mindtree in search of a CFO position in another organization. Another weakness of business smart leaders is that while they can come up with a great vision, they may struggle to execute it, let alone take responsibility if the execution fails.

As you read these descriptions above, did you recognize the color of your own filters? In other words, do you tend to perceive the world as leaders in the blue zone do or as leaders in the red zone do? Revisit your self-assessment in chapter 1 and look at your perspective subscore. Have you built yet your wise leader perspective as a strength (subscore 13–15)? (If needed, redo the self-assessment in chapter 1 or you can go to fromsmarttowise.com for a more detailed assessment of your perspective.)

Now ask yourself: How would I view the world if I were to remove the filters that color or distort my perspective? How would I act differently if I were to be a wise leader and shift my perspective?

THE WISE LEADER'S PERSPECTIVE

Wise leaders tend to pay attention to patterns that connect and ideas that expand their worldview and help them find a larger meaning in life. They focus on bringing out the best in others because they believe that a leader's goal should be to develop followers into becoming better leaders than they themselves are. In doing so, they find shared purpose with their followers and strive to cocreate value with them for the larger society. When they work with others, they keep their eyes open for what connects and integrates each other and their larger purpose. Jim Collins and Jerry Porras, coauthors of *Built to Last*, reported that organizations driven by purpose and values outperformed the market fifteen-to-one and outperformed comparison companies six-to-one.[4] According to Collins, a noble purpose has "the power to ignite the passion and commitment."[5]

We find that just like great organizations that are driven by a higher purpose, wise leaders are driven by a personal noble purpose, which serves as their North Star (a concept similar to what Bill George, former CEO of Medtronic and now a Harvard Business School professor, calls True North). They use their North Star to guide all their decisions and actions at an individual level and in an organizational context. When interpersonal conflicts arise within their team, wise leaders resolve them by framing the conflict in a larger context, using their North Star for inspiration. They enjoy and excel at mentoring others in their process of shifting their perspective and discovering their own North Star.

SHIFTING YOUR PERSPECTIVE

Albert Einstein once famously said: "One cannot solve a problem with the same mind-set that created it in the first place." As the global business environment, driven by diversity and interconnectivity, becomes increasingly complex, we all need a range of skills to deal with the challenges. Both kinds of smart leaders need to identify and understand the limitations of their perspective and then learn to shift it.

We see two critical paths to shifting one's perspective, as indicated in the "What Is 'Perspective'?" section. The common path is that of desperation, which is adopted by leaders who have to radically shift their perspective in reaction to unexpected crisis. In this dire situation, the shift in perspective usually does not last. The second is the path of aspiration: a leader proactively and willingly seeks out and finds a noble purpose that will provide direction when the path ahead is hazy, acting as a kind of North Star.[6] A noble purpose is one that transcends personal gain and ego and is worth pursuing in an honorable manner. It gives meaning to one's life and offers a path with many choices to contentment and happiness. Your noble purpose gives you humility when arrogance announces false victory and inspires you when the outlook seems bleak.[7] We will discuss noble purpose (we call it *North Star* because it fulfills that role for smart leaders) more at length later in this chapter, but it suffices to say here that once you find your North Star, your perspective irrevocably shifts.

Shifting perspective is not a one-off conscious act, but an ongoing process that needs to be undertaken diligently. The goal is to cultivate openness as a way to facilitate a continual reframing. By unlearning and selectively forgetting past successes, wise leaders open themselves to an unknown future. They are humble enough to allow their mind to be shifted by external circumstances. This flexible mind-set enables them to continually reframe and reinterpret events and find new meanings within a rapidly changing external context.

In November 2011, some of the biggest players in Silicon Valley, from venture capitalists to billionaire entrepreneurs, attended a gala event to toast their success and swap stories about their great experiences. Nipun Mehta, the cofounder of ServiceSpace, an all-volunteer organization that leverages technology to inspire public service, gave the keynote address in which he talked about becoming richer—not by earning more money but by giving away one's riches and "serving others"—as the noblest act one can perform in one's life.[8] Mehta explained his concept of the "gratitude économy," or making economic decisions through the lens of gratitude rather than greed.

Mehta was speaking from firsthand experience because ServiceSpace has over 340,000 members who are driven by a desire to transcend their individual selves and serve a larger purpose. These members run a wide range of generosity-driven projects that include a popular daily news service, DailyGood.com, that delivers inspirational news every day—in contrast with the doom-and-gloom events reported in mainstream media (DailyGood. com receives 1 million page views a month.) Members also operate an acts-of-kindness portal, HelpOthers.org, as well as Karma Kitchen, a nationwide network of gift-economy restaurants: anyone can eat there for free in exchange for committing to serve as a volunteer (as unpaid servers, greeters, or cooks) in the restaurant in the future.

During his keynote address, Mehta recounted how the members of ServiceSpace, many of them accomplished professionals, "value" their lives based on the hours they invest in improving the lives of others. They measure return on investment of their time in terms of the joy and satisfaction they bring to others. These volunteers derive their life energy and passion by "giving, receiving, and loving" rather than "taking, taking, and taking," Mehta explained.[9] We heard from people who attended the meeting that these were striking observations for the highly successful, wealth-driven Silicon Valley audience. Some were moved to tears.

The next day the CEO of a well-known tech firm who attended the talk wrote to Mehta about his experience after the meeting. He said that while he was driving home, his wife called to say that their eighty-year-old neighbor was on her way to the emergency room after experiencing dizziness and high blood pressure. The CEO, deciding to act outside his normal behavior, drove straight to the hospital and spent the next hours at her bedside. He comforted his neighbor and friend as the doctors ran tests. "What was relevant to me was that I was granted an intimate and heartfelt audience with another human being that entertained my inquisition on the nature of spirit," the CEO wrote.[10]

Many leaders such as this tech CEO undergo a shift in consciousness in an unexpected way after attending an inspiring talk or reading a moving book or through hearing about an emotional personal experience. Some ignore those insights and remain locked in their traditional mind-set. But others find that such experiences set the stage for them to discover their real purpose in life, perhaps for the first time.

One aspect of wise leadership is about using smartness for the greater good. The CEO who went outside his normal behavior to give comfort to a neighbor could use that experience, and his reflections on it, as a springboard to lead others to court similar experiences. He could start by figuring out a way to spend part of his time in making a difference to others. To take it even further, he could encourage his employees to volunteer and engage in acts of kindness on a regular basis. In our experience, only rarely do leaders take such actions. When they do take such steps, however, they experience an irreversible shift in their perspective as they discover and more deeply connect to their noble purpose.

Serving a noble purpose requires moving outside our comfort zone and discovering our connection with each other and the universe around us. Once we discover a noble purpose, we can transcend our self-centered perspective and adopt a broader perspective that is more inclusive of others.

NOBLE PURPOSE: IT'S YOUR PERSONAL NORTH STAR

Finding your noble purpose isn't always easy. Many leaders have trouble finding it because they look for it externally rather than within themselves. And even when they look outside, they primarily focus on what connects them to the organization they work for rather than what binds them to humanity.

Many business smart leaders we know are strategic thinkers and excel at creating vision statements for their organizations. They often say something like this: "We will become the largest and most profitable company in our industry by 2020." Yet such organizational vision statements are just nicely worded expressions of company goals; they don't define the leader's personal goals, let alone higher purpose. And they are often too closely identified with a leader's personal vision statement.

Functional smart leaders, who are more oriented to tactical decision making, tend to believe that their main task is executing their organization's strategy while others focus on vision and purpose. They believe in execution more than vision and do not feel a need to have lofty vision statements to guide their personal lives either. In our consulting work, when we ask such executives to define their purpose in life, they usually recite their organization's vision statement.

Many business smart leaders confuse vision (what we want in our future) and purpose (why we do what we do). They also sometimes confuse purpose and noble purpose. Noble purpose, as we have defined it, is a purpose that transcends personal gain (and ego) and gives meaning and a path to happiness. For example, we worked with a software company executive whose purpose in life was to be rich and famous, so every action he took was about earning money or becoming known. It was only after he lost half his management team that he began to pay more attention to purpose that transcends his own needs and ego.

Money can't buy happiness, as we all know. But smart leaders can make the mistake of believing that attaining material success is indeed the key to happiness. When you are in the blue zone, you construe physical comfort, pleasures, and material success as true well-being and in that zone, words like *vision* and *purpose* are too abstract and don't make sense. And when you operate in the red zone, you can get caught up with your vision yet rarely ask questions about why you are attached to that vision and what purpose it would serve. When we are in the red zone, nothing ever makes us happy for long.

For Bill Gates, a quintessential business smart leader, satisfaction came when he switched from driving Microsoft to dominance in its industry to helping humanity through the Bill & Melinda Gates Foundation. And now he is going further in this direction with the Giving Pledge, a movement developed in partnership with Warren Buffett to encourage wealthy individuals to give 50 percent or more of their fortunes to philanthropy.[11] In this way, Gates is continuing to connect deeply to his noble purpose and continuing to mature as a wise leader.

Leaders who struggle to integrate their noble purpose into all their actions have created what we call a compartmentalized noble purpose: they do community or volunteer work in their free time but engage in intensely competitive work during their weekdays. They are following a noble purpose in their spare time but not at work, where they spend most of their time. When you find your noble purpose, you must be prepared to live it because you cannot manage it in your spare time. A noble purpose manages you and shifts your priorities. If this isn't the case, then you are not truly engaging with and embracing your noble purpose as the guiding principle of your life.

Recently we coached Jane, a successful former chief financial officer of a Silicon Valley company who asked us to help her identify her next career opportunity. Jane was regarded as a very smart leader and was financially secure. Within a few weeks of a job search, she was ready to pick one of three appealing job opportunities.

Our approach was to ask Jane to outline a five-year vision and then an even longer-term vision of her life, including a noble purpose. During that process, she shifted from focusing on what she wanted for her family to what she was seeking from her new employer, which was even more success. Then she began to move in another direction to consider what it might mean to take a more challenging job with little risk to one with a higher risk–to-reward ratio and a noble purpose. As the conversation focused on noble purpose, Jane realized that her ideal was not to serve the company or shareholders but to make a lasting difference to her community. She had experienced a big shift in her perspective and was thrilled to have found her noble purpose. In the end, however, Jane did not immediately pursue her noble purpose. She accepted a position with a large energy company and postponed her journey.

Jane carried her dissatisfaction to the new job and within three months was ready to move again. Although she had found her noble purpose, her red zone personality was not willing to give up the recognition and financial reward that goes with a job in a Fortune 100 company. She was aware of what would bring her happiness but was not convinced to act on it. (Chapter 3 focuses on maintaining the alignment between one's perspective and one's action orientation.)

Finding One's Noble Purpose

We believe there are a number of ways to consciously and intentionally identify one's noble purpose. The journey can start by learning to pay attention to the limits of perception. Allianz Global Investors, a global asset management company, operates a unique training center at its Munich headquarters, where senior managers from Allianz as well as client companies take part in leadership development programs facilitated by trainers with disabilities. Visually impaired trainers conduct workshops in total darkness—appropriately called Dialogue in the Dark—and hearing-impaired trainers facilitate workshops called Dialogue in Silence by communicating only through gesture.[12]

The goal of these experiential learning programs is to shift leaders' perspective by making them aware of their own limitations and increase their empathy for others. For instance, in total darkness, the sudden withdrawal of eyesight challenges these leaders to rely on other senses. In this new context, blind people become the "sighted" ones and can demonstrate their capabilities better than the sighted participants. This role reversal fosters reflection, confers a sense of humility, and increases empathy. In this dark environment, managers are given team-building exercises, like assembling a railway track of single pieces in total darkness, that force them to adapt quickly and learn to communicate and cooperate effectively with other participants in order to complete the exercise.

Such emotionally challenging experience provides managers with a potent tool to reflect on their own limits and respect for others, while reinforcing a collaborative mind-set and cultivating emotional intelligence. Most important, a new sense of vulnerability helps cultivate humility and a willingness to "receive," the first steps toward overcoming self-centeredness and finding a higher purpose. Managers who have attended Allianz's workshops report that these sessions have helped improve their leadership skills by increasing their capacity to adapt to and learn from adversity, communicate more effectively, and cultivate empathy and openness toward colleagues.[13]

Another technique for connecting with one's noble purpose is coaching, of the sort we did with an employee named Michelle Kelley at Airco, an aerospace company (we have changed its name here). Kelley was helping to design and implement employee development programs at the company. When we first met her, she had just joined her department and needed to select a project that would maximize her contribution. She knew that technical employees at Airco needed more risk-taking ability if Airco was to keep its creative edge in the marketplace, but she didn't know how to go about helping the organization take risks.

While talking with us, Kelley described the need for more innovation at Airco, which led to an invitation for us to speak with the technical staff. We urged them to move outside their comfort zone, take risks, and tap into their own creativity. Participants responded to our call, and each of them identified a project that they would work on for the next three months. As she listened to us, Kelley identified her own noble purpose: to ignite the genius within others by fostering innovation at Airco.

She took the risk herself, even though she did not know yet how to go about developing an action project designed to make Airco's technical workforce more innovative. "My vision was to have at least 5 percent of the technical workforce think outside the box in five years and influence our products and services at Airco," she told us. We ended up working with her closely for the next three years, and soon she was on her way to realizing her vision, with about 3.5 percent of the technical workforce of some seventeen thousand people in the program. For her, coaching and mentoring helped her remove her remaining mental blocks and became the pathway to live her noble purpose.

Gaining clarity and awareness of one's noble purpose in life is only the first step. We then need to act on the self-awareness we've achieved: wise leadership is grounded in action. Unless we act, the moral courage that accompanies our noble purpose will quickly dissipate, and the insights fade as we slide back into our old comfort zone. Once we revert to habitual mental patterns, tunnel vision and risk aversion tend to take over for some functional smart leaders, and overconfidence and impatience tend to take over business smart leaders. Both types of leaders have difficulty taking the leap of faith required to fulfill our purpose in life.

Kelley acted on her North Star to bring a shift in her perspective and develop new capabilities to help others discover their own noble purpose. Action is critical for perspective to stay changed; otherwise, our autopilot responses will pull us back to the red or blue zone quickly.

Steven Milovich is currently a senior vice president of global human resources, talent, and workforce diversity for Disney ABC Television Group. When we worked with him, he was a rising star at Disney after having a very successful career in PepsiCo and other companies before. Milovich is a talented business smart leader who sees opportunities faster than others do and had big visions and goals for himself and the company. During our coaching engagement, he began to work on his North Star and discovered that it is about helping others become successful: his "destiny" is to be a kingmaker, not a king, and to do great work through others.

At first he had difficulty accepting what felt right to him, and he kept going on his path full speed with red filters. Along the way he developed the ability to reflect and spend time better understanding how he could be more effective and more centered. That allowed him to rethink his priorities. He said, "Fundamentally I needed to put some distance between me and my work without becoming disengaged. I had become preoccupied with my goals that were too narrowly set at the time. I needed to reframe my approach and the North Star I developed suddenly made perfect sense."

Milovich started a meditation practice and daily exercise routine. Slowly things began to change, and that process accelerated as he focused on developing next-generation leaders. "My personal transformation over time helped me to bring about an organizational transformation" said Milovich. He worked on various projects, and some of them required persuading his company to make a multimillion-dollar investment in projects aimed at helping employees learn, grow, and develop on the job. It was effortless for him to direct his red zone smartness to make wise decisions for the company. Milovich was so inspired by the process that he now spends more of his time formally coaching executives to improve their personal and their organizations' effectiveness. He also completed additional training as an executive coach and visualizes himself now serving as a full-time kingmaker no matter what role he is playing in the company.[14]

Finding Your North Star

For this exercise in finding your North Star, write down on sticky notes as many memorable moments from your life as you can think of. Identify them by looking back over your friendships and family, career, school, and leisure-time activities—and stick the note to a wall. Then step back and pay attention to feelings and emotions that the collage evokes. Look for patterns—familiar ones and ones you never picked up before. Ask yourself:

- What makes me come alive? Think of specific activities, people, places, behaviors, memories, books, music, or something else that energizes you and uplifts your spirit.
- What do I see in this collage that represents my authentic self? What, where, and when do I operate from my authentic self?
- What values, beliefs, and behaviors indicate I'm operating from my authentic self?
- If there were to be a noble purpose to my life, what would it be? Look for cues not just in explicit words but also in images, sounds, and music that may pop up.
- Where do I find joy and lose myself? What activities engage me completely without any external motivation or compensation?
- What do I need to unlearn and let go to be true to myself?

- What conditioned responses, autopilot behaviors, and past experiences get in the way of my discovering and consistently following my North Star (my noble purpose)?

Finding your North Star is an iterative process; you might have to go through three or more rounds of reflection and introspection before you find your deeper purpose. Whenever you feel you have identified your North Star, express it briefly in writing, in a phrase or sentence—for example: "Help young people in my city realize their full potential," "Build inclusive and sustainable communities in Rwanda," or "Develop 100 social entrepreneurs in my country in the next ten years." Put this statement to the test by asking yourself three questions:

1. Does this North Star give me inspiration, especially when I am down?
2. Does this North Star challenge me when I feel complacent?
3. Does this North Star give me direction when I am lost in my life?

If the answer is no to any of the three questions, dig deeper. If you are satisfied with your answers, explore whether your values, decisions, and actions are all aligned with your North Star (chapters 3 and 4 will show you how to keep your actions and decisions centered on your North Star).

Noble Purpose in Action: Dr. V's Story

Govindappa Venkataswamy, an ophthalmologist known as Dr. V, acted on his noble purpose by creating an institution that has brought a revolutionary new approach to eye care in India and other countries. In 1976, after his retirement from government service, Dr. V started the Aravind Eye Care System. He didn't have a real business plan or much money or resources, except for the equity in his family home in Madurai, India. But he did have an innovative idea for how to enact his noble purpose: to provide high-quality eye care for all and eliminate curable blindness.

To tackle the problem in a country like India, Dr. V knew he had to develop highly efficient, scalable, repeatable processes to treat eye diseases on a massive scale. So he studied McDonald's and its model of fast food service at low prices. "If McDonald's can do it for hamburgers, why can't we do it for eye care?" he is quoted as saying in *Infinite Vision*, a book that delves into the Aravind story.[15] This perspective shift resulted in a process by which Aravind surgeons undertake more than five times the number of cataract surgeries annually than are done by the average Indian eye surgeon (and ten times the U.S. average). Eye care services are broken down into a series of discrete processes that organize patients in operating rooms so that nurses and doctors can quickly move the operating microscope from one patient to another and effortlessly start a surgery (nurses help in surgeries wherever doctors are not essential and are huge contributors to the efficiency of the system).[16] Aravind runs all its hospitals with remarkable discipline and standardized processes, just like McDonald's does.

Aravind has grown dramatically and continues to flourish and stay true to its mission six years after Dr. V's passing. In 2012 around 2.7 million patients were treated, making it the largest eye care provider in the world. Most of these patients were treated for free or at steeply subsidized rates: the financial model is built around the idea that those who can pay subsidize those who cannot (for each paying patient, Aravind takes care of one and a half nonpaying patients). Aravind is a nonprofit hospital but does not apply for grant money or donations as many other nonprofits do; it supports its own growth based on the services it provides and the income it generates.

According to Pavithra Mehta and Thulasiraj Ravilla, close relatives of Dr. V and executives of Aravind, Dr. V's commitment to spiritual practice, based on the principles of Aurobindo Ghose, an Indian philosopher, yogi, and poet of the early twentieth century, led him to develop his noble purpose. His spiritual practice included daily readings of Aurobindo's works and introspection (using journal writing as a reflective practice) and the compassionate practice of offering his services selflessly to others whether they could pay or not.[17]

Although he was driven by a noble purpose, Dr. V was not just a thinker: he was oriented toward action and was pragmatic in his actions. He started small and enrolled many of his relatives and friends to join and support the cause. Once he started acting on his broader perspective, the opportunities for expanding Aravind were limitless. He set bold targets for himself and always encouraged the staff to exceed them. For example, when intraocular lenses (IOLs), an artificial lens used in cataract treatment, were introduced in the West in the early 1980s, many health professionals regarded these devices as a luxury. Dr. V thought otherwise. Recognizing the value of IOLs, he encouraged his nephew Balakrishnan, who was living in Michigan at the time, to return home in the 1980s to start manufacturing them in India (this was long before India had become a mecca for outsourcing). Dr. V's nephew set up Aurolab, Aravind Eye Care System's manufacturing unit, to mass-produce high-quality IOLs priced at $10 (in 1992), a fraction of their $150 cost in Western countries. Today Aurolab accounts for 7 percent of global IOL implants.

Dr. V was relentless in his efforts to influence others and bring the best out of them. He inspired confidence in others, like Balakrishnan, a mechanical engineer who did not have any knowledge of or interest in eye care but was convinced by Dr. V to return to India to create Aurolab. Dr. V also focused on what works for others while serving his noble purpose. He paid attention to the context he was in and tried to shape the solution to fit the problem. When patients refused free eye care, he wanted to know why, and then he systematically addressed whatever issues were necessary to make eye care available, whether it was transportation or accommodations.

Dr. V consistently acted and led with wisdom and was guided by a noble purpose—with which he worked daily to maintain contact. His purpose gave him both inspiring and concrete work to do each day ("provide high-quality eye care for all") and a goal that would never let him be complacent ("eliminate curable blindness"). He constantly expanded his worldview and was open to learning from everybody he met along the way. As a result, he created one of the most highly efficient health care systems in the world and reduced the number of people suffering from blindness and eye diseases.

Reflecting on the remarkable journey of Dr. V, we see that discovering a noble purpose is the first step, and acting on it constantly to move steadily into wise leadership is the second. Finally, Dr. V went one step further by establishing an institutionalized structure and framework for his noble purpose. This is how you can create a legacy or purpose that can thrive beyond your leadership.

According to Kris Gopalakrishnan, cofounder and co-executive chairman of Infosys, a global information technology consultancy, shifting one's perspective cannot stop with finding one's North Star or pursuing it independent of one's core work. Rather, Gopalakrishnan believes that corporate leaders need to emulate Dr. V by finding ways to integrate their noble purpose into their core business as part of their wise leadership journey. As he points out, "Many corporate leaders strive to serve a larger social purpose through their company's corporate social responsibility initiative, and yet their core for-profit business continues to focus on maximizing shareholder value. Rather than viewing these activities as separate, leaders should ask themselves: 'How can we combine social consciousness and business performance? How do we redefine the key performance indicators for business to shift its focus beyond shareholder value and serve a larger purpose?' "[18]

A MINDFUL MIND-SET

Wise leaders don't always consciously and intentionally try to broaden their perspective. Rather, they allow shifts to occur naturally by staying open to such shifts. In Buddhism, this state of openness is called *mindfulness,* and it is defined as the ability to be conscious of changes occurring in internal and external contexts without judging them, let alone trying to control them (Buddhists believe in impermanence, the notion that stability is an illusion). This openness or awareness provides three main benefits to leaders: they can accept and welcome changes in a nonjudgmental fashion; they can see the bigger picture and detect new patterns, including major opportunities in a fluctuating situation; and they can respond appropriately to changes using an integrated, holistic perspective rather than reacting to them using a fragmented perspective. More important, by staying in a state of openness, leaders improve their ability to continually reframe—that is, bring new meaning to—an external context that is always changing.[19]

We are acquainted with a well-known Silicon Valley CEO (let's call him Janus) whose daughter attended Nueva Center for Learning, a school for gifted children. In one class, parents were invited to build models with their kindergarten children using erector sets. They were given twenty minutes to complete the task. Being extremely creative and a hard-core business smart leader, Janus helped his four-year-old daughter construct an elaborate and stunning model in much less than twenty minutes. They didn't even use all the pieces in the erector set. Janus beamed with pride as the other parents and the teacher heaped praise on the father-daughter team for demonstrating amazing creativity.

As the class drew to a close, the teacher, Mary, instructed the parents and children to take apart their models and put away the erector sets. At hearing this, Janus looked offended and asked Mary why it was necessary to disassemble his unique creation. "That's a work of art," he declared. "It needs to be put in a showcase to inspire other students." To which Mary replied, "Janus, what makes you think that this model is one of a kind? If your mind is creative enough to come up with that one-of-a-kind piece in less than twenty minutes partnering with a four year old, it can definitely conjure up many more wonderful artifacts in the future." Janus sheepishly disassembled his creation.

Mary said to us later that for Janus, that was a turning point. In our analysis, Janus had been exhibiting the classic characteristics of a business smart leader: he had become attached to his creation, believing it was unique and could not be replaced. Once he reframed what had happened, he opened up and recognized that his creativity is limitless and that he should enjoy the process of creating something new rather than getting attached to its uniqueness. Having worked with and observed Janus for over twenty-five years, we were amazed to see him evolve from being a leader with an impulsive need to show off his creative genius to a wise master who taught other creative geniuses and in doing so took his company to even more success.

Many of us are not very different from Janus, in that we make decisions based on a fragmented perspective and then get upset when our view is challenged. You can become open to a different perspective through reframing by others (as the astute teacher did for Janus) or becoming more aware of your own mind-set.

OPENNESS THROUGH REFRAMING

What Dr. V, Raj, and Kelley have in common is their belief that they can change and learn. This is a growth mind-set, as defined by Stanford University professor Carol Dweck.[20] Leaders with a growth mind-set, a key characteristic of wise leadership, believe that their basic qualities can be nurtured and improved through effort.[21] This malleable and highly adaptable mind-set allows them to stay open to changing contexts and learn what they need to in order to change their behavior appropriately. Leaders who operate without any filters live as if life were a kaleidoscope: they are open to let their perspectives, conditioned by beliefs and experiences, be re-formed not just once but again and again. Wise leaders are open to change because they understand that without personal change, they will get stuck, and they are aware that the context around them is changing constantly. Openness could mean vulnerability for some business smart leaders because they are reluctant to acknowledge that they don't know what they don't know. Being open is considered too risky for some functional smart leaders, because they become insecure when they are exposed to new and unknown contexts. But for wise leaders, openness means an opportunity to demonstrate their context sensitivity and gain a new perspective.

You can cultivate openness in a number of ways. Reflection and introspection are critical tools that allow you to become more open to the changing context and balance and leverage your smartness toward serving a higher purpose. When you take time to be reflective and introspective, you will consciously know when to rein in the intensity of your engagement with the world (if you are a typical business smart leader) and when to increase that intensity (if you are a typical functional smart leader). When we can stay mindfully in the present moment and dynamically recalibrate our level of engagement, we become open to all outcomes and carry out our actions with emotional detachment. Staying grounded in the present and maintaining equanimity—a composed, nonjudgmental attitude—in the face of great challenges is a critical capability for leaders whose job is to deal with a multiplicity of issues in a time of increased complexity. Indeed, emotional detachment and equanimity enable leaders to see things as they really are without being clouded by strong emotions that filter their perception of reality, and they take appropriate actions and make wise decisions.

Another way to develop openness is to be intellectually curious. Children are often filled with a sense of wonderment and stay open to and learn from new experiences. Studies suggest that very young children excel at divergent thinking and can easily combine unrelated concepts from diverse domains and come up with unusual solutions in the process.[22] Divergent thinking is vital for creative problem solving. Sadly, we mostly lose this ability as we age and fail to nurture this inquiring mind. One leader who has used his intellectual curiosity and boundless energy to cultivate openness at his company is Alan Mulally, CEO of Ford Motor Company.[23]

Prior to joining Ford in 2006, Mulally spent thirty-seven years at Boeing, which he had joined right after college as an engineer. During his time as a leader there, he led many groundbreaking initiatives, including the development of the Boeing 777, at the time the world's largest twin-engine commercial plane conceived entirely with computer-aided design and modeling. Mulally is well known for his large-scale project management capabilities and built the 777 working with over twenty thousand suppliers who were providing millions of parts that needed to match precisely to create customized planes one at a time. His remarkable leadership in developing the 777 helped him get promoted to the role of CEO of Boeing's Commercial Airplanes division.

Ford was in trouble when Mulally took over. The company was losing market share and brand equity and faced deep losses because of increased competition and globalization. At the time, he made a bold but controversial decision to mortgage all of Ford's assets to secure a $23.6 billion loan, which he said was needed to invest in R&D and serve as "a cushion to protect from a recession or other unexpected event." This decision was widely criticized and deemed unwise at a time when the economy was doing well. But Mulally maintained his composure and focused on the path that he believed was right for the long-term good of the company. "We have to control our own destiny," he noted.[24]

Two years later, at the height of the recession, Mulally's decision proved to have been wise—for totally different factors. Chrysler and GM filed for bankruptcy and were bailed out by the government, while Ford, thanks to the loan, could weather the recession without taking federal bailout funds.

In addition to a financial investment, Ford had to stop the decline of its market share. Mulally came to recognize that neither a product nor a business model innovation would be able to stem the company's decline. What Ford needed was a mental model innovation—that is, a fundamental shift in the mental models that its senior leaders used.[25]

Mulally's realization was inspired by a chance event. One day when he was walking through the parking lot at Ford headquarters in Detroit, he noticed the hodgepodge of Ford brands that had no common attributes in shape or style. Mulally realized that the time had come for Ford to prune its oversized product portfolio. Fewer brands, he figured, would help it concentrate on improving the engineering quality of a smaller roster of models. It would allow the company to reuse components across brands, reaping big savings on supply chain costs. Mulally also articulated another big benefit of reducing the number of models: "It helps all of our distribution, Ford store owners, suppliers, employees and consumers to know exactly what they're getting."[26]

By reframing *focus* as a new mantra and helping managers understand that quantity doesn't always equal quality, Mulally trimmed Ford's bloated portfolio to about twenty models from ninety-seven. In particular, Ford sold off Jaguar, Land Rover, and Aston Martin—all luxury brands that were bleeding money— and pulled the plug on the seventy-one-year-old Mercury line. Instead of gas guzzlers, Ford would focus on smaller, more fuel-efficient cars.

After trimming the product line, Mulally convinced his management team to reinvigorate some older models like the Taurus. The Taurus had been America's best-selling car in the 1980s, but its poorly designed successors did not impress car buyers. The brand had withered and was eventually discontinued. But Mulally ordered a fully revamped Taurus sedan—one that would be "the coolest vehicle" Ford had ever made—and this new Taurus roared back in 2010 and became an instant commercial success.

Mulally succeeded because he had the capacity to reframe, and he reframed Ford around a unified message that was captured in a new slogan, "One Ford," which inspired and encouraged Ford managers to work together and focus on making Ford successful. Profits, sales, and share value under Mulally have increased dramatically. In its ads, Toyota now compares and contrasts its cars with Ford vehicles, not those of its archrival Honda.

You don't need to be the chief executive of a global business to apply lessons from Mulally's wise leadership at Ford. Wherever you lead, focus on helping people gain a larger and more holistic perspective and lead by example by demonstrating such a broad perspective yourself. In Mulally's own words, you have to help your team see the bigger picture, as exemplified in this story he once told us:

> A reporter went to a construction site and interviewed three bricklayers. He asked the first bricklayer about his work. The bricklayer said, "I'm making a living laying these bricks." The reporter asked the same question to the second bricklayer, who replied, "I am practicing the profession of bricklaying. I'm going to be the best bricklayer ever." When the reporter queried the third bricklayer, he responded: "I'm building a cathedral." . . .
>
> We all want to contribute to making a cathedral. The more we find meaning in our work and the more we help others find meaning in their own work, the more we can move our team performance to a whole other level of excellence.[27]

CONCLUSION

Our perspective or worldview is based on the sum total of our knowledge and experiences. It defines us, shaping our thoughts and actions, because it represents the way we see ourselves and situations, how we judge the relative importance of things, and how we establish a meaningful relationship with everything around us. If you primarily operate in the blue zone, your perspective can skew toward being too narrowly focused; if you mostly operate in the red zone, your perspective may become too self-centered. Once you remove the perceptual filters and step out of the blue or red zone, you have an opportunity to shift your perspective.

A wise leadership perspective is oriented toward one's North Star, which represents one's noble purpose. A noble purpose transcends personal gain and ego and is worth pursuing in an honorable manner. It gives meaning to life and offers a sure path to contentment and happiness. Being able to move from a smart leadership perspective to a wise leadership perspective entails finding and following your North Star.

Shifting perspective is rarely a single, conscious act. Rather, it's a series of reorientations toward a changing reality. Being open to changes in the internal as well as the external context and cultivating a growth mind-set will open the way for you to let these shifts unfold repeatedly in a graceful and natural manner.

When you seek to shift your perspective, start by identifying where you are: the zone in which your perspective is predominantly anchored. You can do this by using the self-assessment in chapter 1 or the assessment on our website (fromsmarttowise .com). Next, find your noble purpose—your North Star—and try to identify it in words. With knowledge of your starting orientation and a formulation of your noble purpose, you can begin to cultivate a growth mind-set. This involves remaining open to changes and experiences that are new, are emotionally charged, or make you feel vulnerable; it also means consciously reframing situations to create more meaning and interconnectedness. You can use the wise leadership dashboard on our website to keep track of your progress toward developing a wise perspective.

To get the most out of this chapter, we recommend that you ask yourself the following questions, depending on which zone you more closely identify with and reflect on them in as curious and nonjudgmental a manner as you can. If you are in the red zone, you may need to slow down to shift your perspective and learn to reflect and look inward as a balance to your rapid, full-throttle approach to your work. If you are in the blue zone, you may need to stretch yourself outside your comfort zone to get a broader perspective, not defaulting to tactical or operational solutions too quickly. In either case, a good grasp on your North Star will help you reach beyond your default set of ideas and answers.

Red Zone

- Are there times and situations when I tend to make decisions too rapidly and without a balanced perspective? What are they, and what are the consequences I can foresee when that happens?
- Do I worry that I'll miss out on something if I slow down or pull back from my work? What might I gain by trying to bring more balance to my life and my work and to my decision making?
- Vision is not the same as purpose. Do I confuse vision, which arises out of "what" questions, and purpose, which arises out of "why" questions? If so, when do I do this and why?
- Not every action or decision is at the same level of importance. Do I get overwhelmed because I'm not prioritizing enough? In what situations does this happen? Do I lack project management skills?
- What is my attitude about personal change away from my areas of strength?

Blue Zone

- Do I have trouble stepping back from my areas of strength— my tactical or operational perspective? In what conditions or situations is this the most difficult for me?
- What is my attitude toward risk and failure? When I think of taking a risk or trying something new—professionally or personally—and failing, is the mere thought of failure enough to keep me from taking the risk?
- Think of a time you experienced failure. Then ask what failure meant to you. Do I tend to take it personally? How might I

learn to reframe failure (this particular one or failure in general) more constructively?

- Think of a time when you defaulted to a tactical or operational solution, perhaps too quickly. What was the outcome, and what were the opportunity costs?
- What is my attitude about personal change away from my areas of strength?

Having a clear noble purpose and a broadened perspective are important first steps to wise leadership. The next is to pay attention to your orientation to action and find ways to act authentically and appropriately. This is the topic of chapter 3.

CHAPTER THREE

BE AWARE OF YOUR ACTION ORIENTATION
Act Authentically and Appropriately

Gaining a wise perspective—by shifting and broadening one's perspective—is the first step of attaining wise leadership. But unless this wise perspective is followed up with appropriate action, it becomes a missed opportunity. In our view, practical wisdom is always rooted in action. Metaphorically, wise leadership means taking off the colored glasses; experiencing the world as it is; and, based on what you see, identifying actions that are both an authentic expression of who you truly are and appropriate to others at the same time. Wise leaders are sensitive to the context they operate in and fine-tune their actions accordingly while continuing to serve their noble purpose. This balance of context sensitivity and groundedness is often tested by challenging events, as it was one spring day in 2011 for V. R. Ferose, managing director of SAP Labs India.

At five in the morning, Ferose woke up to a phone call from his human resources director, who informed him that one of their young employees had died unexpectedly. Ferose, shaken by the news, hurried to his office while reflecting on his own young life and the journey he had taken to reach the position of managing director.[1]

SAP Labs India, one of the fifteen global R&D labs of the German software giant SAP, is made up of two R&D centers—one located in Bangalore and one in Gurgaon. In 2008, Ferose took over the Gurgaon center as managing director when he was only thirty-three years old, making him the youngest managing director of a global multinational company in India. In April 2010, he was also put in charge of the Bangalore center. Among his many responsibilities, he had a clear mandate to boost employee morale at SAP Labs India, where employee turnover was running as high as 19 percent. SAP's senior management wanted Ferose to bring that attrition rate below 10 percent within two years.

Ferose had a long list of goals. Yet he felt it was important to take time to understand the culture of his company better by paying attention not only to what employees were saying but also why. He read all the posts on the Indian lab's internal blog, where disgruntled employees were making disparaging comments about SAP and its local management team. Then he reflected on the comments to identify the root cause of the discontent.

Ferose believed that SAP Labs India needed to shift gears and introduce new ways of engaging with employees who were feeling frustrated and dissatisfied with the work environment. For instance, there were no child care facilities for employees on campus, the process for expense reimbursement was long, and the list went on. Recognizing that he did not necessarily have smarter solutions to provide, Ferose invited about ten of the disgruntled employees, along with other interested employees, and encouraged them to find solutions that would work for them and for the company. Ferose got their managers to free up time for the group to work on solving their own problems.

With this support structure in place, employees organized themselves into teams of five to address the problems. One team developed a system to process expense reimbursement claims in less than twenty-four hours. Another team designed and set up a day care facility. Amazingly, these two high-priority projects were implemented within one week with a very limited budget, thanks to motivated employees who volunteered their time and found ways to implement these two projects quickly and cost-effectively. Then these empowered and engaged employees took on more projects. During Ferose's first year as managing director, employees at SAP Labs India successfully implemented an amazing fifty-two projects, and productivity and creativity shot up. Not surprisingly, Ferose felt he was on the right track.

On the morning when he heard the sad news about his young employee, Ferose wondered both what had happened and whether he could have done something to prevent it. By chance, two significant events were scheduled to take place at SAP Labs India that day. In the morning, a leading Indian business magazine that publishes an annual ranking of the best employers to work for was coming to interview some employees at SAP Labs India as part of the evaluation process (the ranking is highly regarded by Indian employees, and Ferose thought a high ranking would boost morale and help attract motivated future employees). Later that same day, the renowned Oscar-nominated film director Shekhar Kapoor was scheduled to deliver a talk as part of a monthly lecture series that Ferose had initiated to help broaden his tech-focused employees' perspective. The idea was to introduce them to the unique leadership styles of famous people in the arts, culture, sports, and politics. *But given the shocking news, should these events still take place?* Ferose wondered. Ferose needed to act both quickly and with delicacy.

Rather than worrying about what he could have done, he decided to focus on what he could do that day. First, he arranged for the parents of the deceased employee to be flown to Bangalore; he also personally offered moral support to members of that employee's work team, who were devastated. He sent a short, heartfelt e-mail to all lab employees informing them of the death. He also decided that the evaluation process by the business magazine must go on as planned, and he encouraged employees to be open and transparent in their interviews with the magazine representative. He also kept the film director's lecture on the schedule. Then Ferose retreated to his office and collapsed in a chair. He realized that he had made all these decisions spontaneously, but now that they were made, he started having doubts. He was in a pensive mood when he heard a gentle knock on the door.

A young man in his twenties with a warm smile was standing at the door. "I am Ramesh, and I want to let you know that I am proud of you," the man said. "I really like what you have done in the past year and feel that you really care about us. I know today is a difficult day for all of us. But I want to tell you that my colleagues and I are committed to this company as long as you are here."

Ramesh's genuine words lifted Ferose's feelings of doubt and, reflecting further, he reached a number of conclusions. He realized that his actions were consistent with his perspective of doing what is right for the employees and the company. Through his actions, he was trying to simultaneously address short-term priorities—shoring up employee morale against a strong blow—while also participating in the evaluation, which would bring long-term benefits. Ramesh's comments helped to confirm Ferose's belief that he was acting with authenticity and in a way that was appropriate for the challenging context of the day's events. He thanked Ramesh and went on to host the film director's lecture, which under the circumstances was recalibrated to be an uplifting and insightful talk on the link between creativity and spirituality.

With hindsight, it's clear that the way Ferose acted is grounded in sound management principles, if not sheer common sense. Still, his thoughtful actions conveyed leadership maturity despite his young age, and they were unusual because he used his intuition rather than following a policy manual or a strategy learned in a management training class.

When the annual ranking of best employers in India was published in 2011, SAP Labs India made it to the top five—with an impressive #4 ranking.[2] Under Ferose's leadership, employee motivation had improved significantly, with the India lab now ranking first in employee satisfaction among SAP's fifteen R&D

labs worldwide. In addition, the attrition rate dropped from 19 percent in 2009 to 10 percent in 2011 and is projected to be as low as 7 percent in 2012. By April 2012, two years after becoming managing director of whole SAP Labs India, Ferose was credited with the dramatic improvement in the company morale and overall productivity. In late 2012, in recognition of his significant achievements, Ferose was promoted to a larger role within SAP as the head of its globalization services organization.

AUTHENTICITY AND APPROPRIATE ACTION

Reflecting on the story of Ferose and that difficult day at SAP Labs India, we see a number of challenges that he addressed deftly by acting wisely. He needed to shift his perspective on several levels to determine the appropriate actions for dealing with the deceased employee's family and work team, as well as the right actions for SAP Labs India in both the short and long terms. Ferose needed to act authentically by remaining true to himself and leading appropriately in an entirely new context.

The dictionary definition of *authentic* is "not false; true to one's personality, spirit, or character." *Authenticity* means "the quality or condition of being trustworthy, genuine, credible."[3] In studying the lives of many authentic leaders, we have found Mahatma Gandhi to be an authentic leader who embodied his philosophy of frugality by leading an austere, near-monastic lifestyle. Steve Jobs was also authentic: he always followed his heart and acted according to his own intuition. Ford's CEO, Alan Mulally, is another authentic leader with whom what you see is what you get.

Today authenticity is touted as a virtue that leaders need to cultivate. While we agree with that, acting with authenticity alone isn't enough—and could sometimes even backfire—unless a leader also acts appropriately, that is, in a way that is suitable or fitting for a particular situation.[4] Steve Jobs was authentic, but his actions were not always appropriate. He denied giving stock options, for example, to his long-time friend Dan Kottke (and Mike Fernandez) who had worked on early versions of Apple computers in Jobs's garage (Jobs claimed Kottke was just an hourly employee).[5] Steve Wozniak, the other cofounder of Apple, was authentic as well as appropriate when he recognized the need to give stock to Kottke and Fernandez because they had contributed to Apple's early success. When Jobs refused to agree, Wozniak gave some of his own stock to Kottke and Fernandez.

Practical wisdom involves learning how to be appropriate—to both oneself and to others—in one's action without losing one's authenticity. Manu, one of the early thinkers of social law and customs in Indian philosophy, said that wise leadership is about having the discernment to know how to balance authenticity and appropriateness.[6] To put it plainly, there are times when you need to act in accordance with your nature (who you truly are) and times when you need to act against your nature when circumstances require it—for your own benefit as well as the larger good. But it is not just about acting in a way that is appropriate to oneself as much as it is about acting in a manner that is appropriate to others. Leaders must allow both the internal and external contexts to shape what is appropriate in their actions.

We know that many leaders don't act out of authenticity, let alone act appropriately, in that their actions are incongruent with who they are or with their noble purpose. In this chapter, we discuss how wise leaders can use their context sensitivity and discernment to maintain a balance between authenticity and appropriateness in their actions.

How do we become authentic, and where does authenticity come from? Finding one's source of authenticity can be tricky. In his book *Authentic Leadership*, former Medtronic CEO Bill George suggests that leaders can derive and demonstrate their authenticity by "being yourself—being the person you were created to be."[7] George believes that many leaders embody a leadership style that is either "fake" (because it is about keeping up appearances) or "borrowed" (because the leaders were trained in business school or by a mentor or coach to act and lead in a certain way). This lack of authenticity in leadership, George believes, compels many CEOs to take actions that make them look good and deliver personal gains, but fail to contribute to the organization's long-term sustainability. Self-deception is a major stumbling block to wisdom; it's a mental filter that limits our ability to be authentic and appropriate.[8]

In our experience, wise leaders are authentic when they emphasize character and substance over style. In this way, their actions are always aligned not only with what they are feeling; more important they are aligned with their being, their authentic self.

When Ferose became the managing director of SAP Labs India, he showed up on the first day at the office wearing jeans and a casual shirt. He blended in perfectly with the young workforce of SAP Labs India, whose average age is twenty-nine, and its laidback lifestyle and dress. Ferose recalls that some senior managers weren't amused and suggested that he live up to his title by wearing a suit and even growing a beard to hide his boyish features. Ferose was unfazed. "I wanted to act and lead like Ferose, not as someone else I can't recognize in the mirror," he explained. Except when meeting clients, Ferose has maintained his casual dress code (and kept his face clean shaven) and has extended his informal leadership style to major corporate events. At the annual employee meeting in 2011, Ferose and senior management scrapped the usual speeches and improvised a show in which they assumed the roles of Bollywood actors or self-deprecating political characters. At the end of the performance, they received a standing ovation from their delighted employees.

But acting with authenticity isn't enough to cultivate wise leadership. Rather, wise leaders know when and how to keep their authenticity in check and act appropriately whenever circumstances require it. For example, although Ferose dresses casually while in India, he does wear a suit and tie when he meets with senior management at SAP headquarters in the more formal business environment in Germany.

As you continue on your wise leadership journey, the next step after shifting your perspective and finding your noble purpose is to start aligning your new perspective with authentic and appropriate actions. Identifying your noble purpose is only the beginning. You must then act consistently in alignment with that noble purpose as well as on the insights and discoveries it brings.

AUTHENTIC AND APPROPRIATE ACTION IN THE AGE OF COMPLEXITY

Acting authentically and appropriately is vital in a world dominated by diversity, velocity, and interconnectivity. The fact is that no one can hide anymore. The tools of social media open all our actions to instant analysis and massive scrutiny. Any inauthentic or inappropriate action is quickly spotted and called out—or digitally chased—by customers or competitors. (And conversely, authentic and appropriate actions can gain an instant following with the viral impact of social media.) Keep this in mind as you consider your company's advertising and marketing budget. According to Forrester Research, 95 percent of consumers consider advertising messages to be disingenuous.[9] This information led Kevin Roberts, CEO of the global advertising agency Saatchi & Saatchi, to conclude that the days of pitching to customers are over. He believes that marketing leaders must learn to engage customers in a meaningful and authentic conversation.[10]

Yet it can be difficult for many leaders to be open and transparent with employees and customers, according to Charlene Li, author of *Open Leadership*, who explains that "leaders equate openness with vulnerability. They are indoctrinated in the C-suite that it's taboo to appear vulnerable. But in the eyes of your employees and customers, being vulnerable will make you look authentic—

not weak. Authenticity is priceless—but lack of genuineness can cost your job."[11]

In addition to acting authentically, leaders are facing pressure from customers and employees to act appropriately by looking well beyond maximizing shareholder value. The context in which leaders act is no longer limited to the boardroom: it increasingly extends to the entire organization and the broader world of public opinion and trust. Indeed, more than ever before, customers and employees want to engage with organizations that seek to serve a higher purpose and contribute to society rather than focusing entirely on keeping shareholders happy. A Burson-Marsteller survey found that more than 75 percent of consumers believe that social responsibility is an important factor in their purchase decisions, and 70 percent are willing to buy products at a premium from a socially responsible company that, among other things, strives to protect the environment.[12] "Consumers want a better world, not just widgets," Simon Mainwaring, author of *We First*, has pointed out.[13] Hence, it's vital for leaders to pay attention to the changing context and fine-tune their actions accordingly.

Acting authentically and appropriately means different things to different leaders, depending on whether they operate predominantly from the blue zone (functional smart) or the red zone (business smart). Leaders act very differently in different zones, and there are different reasons for why they do so.

THE LIMITS OF A SMART ACTION ORIENTATION

Many functional smart leaders are challenged to act authentically and appropriately because they generally focus more on doing things "the right way" rather than doing "what is right." Risk averse by nature, they prefer to play by the book by following predetermined processes or their own proven best practices. Such action orientation serves them well when the goal is to optimize the performance of an existing system or function—say, a sales department that has been selling the same products for the past twenty years.

But these leaders are at a loss when the external context changes and the playbook itself needs to be updated or even replaced. Due to their static notion of what is appropriate, they can't dynamically adapt their actions to reflect what is appropriate across different contexts. Also, because they are more focused on what is appropriate in the short term, like meeting the numbers in the following quarter, they may not address issues or pursue opportunities that are appropriate for their own or their organization's long-term success. Similarly, they struggle with authenticity: sometimes they may feel or intuitively know what is the right thing to do but can't muster courage to actually do it; instead, they revert to their habit of doing things in what they think is the "right way."

Business smart leaders tend to grapple with their own set of challenges when it comes to acting authentically and appropriately. Because they are impulsive by nature, their emotions—especially emotions that come up around their innate need to always feel successful—dictate how they choose to act rather than what is objectively appropriate in a particular situation. Intense and laser focused, they tend to do whatever it takes to get the job done and obtain what they want. But this end-justifies-all-means perspective could lead them to act inappropriately and even engage in questionable practices. Quick thinkers and actors, they can swiftly pick up changes in the external context and adjust their actions accordingly, but they may not bother communicating their abrupt course corrections to their teams or organizations, leaving them frustrated. Although they are authentic to themselves—by aligning their own actions with their perspectives—they may not always be genuine in expressing their true feelings and thoughts to others. They could be too proud to acknowledge the contribution their collaborators made to a project, let alone credit them for the project's success.

HOW WISE LEADERS ACT

While mulling their next moves, wise leaders are neither excessively cautious nor risky. They use their noble purpose as a touchstone to assess which risks are appropriate and think systemically. They pay attention to the larger context before taking action. They enjoy their work but don't lose themselves in their job; in other words, they never lose perspective while working. Wise leaders are not workaholics: they take time off from work to relax and enjoy their life with their families more often than leaders in the blue or red zones. Once a project is completed, they don't keep on thinking about it. Rather, they move on, knowing that they have done the best job they could. They measure their effectiveness based on their thoughtfulness and action orientation rather than the results. Similarly, when wise leaders set goals for themselves, they make sure those goals are aligned with their North Star (their noble purpose) and will help meet the promises that they have made to others instead of taking spontaneous actions or competing with others. When given a choice about the next project, they take time to reflect and identify one that creates maximum value for others and the organization instead of maximizing their own chances of success. Their logic for picking a task or a project revolves around learning and value creation to others instead of urgency or opportunity value for self.

In our research, we found that wise leaders balance the action orientations of leaders in the red and the blue zones—strategically oriented for the former and execution focused for the latter—by consistently demonstrating the six key attributes in their actions: alignment with a noble purpose, prudence, context sensitivity, maintaining equanimity and having fun, intuition, and integrity. Of these, we regard integrity—the congruence between your true being and your actions—as the most difficult to develop. Toward the end of the chapter, we elaborate on how to cultivate integrity, which is the cornerstone of authentic and appropriate action.

Align Actions with Noble Purpose

Many business smart leaders align their actions with a strategy or a vision, while functional smart leaders tend to align their actions with execution. But neither action orientation can entirely sustain your inspiration through complexity or challenge you to make bold moves and change the status quo in good times. Based on our work, we have found that wise leaders align their actions with a noble purpose, which confers authenticity and appropriateness.

Understanding changing consumer needs and industry trends, Indra Nooyi, chairman and CEO of PepsiCo, has aligned her actions around a noble purpose: creating value for all stakeholders. Central to PepsiCo's business strategy is what Nooyi and nearly 300,000 employees call "Performance with Purpose." It's the company's promise to provide a range of foods and beverages for local tastes and needs around the world; to find innovative ways to cut costs and minimize impact on the environment through energy and water conservation and reduction of water volume; to provide a great workplace for the company's employees; and to respect, support, and invest in local communities where the company operates. And the company is making great progress: making more nutritious products, becoming the first major U.S. food company to eliminate trans fats from cooking oils, leading water conservation programs in water-distressed areas, organizing massive recycling efforts, limiting their carbon footprint in operations, developing and training a diverse global workforce, and supporting local communities through the PepsiCo Foundation. Under Nooyi's leadership, PepsiCo is focused on multiple stakeholders and is showing how to do what's good for consumers and deliver returns to shareholders for the long term.

Act with Bold Prudence

While red zone leaders take too much risk since they like to explore all options, blue zone leaders take too little risk because they are too worried about failure. Wise leaders instead take calculated risks. Guided by their noble purpose rather than raw emotions, they act prudently. Rather than reacting in a knee-jerk fashion to external stimuli, they devise an appropriate response and act calmly and thoughtfully. They use discernment when making their judgment calls, especially when confronted with adverse circumstances, and they bounce back from failures with resilience. Ferose at SAP Labs India could have decided to cancel all corporate engagements when the young employee died. But he intuitively decided that a more prudent approach would be to allow the events to take place.

Although wise leaders are careful in their actions, they are not risk averse. In fact, some of their actions may in fact be bold. Take the case of James Parker, former CEO of Southwest Airlines. In the aftermath of the 9/11 terrorist attacks, as consumers stayed away and the industry contracted, many airlines started cutting jobs. Instead of following the trend, which he viewed as not being prudent, Parker took an intuitive and bold action: he announced that Southwest would keep all of its employees and initiated a $179.8 million profit-sharing program for them. Parker's counter-intuitive action was shaped by his belief that although a restructuring would yield short-term benefits, it would irremediably hurt the company's legendary trust with its employees.[14]

Act with Context Sensitivity

Both blue zone and red zone leaders tend to indiscriminately apply the same success formula regardless of the context in which they operate, which can lead to ineffective action and sometimes catastrophic consequences. Wise leaders use discernment to adapt their actions to different contexts.

Ramón Mendiola Sánchez is the CEO of Florida Ice & Farm Co., a leading food and beverage company in Costa Rica.[15] In the mid-2000s, he recognized that his industry context was shifting: customers wanted manufacturers to adhere to environmentally sustainable business practices. Meanwhile, the Costa Rican government wanted to impose some regulations on manufacturers to make their supply chains sustainable.

Heeding the shift in the industry context, Mendiola decided to enshrine sustainability in his firm's core business model. He recognized that the triple-bottom-line approach of striving to add value simultaneously to shareholders, society, and the environment was the best course of action for his organization.[16] As a result, he implemented a set of key performance indicators (KPIs) that measure how well the company is improving its triple bottom line. As an incentive, Mendiola tied these KPIs to senior management compensation: 50 percent or more of their pay is linked to their meeting or exceeding the KPI goals (65 percent of his own compensation is linked to achieving these goals). Adherence to these KPIs helped shift the perspective of all Florida Ice & Farm employees, from senior executives to factory workers and delivery truck drivers. They realized how everything they did had a broader social and environmental impact. That awareness led each employee to find innovative ways to achieve a sustainable supply chain, like reducing water use or solid waste.

The highly motivated employees also encouraged suppliers and distributors to adopt ecofriendly practices to reduce the carbon footprint and save water. This increased awareness and support among all members of Florida Ice & Farm's extended value chain helped the company dramatically cut water use from 12 liters to 4.7 liters per beverage and increase productivity. Its operating income grew at a compound annual growth rate of 6 percent from 2008 through 2011, to a total of $140 million. This contributed to a compound annual growth rate of 25 percent between 2006 and 2010, twice the industry average. In 2012, Florida Ice & Farm became "water neutral": it returns every drop of water it uses to the community through conservation and provides clean water to communities in Costa Rica.[17] As Mendiola notes, "Rather than optimizing our performance for short-term gains we started managing our business for long-term value. In doing so, we successfully eliminated the trade-off between sustainability and profitability."[18]

Maintain Equanimity—and Have Fun

Many business smart leaders work hard to produce results and can have a difficult time enjoying their work. They tend to focus more on the results than the effort itself. Because of their attachment to outcome, they can be overwhelmed by emotions. Functional smart leaders in general focus on execution, and as long as they don't have to pay attention to the big picture, they feel that there are few emotional entanglements. They tend to experience work and play differently and don't generally mix them.

Wise leaders both enjoy what they do and maintain their perspective. They avoid the trap of an emotional roller coaster, remain poised, and maintain equanimity. For instance, whenever we met Ford's CEO Alan Mulally, we always found him to be cheerful, energetic, and level-headed.[19] He was always well prepared for meetings and rarely allowed interruptions, and he always appeared to be in a good mood—even in the midst of what most leaders would consider as stressful circumstances. He peppered our meetings with him with self-deprecating jokes. Humor is an essential part of his presentations, and he tends to extemporize even when giving public speeches. For example, when Mulally was invited to give a formal talk to students at Stanford Business School, he opted instead to engage students in a lively case discussion about Ford.[20]

Heed Intuition

Once you internalize your noble purpose, you no longer crave validation because your self-esteem is not dependent on outside sources, and that reflects in your actions. You intuitively do the right thing and don't care how others judge you. For instance, Steve Jobs was so aligned with his noble purpose that he often disregarded the opinions of investors, analysts, the media, and even customers—anyone, for that matter, who tried to judge or question his bold actions. Jobs always followed his intuition.

We think that intuition is not the same as either instinct or vision, though many people don't seem to see the difference between instinct and intuition.[21] When we operate in the blue zone, we tend to rely on our instinct: it gives us signals and guides our decisions based on our accumulated experiences, both good and bad. When we are in the red zone, we can envision the future and act according to our vision. Wise leaders, however, do not operate out of either their instinct or their vision. They are guided by their intuition, which is facilitated by mindfulness: the ability to fully experience the present moment with total awareness and without judgment.[22] Hence, their intuition is anchored fully to the present moment even though it may be influenced by past instincts and visions of the future.

Act with Integrity

Integrity relates to completeness or wholeness. The Sanskrit expression for integrity—*trikarana suddhi*—denotes the alignment of our words, actions, thoughts, and feelings. We would add an element to this definition: the alignment between who we are— that is, our essence or being—and what we do.[23] A leader with integrity stands out in the crowd and has character. Integrity helps to differentiate one person from another with similar backgrounds, experiences, and competencies. A leader who does not act with integrity appears inauthentic and can lose the trust of employees and shareholders.

We have observed a lack of integrity in many leaders whose actions are not aligned with their thoughts or feelings, let alone with their essence. In contrast, wise leaders tend to rely on an innate moral compass to guide their actions. Hence, their actions are infused with a high degree of integrity. Mahatma Gandhi, who ended British colonial rule in India and guided the country toward independence, was advised by many people on what actions to take. As a wise leader, he listened to them and reflected on what they said, but ultimately he let his inner voice or intuition determine what actions would be appropriate. For example, when Gandhi returned to India from South Africa in the early 1900s, the Indian National Congress, India's oldest political party, was merely seeking home rule. But after traveling across the country to observe the living conditions of ordinary people, Gandhi believed that only total independence from the British would enable India to progress as a nation. Gandhi spoke and acted in alignment with his noble purpose and his observations and reflections, and he persisted for many years: India became an independent country in 1947.

BRIDGING THE INTEGRITY GAP

Many leaders in business or politics have integrity issues. Just read the news: they break promises, suppress their true feelings, and don't have the courage of their convictions. There is a misalignment of their words, feelings, their authentic self, and their actions. They are perceived as being inauthentic, and their actions are often judged as inappropriate. Becoming a wise leader entails cultivating self-awareness by minding the integrity gap and then bridging it. In doing so, you will improve your credibility, commitment, and courage.[24]

Credibility: Bridging the Saying-Doing Gap

A credibility gap emerges when what you say is misaligned with what you do. For example, most organizations have articulated a vision, values, and objectives, and often they prominently display these principles in their offices. But in fact, leaders don't always follow them. The resulting problem is that the leaders and their company lose credibility, and nobody will listen to a leader who lacks credibility. As Doug Conant, former CEO of Campbell Soup Company and coauthor of the best seller *TouchPoints*, explains: "A company's vision is not just a nice statement you post on the wall. It needs to be a living thing: all employees must understand how that vision connects to their job. It is a leader's responsibility to help make that connection explicit—they need to lead by example."[25]

We once consulted with a senior executive in a large high-tech firm in Silicon Valley who promoted teamwork through all his messages but was unable to nurture a collaborative team spirit. When we interviewed team members, they told us that the executive uses every opportunity to put down his peers. As a result, his subordinates emulated his actions rather than his words, leading to an absence of collaborative spirit despite the executive's lofty messages.

Remember that your words are important. They might sound like mere words to you, but to others, they are promises. To bridge the gap between what we say and what we do—to be credible—we must always be aware and conscious of what we are saying and the context of our words. And if we fail to follow through on promises, we must learn to seek forgiveness, because our credibility is at stake.

Before speaking, keep the following in mind:

- Is what I am about to say aligned with what I want to do?
- Does it imply a promise that cannot be fulfilled?
- How could I articulate my ideas and concerns in a way that doesn't give someone a false expectation?
- When I make a promise, what is an effective way to see it through?

Commitment: Bridging the Feeling-Doing Gap

A commitment gap arises when what we say or do is not aligned with what we truly feel. People hesitate to share their true feelings and thoughts. If we perceive that a team member is not doing a good job and spending more time focusing on his personal projects at work, we have three choices: let the person know it is unacceptable, complain to the project leader behind the back of the person, or keep quiet and take up the extra load but resent it. Many functional smart leaders tend to keep quiet and become resentful, while some business smart leaders are quick to complain and bluntly let the person know it is unacceptable—often in an unclear and emotional tone that prevents the person from hearing the content of the message.

When we don't give honest feedback to our coworkers because we feel uncomfortable doing so, nobody experiences growth. Interestingly, our commitment in this case is to "look good" by avoiding giving honest feedback but not necessarily to "feel good" by helping others grow. Authentic and appropriate commitment helps a relationship blossom. Without it, relationships fade.

We recently attended a board meeting of a large company and were amazed to see how various executives agreed to the requests of others without any commitment to keep them—as we inferred from the conversations we overheard during the coffee break. These people suggested that the CEO did not track promises that were made but instead would track people who challenged him or disagreed with him in the meeting. Over time, executives in this company learned that a polite "yes, I agree" was the best answer to give when the boss asked for their opinion. When they were asked to make bigger commitments to sales, cost cutting, or quality, they made unrealistic promises just to please their boss, knowing there would be no serious penalty for missing those deadlines. When we later challenged their CEO in private and raised questions about accountability, he fired us as his consultants.

When senior leaders in your organization are not interested in honest feedback but rather reward sycophancy, as in the example, you have two options: speak up and tell the emperor he has no clothes or toe the line. In this situation, being authentic is about mustering the courage to tell your superiors what you truly think about their plans, decisions, or actions. Don't confuse commitment with allegiance: your commitment is to the larger organization and its growth rather than to individual leaders and their personal success.

To bridge the gap between feeling and doing—to act with commitment—we often have to choose carefully when, where, and how to communicate our authentic feelings to others. Disagreeing without making a scene or becoming disagreeable is an art worth learning. Try to separate the person from his or her actions and communicate that there is a conflict with the action but not with the person (this can be especially challenging for many business smart leaders to say and hear). This will keep your criticism from being experienced as a personal attack. Ask yourself these questions to help identify and overcome a commitment gap:

- In which relationships do I have the biggest commitment gaps?
- Why don't I express my thoughts and feelings in that relationship?
- What is the worst that can happen if I share my concerns?
- What is the best that can happen if this other person understands and appreciates my feelings and thoughts about him or her?

Courage: Bridging the Being-Doing Gap

The courage gap is the disconnect between who we are and what we do. Here, "who we are" represents our true personality and our real identity—our unique being. Sometimes others perceive and appreciate this uniqueness, but we often don't see that. Rather, we suppress this uniqueness in order to gain approval or to fit in with the group. It takes courage to be different and raise issues that may be sensitive to others.

John Mackey, co-CEO of Whole Foods Market, has always known who he truly is and has dared follow his wildest dreams no matter what others say, as when he opened his first market with forty-five thousand dollars simply to satisfy his own passion for healthy foods and healthy lifestyles.[26] Mackey credits that courage to several formative experiences in his youth. For instance, when he was nineteen, he dropped out of the University of Texas in Austin and decided to hitchhike to New York City. His parents were upset about his decision. The day he was about to leave the house, his mother tried to dissuade him: "If you walk out of that door, you can never come back into my house." Mackey replied to her: "If this is how you think about me and our relationship, then I would rather not stay here any longer." And he left. That day, Mackey says, he was true to himself and his destiny: "I found the courage to forgo the security of my family in pursuit of my dreams. I was liberated by going forward rather than staying back. From that point on, I began acting to meet my own expectations rather than others'."

In our experience, the courage gap is the one that most leaders pay the least attention to, and yet when it is bridged, it can yield the biggest payoff. Self-deception or lack of self-awareness, or both, generally prevent leaders from discovering their deeper desires and intentions. According to Ken Anbender, a clinical psychologist and CEO of Contegrity, a leadership development consultancy, three factors—projection, protection, and abject fear—get in the way of discovering the kernel of integrity that is authentic to us. To find the courage to follow your authentic self, consider these questions:

- What have I given up for my current job or relationship?
- Have I been ignoring my passions just to make money or be successful?
- How do I find the courage to follow my dreams?
- Am I supporting others to pursue their own passions?

CONCLUSION

In chapter 2, we explored how leaders can discover their North Star—the noble purpose that provides an ethical compass to guide our actions. Finding your North Star, however, is only the first step in the path toward wise leadership. The next step is to systematically align your actions with that North Star. Otherwise, you may act authentically—being true to yourself by acting too much out of self-interest and in the process demotivating others around you—or try to act appropriately in a context-sensitive manner—pleasing others or filling a perceived role that is either fake or borrowed and in the process sacrificing your own authenticity.

Smart leaders struggle to act both authentically and appropriately at the same time. Leaders who tend to operate in the blue zone generally act with prudence by following a textbook approach to ensure that their actions are appropriately aligned with established norms and prescribed best practices. They may repress their authentic feelings in order to get the job done according to what others (e.g., their superiors) believe is the right thing to do. Hence, they may struggle to make rapid course correction or take bold actions that will compel them to step out of existing boundaries—even if their intuition tells them that's the most appropriate thing to do. Leaders operating in the red zone are bold and quick in their actions: they can spot the changing external context and rapidly adapt their actions. But given their potential intensity and tendency to be self-centered, they can become reckless and undertake inappropriate actions that could hurt their credibility in the long term.

Wise leaders strive to simultaneously act with authenticity while also taking appropriate actions that serve a larger purpose and to act with both prudence and courage while paying attention to the changing context. They tend not to get so caught up in their work that they cannot maintain equanimity and act with poise even in highly stressful circumstances. They heed their intuition and demonstrate great integrity by aligning their actions with their true words, feelings, and authentic selves.

Integrity is the cornerstone of wise leadership. You can cultivate it by working to bridge three gaps: credibility, commitment, and courage.

Wise leaders are consistently thoughtful in how they act. In the next chapter, we will see how they are also thoughtful in choosing the correct roles to assume. The idea of roles may seem to go against what we've been saying in this chapter about authenticity and integrity, but it is not. Instead, it is a facet of authenticity that acknowledges that "leader" (for example) is a role that is not the same as a person's identity. Indian philosophy identifies a state of detached engagement wherein one is fully engaged in an action while recognizing that one is merely playing a role; this awareness allows one to stay detached from the action in terms of emotion even while choosing to fully engage in terms of the action. Being conscious in picking your role and performing that role with detached engagement is the topic of the next chapter.

CHAPTER FOUR

GAIN ROLE CLARITY
Lead from Any Position

R ole clarity is the capability to perform a chosen role convincingly and with enthusiasm, and without losing sense of who you are behind your role. Think of an actor who in one movie is the romantic hero and a villain in the next. A leader with role clarity can step in and out of different roles in different contexts with ease and be fully engaged in any one of them, knowing that it is just a role. With role clarity, there is equanimity and clarity in crisis situations and a lack of emotional attachment—that is, you are able to experience your emotions without judging or getting attached to them.

As an example, Raj, the start-up CEO introduced in chapter 2 who was consumed by his job, was emotionally attached to the role of the start-up CEO: he was very successful in that role and valued it highly. Once he gained role clarity, however, he recognized the real value of his family roles, and his unconscious judgment that one role is better than the other disappeared. He also realized that ultimately he was more than his roles—he was first and foremost a human being—and that shift in perspective led to his sense of equanimity and happiness.

In a business context, role clarity means knowing that your role as leader is just that: a role. Today you are a director in one company, next you could be a vice president in another company, and a year later, you could be an entrepreneur—and these are merely roles you play to contribute to your organization and to yourself. Business smart and functional smart leaders tend to attach a meaning and judgment to their role—and those of others—by, for example, viewing an entrepreneurial role as being more exciting than a corporate executive role or a vice president position being more prestigious than a director title. This is because smart leaders view roles through the red or blue lenses they wear. As long as they wear these filters, they risk mistaking their role as their identity, and in doing so, they lose their perspective and act without authenticity and appropriateness. When you remove your filters, you gain role clarity, and recognize that you have the choice to step out of that role whenever you want. You will put your ego aside and begin to pay less attention to your own title and perks and more attention to the needs of others in the organization. You will even recognize that it is your role or your title that confers your power and responsibility, and when you play that role, you inherit them only temporarily. Wise leaders are able to remove their blue or red filters and enthusiastically assume the most appropriate role that they need to play to get the job done—and they do this without emotionally getting caught up in that role. In other words, leading from any position means sometimes being a leader who serves others as a servant leader.

In fact, role clarity as we define it in this book is closely related to both the concept of servant leadership popularized by Robert Greenleaf and the stewardship concept of Peter Block.[1] The concept of servant leadership itself has ancient roots not only in Western culture, particularly in Christian spirituality, but also in the Eastern traditions. Chanakya, an Indian philosopher and royal advisor in the fourth century B.C.E., wrote in his book *Artha-shastra*, "The king shall consider as good, not what pleases himself but what pleases his subjects. The king is a paid servant and enjoys the resources of the state together with the people."[2]

As a wise leader, you take full responsibility for the leadership role but don't let your ego or personal needs or emotions get in the way. These factors still exist, but when you are within the leadership role, you don't let them take over. You are open to either leading from the front or playing a supporting role to let others shine. And when the time is right, you willingly relinquish your role.

Some leaders in the red zone have difficulty executing their role with emotional detachment. A good example of such a leader is Bob Diamond, who in July 2012 stepped down as CEO of British banking giant Barclays after the British government fined the bank £290 million ($452 million) for manipulating between 2005 and 2009 a key interest rate, the London interbank offered rate (LIBOR), which serves as a benchmark for global borrowing.[3] David Cameron, the British prime minister, ordered a parliamentary inquiry after the financial scandal raised serious questions about the integrity of the entire banking system. The government also wanted to know who was responsible and who would take accountability for damaging Britain's financial sector.[4]

Diamond, who led Barclays to grow at a faster pace by deepening the bank's presence in investment banking and the bonds market, was known for having instilled an "extraordinarily competitive and aggressive atmosphere" at Barclays since he joined the bank in 1996.[5] He had been a member of the executive committee of the bank since 1997. In 2008, he led the Barclays team that acquired the U.S. securities business of Lehman Brothers— the financial services giant that filed for bankruptcy in 2008—a move that beefed up Barclays' investment banking business. At that time, Diamond was reporting to the CEO of Barclays, John Varley. It was an e-mail that Diamond sent to Varley, which was copied to Jerry del Missier, Diamond's lieutenant at the time, that sparked the whole LIBOR issue. Del Missier misconstrued Diamond's comments, interpreting them as an official request to manipulate the LIBOR rates and instructed traders working for him to do exactly that. Although he authored that fateful e-mail,

Diamond initially denied any wrongdoing in the LIBOR scandal. But then, in an open letter to Andrew Tyrie, a Conservative member of the British Parliament, Diamond condemned the inappropriate behavior of "a small number" of Barclays employees who had allegedly tried to benefit personally from the manipulation. According to Diamond, "The authorities found no evidence that anyone more senior than the immediate desk supervisors was aware of the requests by traders, at the time that they were made."[6]

Not surprisingly, this statement did not end the firestorm engulfing the venerable British bank. Diamond was eventually forced out amid finger pointing and charges that the bank CEO was either complicit in the scandal or incompetent—since, after all, it was Diamond's e-mail memo (in which del Missier was copied) that led del Missier to ask his traders to misreport the LIBOR rate. The Barclays story is still unfolding, and investigations are continuing. In late October 2012, a high court judge ordered Barclays to face trial over damages caused by the LIBOR manipulation. The case is a first of its kind to be heard in a British court.[7] The lesson here is that when the leader at the top refuses to take responsibility for his or her own actions or errors, subordinates at every level in the chain of the hierarchy lose direction. Then when something goes wrong, nobody in authority holds himself or herself accountable and everybody suffers in the end, as we saw in the Barclays case.

Diamond appeared to be more upset about his reputation being tarnished by the scandal than about the fallout on the bank employees and investors, according to a CBS News report.[8] Diamond turned defensive when some British politicians accused him of a lack of candor and accountability, saying that those negative comments "have had a terribly unfair impact on my reputation, which is of paramount concern to me." And though his actions were hurting rather than helping the bank's recovery, Diamond did not give up his role easily. In fact, he was forced out.

Let us examine the Barclays case from a functional smart leadership perspective. Functional smart leaders sometimes give up their role too easily—or become disengaged too quickly—without thinking through the implications. Jerry del Missier, who was Diamond's lieutenant for a long time, was appointed chief operating officer in June 2012 in the middle of the investigation. As the LIBOR scandal unfolded, Barclays singled out del Missier as the key executive who was responsible for ordering false reports of borrowing costs in 2008.

In July 2012, Diamond told a British parliamentary committee that on October 29, 2008, he sent a memo to John Varley, CEO at the time, about a phone conversation he had just had with Paul Tucker, the deputy governor of the Bank of England. Tucker is supposed to have said (apparently falsely) that other banks were quoting lower rates than Barclays, and that created an appearance that Barclays had trouble borrowing money. According to Diamond, del Missier, who was copied on the e-mail Diamond sent to Varley, misunderstood this memo as an order from the Bank of England to make the rates different, and passed it on to brokers who in turn falsified the LIBOR rates. Del Missier resigned from Barclays the same day Diamond left.

Diamond's red zone personality was brash, whereas del Missier was low key, quiet, and unassuming.[9] Del Missier apparently operated in the blue zone in that he simply followed his boss's instructions without raising questions about them. According to his testimony, he was instructed by Diamond to cut LIBOR rates and he did.[10] He felt his role was to be an executor for Diamond's directives—and not, apparently, a leader responsible for the well-being of his bank. His lack of role clarity could have stemmed from an allegiance to Diamond. Del Missier applied for a job at Barclays in 1987 and was sent a rejection letter. After two more jobs, he caught the eye of Diamond and joined Barclays in 1997. He hung the rejection letter framed on his wall because it was a reminder of "persevering through life's challenges."[11]

Leaders stuck in the blue zone might find it difficult to engage actively with their appropriate role, and when a crisis hits, they tend to disengage quickly and recede into the background. This is as harmful to their organizations as the actions of red zone leaders who identify themselves with their role so much that they can't separate themselves emotionally from it. Wise leaders know when to lead and when to let others do so—and they never get caught up in any role they choose to assume, as we see next in the case of N. R. Narayana Murthy of Infosys.

Murthy, cofounder of the Indian software service provider Infosys, is a widely admired business leader in India. He is in fact an exemplary wise leader in his actions and words. Murthy believes that leaders must put the priorities of their team members, customers, and employees ahead of their own and serve them with humility as servant leaders. He also believes that leaders are part of a bigger society and have responsibilities that extend beyond their day-to-day role in their organization to serve a larger purpose. Murthy demonstrated this role clarity and commitment to the concept of a noble purpose throughout his own career.

While working in France in the early 1970s, Murthy was strongly influenced by principles of socialism.[12] While he was visiting communist Bulgaria on vacation, he was arrested for having talked to a girl in French. He was locked up without food and water for ninety-six hours and charged with espionage. Bulgarian authorities told him later that he was released because he was from India, which was considered a friendly country. Murthy shuddered to think what would have happened to him if he had not been from a friendly country. That incident disillusioned him with communism as a political system, although the socialist economic principle of sharing one's wealth with society continued to resonate with him. Realizing that he was "a capitalist in mind, [but] a socialist at heart," he went on to start Infosys in 1981, describing his company as an "experiment in entrepreneurship to create wealth legally."[13] It was Murthy's socialist belief in the distribution of wealth that made Infosys one of the first

Indian companies to offer employees stock-option plans and helped create thousands of millionaires when Infosys went public in 1991.

Over the years, Murthy diligently groomed and mentored future leaders at Infosys. He was also known for delegating power and giving credit to others whenever appropriate. Rather than clinging to his CEO role, he voluntarily stepped down from his position in 2002 (when he turned fifty-six years old) and became Infosys's chairman, a role that he relinquished in 2011 when he turned sixty-five. Since 2002, Infosys has had an orderly transition of power at the CEO level.

Despite being a billionaire, Murthy maintains a frugal lifestyle: he has lived in the same two-bedroom house in Bangalore for decades. Murthy and his Infosys cofounders walk or use scooters for short distances instead of cars. They take short showers to save water. After a number of kidnappings of prominent businessmen in India, the police top brass who manage security in India offered Murthy protection, but he declined, saying he didn't want to annoy his neighbors and block traffic. He has given away tens of millions of dollars to charities, which is in line with his concept of "compassionate capitalism."[14]

When Infosys became the first software company in India in 1999 to receive the highest level of capability maturity model (CMM level 5) certification from Carnegie Mellon University, Murthy did something unusual: he decided to share the company's experience of the certification process with all its Indian competitors.[15] Murthy believed that by helping his rivals receive certification at the same level, the entire Indian information technology (IT) services sector would become globally competitive and attract more investments from multinationals, and that in turn would also benefit Infosys. It was clear to Murthy that letting other Indian companies excel would lead Western companies to pay attention to India—a country that in the 1990s hadn't yet made its mark in the global IT outsourcing sector—and by so doing would help increase the overall Indian market share and not just Infosys. India is now a prominent player in the global IT market.

Although he cofounded Infosys, Murthy led his company as if he were a trustee—an individual who holds or manages assets for the benefit of Infosys customers, partners, employees, and shareholders. Recognizing that the role of trustee is that of a short-lived caretaker, Infosys has given away stock options worth $10 billion to employees. "Every Indian employee at all levels of the company joined on or before March 2010 is a stock holder of Infosys," Murthy wrote in the company's annual report for 2010–2011. With these steps, he has helped over two thousand Infosys employees become millionaires.

Wise leaders like Murthy are willing to cede their power voluntarily. They are not caught up in their role and the power that usually comes with that position. Seeing himself as a trustee, Murthy had no qualms about letting go of his position and in fact saw it as part of his duty to ensure a smooth and well-considered transition. Kris Gopalakrishnan, another cofounder and current cochairman of Infosys, told us that when Murthy was CEO, all of his senior executives had an equal voice.[16] Murthy encouraged debate and listened to multiple perspectives before making a decision. When he was chairman, he might argue with the CEO about a decision, but he enthusiastically supported whatever decision the CEO made in the end. Murthy felt that as a senior steward of the organization, he should fully support others in leadership roles. He consistently demonstrated simplicity and humility by maintaining a low profile without letting money and success go to his head. He also knew how to play a larger role in his industry and in Indian society.

We regard Murthy as a wise leader because he has demonstrated all six capabilities of wise leadership discussed in this book. In particular, he has demonstrated remarkable role clarity throughout his career and used that clarity to make wise decisions and actions.

THE LIMITS OF SMART LEADERSHIP ROLES

The level of enthusiasm and willingness of leaders to play different roles in different contexts depends on whether they operate from the blue or red zone. Leaders perform their role in very different emotional states and with very different expectations in each zone. Reflect on the zone in which you most often find yourself, and keep this in mind as you read the rest of the chapter so that you get personal clarity on what you could do to lead more from the front or more from behind—and do so without emotional attachment.

Leaders operating in the blue zone are generally challenged in the area of role clarity because they like to lead within their domain of control and leave bigger philosophical or ethical questions that cut across domains to their superiors. In other words, they focus on the "what" and "how" of their role rather than worrying about the "why." For instance, at Barclays, when del Missier saw the note from Diamond about lowering LIBOR rates, he simply followed it without questioning—even though what he was doing was probably unethical and potentially illegal.

In addition, blue zone leaders tend to leave their personal emotions aside in favor of focusing on getting the job done and producing results. For example, when Tim Cook was chief operating officer of Apple, he focused primarily on boosting his company's operational efficiencies and overlooked the poor working conditions of factory workers at Apple's Chinese subcontractors. Only after he became CEO did he pay attention to the ethical concerns raised by the media about Apple's supply chain. Cook went to China to inspect his subcontractor's factories and then had Apple join the Fair Labor Association. Moreover, leaders in the blue zone tend to stick to the same role because over time they get proficient at it and feel comfortable to the point where they become reluctant to take on additional roles. They may even lose their identity in the process.

Leaders in the red zone often struggle with role clarity because their pride gets attached to the role they are playing. But unlike blue zone leaders, they still have a strong sense of ego boundaries and retain their identity even when they are fully immersed in a role. Also, their attachment to certain ego-based outcomes makes it difficult for them to give up the role and perks associated with a particular role. Bob Diamond, who is said to have ruled Barclays in an imperious way, was paid £30 million in salary in 2011. As the LIBOR scandal broke, a defiant Diamond refused to quit his CEO role. Eventually he was forced to resign under pressure from the British government, but then Barclays offered him a £20 million severance package. The resulting public outcry led him to forgo £20 million of that package and settle for £2 million.[17]

Furthermore, business smart leaders tend to believe that the end justifies all means: when they are performing a role, ethical and legal concerns take a back seat to what needs to be done to produce the desired outcome. Nearly a quarter of all Wall Street executives believe that "wrongdoing at the work place is key to success."[18] Even if red zone leaders have some doubts about the ethical basis of their planned action, they tend to override their inner voice, as Harvard Business School professor Clayton Christensen explains: "Unconsciously, we often employ the marginal cost doctrine in our personal lives when we choose between right and wrong. A voice in our head says, 'Look, I know that as a general rule, most people shouldn't do this. But in this particular extenuating circumstance, just this once, it's ok.' The marginal cost of doing something wrong 'just this once' always seems alluringly low."[19]

Interestingly, in our research as well as consulting experience, we found that some leaders—those who operate sometimes from the red zone and other times from the blue—can display two different levels of engagement depending on what zone they are operating from. When they are in the red zone, they play their role with passionate attachment, and when they are in the blue zone, they can become disengaged from their role.

HOW WISE LEADERS DEMONSTRATE ROLE CLARITY

Wise leaders perform whatever role they take on without emotional attachment—assuming that role with what one might call detached engagement. They have no qualms giving up their existing role when circumstances require it. Kiran Mazumdar Shaw, the CEO of Biocon, a leading Indian biotech firm, is a good example. She has dedicated her life to finding a cure for diabetes. She invested many years and millions of R&D dollars in developing an oral insulin solution that might have been a breakthrough in the field of diabetes care. But when some of the clinical trials failed to validate the effectiveness of the oral insulin solution, Shaw was willing to reevaluate the whole R&D project without any emotional drama, including the possibility of terminating the project if the clinical data did not justify continuing the research efforts.[20] Although she was willing to give up her role leading the oral insulin project if the clinical data so indicated, she remained committed to her purpose: to find an affordable cure for diabetes.

Wise leaders are able to consistently demonstrate role clarity in that they lead with enthusiasm and clarity from the front or, conversely, they mentor others in the leadership position to succeed, taking a supporting role with the same enthusiasm and clarity. Many wise leaders seem to feel that each role they play has an opportunity for leadership—to be a traditional leader or a servant leader.

Because wise leaders have no role confusion between what needs to get done and who is best at carrying out that role, they act as trustees or servant leaders in whatever actions and roles they accept. As we mentioned earlier, N. R. Narayana Murthy, cofounder of Infosys, stepped down as CEO when he turned fifty-six years old and relinquished his chairman role when he turned sixty-five because he wanted to give others a chance to lead the company. Murthy then assumed many other professional roles, including government advisor, board member, philanthropist, investor, and mentor to young entrepreneurs in his career, and in each role, he exhibited integrity and thoughtfulness with a strong commitment to serve. Many people who interacted with him across these roles, as well as in private, have told us how amazed they were by the consistency of his character and commitment to contribution. They describe his warmth, empathy, and lack of ego, echoing our own impressions of him.

Acting as a steward or a servant leader is one of the most difficult roles to play for leaders who tend to operate in the red zone because they know they have great influence and power in swaying others and it feels good and appropriate to do so. To allow others to make their own mistakes and help them without any judgment, and to learn from their mistakes and guide them with empathy and compassion to discover their own genius, requires red zone leaders to let go of their ego. Peter Block, the author of *Stewardship* and a consultant on leadership to many large organizations, gave us advice a few years ago as we prepared to host a large international conference at the Indian School of Business in Hyderabad, India. "You might be the convener and think that participants and speakers are coming for your conference," he told us. "But it is actually their conference and you have been given the privilege to convene. Remember that your job is to serve them and make this experience the best they had, and when you do that *well*, then you have done your duty."[21]

Wise leaders are great team players: they seek partnerships and collaborate with others instead of wanting all the glory and rewards that go with a leadership position. They recognize that leadership is primarily a stewardship role that consists of developing others and producing value through others. There are times when one does not have to let go of power but can share it with others or collaborate with others, as wise leaders seem willing to do to serve a larger purpose. Guided by their noble purpose rather than their ego, wise leaders strive to create a sense of shared ownership and common purpose across their span of control.

President Abraham Lincoln famously appointed four of his political rivals to his cabinet (three of them had previously run against Lincoln in the 1860 election). Historians point out that he didn't mind giving them major roles in his government because he felt the country needed a government with a well-rounded perspective. Throughout his professional career as a lawyer, Lincoln had cultivated and maintained cordial relationships with his rivals: he believed that by staying engaged with those with opposing perspectives, he could hone the logic of his positions and better defend them. When he ran for president, he staffed his campaign team primarily with his legal rivals, who helped craft his strategy for nomination and election.[22] President Obama did the same by appointing former senator Hillary Clinton, his rival for the Democratic nomination in the 2008 U.S. presidential elections, as secretary of State. He also asked Secretary of Defense Robert Gates from the previous Republican administration to retain that role.

In addition, wise leaders are discerning about the role they want to play and have the self-awareness to know which roles they are fully qualified to assume and which ones are better taken by others. Legendary investor Warren Buffett, for example, realized that great investors don't necessarily make great philanthropists. Rather than setting up his foundation and running it himself, he instead chose to donate tens of billions of dollars of his personal fortune to the Bill & Melinda Gates Foundation to be used for charitable work (he pledged to donate 99 percent of his wealth to the foundation).

Moreover, wise leaders infuse their role with enthusiasm and authenticity. Whatever role they choose to perform, they project their authentic self—the true essence of their being—through that role and show genuine enthusiasm and determination to get the best job done. In artistic terms, wise leaders bring credibility to their professional role by projecting their personal charisma and energy. The celebrated actor Robert De Niro brings his movie roles to life by disappearing into the character. Commenting on

De Niro's performance as a restless young hoodlum in the film *Mean Streets*, the British film critic David Thomson noted: "It looked as if a rogue had come in off the streets." De Niro is known for extensively and meticulously studying his scripted characters before playing them, and yet when he performs in front of the camera, he taps into his innate creative talent—and his signature intensity—to bring these characters to life by infusing them with his own genuine self. "When De Niro walks on the set, you can feel his presence, but he never behaves like a movie star, just an actor. And when he acts, his sheer concentration permeates the whole set," noted director Alan Parker.[23]

ROLE CLARITY AND BECOMING A WISE LEADER

Everybody seeks a role model who represents the idealized embodiment of a particular role one wishes to play. Self-help business books are filled with recipes for success to make you the best leader in your field. Others teach you how to be the best chef or the best parent. Yet it's a futile exercise to attempt to be someone you are not. As long as you keep trying to become your role model, someone will always be ahead of you. Instead of imitating people you look up to, strive to develop your own practices rather than following others' so-called best practices, so that you might end up as a role model to others one day. In other words, if you work on becoming a smarter leader, you can imitate others and perform better by their standards, but if you focus on becoming a wiser leader, you create your own playbook and lead by your own standards. In doing so, you will perform with better role clarity, since your authenticity will shine through your actions.

Several of our coaching clients and leaders who attend our leadership workshops are eager to discover their true selves. But during our initial interaction, they also often ask us: "How can I lead like Jack Welch or Steve Jobs?" or any other highly celebrated executive. We can't help them with that, just as we can't help you become somebody else by reading this book. We can only help you uncover your authentic self and your North Star (your noble purpose). It is up to you to use that insight to define your personal leadership style that is aligned with your North Star.

A decade ago while consulting for a large computer company, we met a high-level African American executive who felt that what she had to say was not taken seriously and that she was excluded from the decision making in her division, even though she was a member of the management team. She even adopted certain behaviors of her successful colleagues, but this did not change anything. She had no idea that the more she imitated her colleagues, the less respect she received from them. Once she became aware of this and developed her own approach to dealing with issues, she become much more comfortable with differences of gender and race and was able to project her own voice and ideas confidently.

Parents can find themselves in a similar situation of seeking authenticity. A friend of ours, Rachel, who is an attorney and mother of a two-year-old son, decided not to blindly follow child rearing philosophies defined by her mother or others in self-help books. Such books, like *Battle Hymn of the Tiger Mother*, which looked at one Asian woman's strict parenting model, lay out formulas for raising children that the authors suggest will result in a certain outcome—that the children will be smarter or perhaps a great athlete. Instead of following one of these books, Rachel said she wanted to be a parent "in a way that is aligned with who I am, with my own perspective and principles." In other words, rather than following the parenting advice of others, Rachel is attempting to develop her own wisdom through experimentation. She encourages her son to explore and experiment without placing too many restrictions on him, allowing him to grow in an atmosphere of security and safety. Rachel told us that she is open to receiving parenting suggestions from friends and family, but she tries them out first and selectively adopts new practices that are aligned with her perspective and prove to have a positive impact on her son. In that sense, Rachel is acting with enthusiasm and excitement and discovering her role as a parent everyday.

Rachel is seeking authenticity in being a parent just as others do in being business leaders. Whether you are a parent or a leader, strive to infuse authenticity in the role you are performing. Wise leaders don't lose themselves in their role; even while they are fully engaged in their role, they maintain emotional detachment. They don't let the ups and downs or the successes and failures of their role affect their mood or their personality. As a result, they do what they think and feel is "the right thing to do" to serve a noble purpose instead of just doing "what is right" according to their job description—or their position in the organizational hierarchy. In other words, they don't play their role in a way intended to please others—their boss or customers or investors, for example—but in a way that feels authentic to them.

Mark Milani, a former senior vice president at Oracle Corporation, is one such wise leader. In his role at Oracle, Milani had to manage the conflicting needs and expectations of several stakeholders: his top boss, Larry Ellison (founder and CEO of Oracle), who is a big picture leader and usually operates out of the red zone; his immediate boss, who was a committed operations leader and hence tended to operate in the blue zone; and his customers, who wanted everything to be delivered yesterday. Rather than trying to please all stakeholders at the same time, which would have emotionally and physical drained him, Milani learned to prioritize these stakeholders' requests and manage their expectations differently. Here is how he put it: "I always did what I personally felt was the appropriate thing to do. I learned to sort out my priorities and address what is in the best interest of the company. I never let myself lose in the role I was playing or get emotionally engaged with what my boss wants me to, or what my customer wants me to do. Had I done that, I would not have lasted as long as I did in my job."[24]

Wise leaders like Milani discipline themselves to focus on what works and tune out the noise. In doing so, they cultivate staying power in their role without getting emotionally drained by it.

CULTIVATING ROLE CLARITY

Based on our experiences and research, we have identified a path to gaining role clarity that leads through cultivating mindfulness, gaining a larger perspective about one's role, performing one's role with a beginner's mind, and sharing one's role and its rewards with others.

You Are Bigger Than Your Role

Mindfulness allows you to see the role and the person playing the role distinctly and without internal criticism. By cultivating mindfulness, you will develop discernment and learn to perform your role with detached engagement as you recognize that you are bigger than your role. Jon Kabat-Zinn, author of *Wherever You Go, There You Are: Mindfulness Meditation in Everyday Life*, defines *mindfulness* as "paying attention in a particular way; on purpose, in the present moment, and non-judgmentally."[25]

Mindfulness facilitates self-awareness by allowing you to simultaneously focus your attention in a deliberate manner on your body, thoughts, feelings, and external context. Being mindful, you see things as they are and observe yourself. This ability to perceive clearly without judgment helps you gain a deeper understanding of who you are as a whole person in relation to the world around you.

The first major benefit of mindfulness is that it gives you the discernment to choose appropriate roles. By being mindful of your strengths and weaknesses, you gain discernment in choosing right roles that leverage your real strengths. All leaders have the ability to act appropriately and choose right roles based on the context, and if they are in a wise state of mind, their emotional attachment to a particular role and ego issues are minimized. They are able to play multiple roles with ease without getting caught up with any one of them. Moreover, they know how to cast other leaders in complementary roles in order to serve a larger purpose. Gaining and maintaining the clarity that you are only a trustee and not the owner of the organization you are leading—even if you are the founder of that organization—is one of the key differentiators between smart leadership and wise leadership.

We have found that many leaders often step into a role feeling confident that they have the right skills to perform that role when in fact they don't. As a result, they have to stretch their skills to make up for this deficiency, which can lead to failure. Other leaders shy away from a challenging role even though they are perfectly qualified for it because they don't want to take the risk of potentially failing once they assume that role. They are more likely to pick a role they are comfortable with, but then they quickly become dissatisfied or bored because it is not challenging enough. Mindfulness helps you find a role that fits your skills and yet challenges you and gives you an opportunity to learn and grow.

Another major benefit of mindfulness is that it will help you perform your chosen role with poise and detachment. We once consulted with Ray Hayachi (not his real name), the cofounder and CEO of a start-up that eventually became a $100 million company. In time, the company investors suggested that Hayachi step aside and bring in a seasoned CEO who had more experience in the types of clients the company had and with multiple product lines. We advised Hayachi to let go of the CEO role and become the chairman of the board, a role in which he could continue to contribute to the growth of the company. Hayachi didn't agree: he felt he could prove his mettle in running a large organization and scaling it up further to make it a billion-dollar company. In the ensuing battle of will, the board won: it brought in a seasoned CEO and made Hayachi chief operating officer. Hayachi resented the board's decision and refused to assume that role. His lack of poise and unwillingness to listen to and learn from the new CEO sabotaged his career: he was forced by the board to leave the very company he had cofounded.

We see many leaders like Hayachi who get caught up in a particular role and are unable to gain a broader perspective and assume that role in an emotionally detached manner because they identify too closely with it. If you are mindful, it is easier to cultivate detached engagement because you can see yourself as being bigger than that role. Over time, this detached engagement helps you deal with failures effectively and build resilience, which helps you maintain your equanimity. You won't cling to that role or become attached to the pleasures derived from it.

This detached engagement will provide you with several benefits. First, you will develop the ability to observe your performance—like watching an actor on stage—and objectively identify areas you need to improve. Second, you won't feel the burden of the leadership role since you are aware of being merely an instrument of a larger purpose. Third, you will carry out your role with consistency and resilience without craving validation. Finally, since you are not attached to the outcome, you will be willing to share in the rewards and become a better team player.

In addition to helping you cultivate detached engagement, mindfulness keeps you grounded in the present. It is a popular notion that we spend too much time thinking and reminiscing about the past or worrying about the future and too little paying attention to the present. Mindfulness keeps you grounded in the present by focusing your attention on what's happening here and now, and this allows you to perform better, according to Mihaly Csikszentmihalyi, a professor of psychology at Claremont College.[26] He has demonstrated that artists and athletes tend to perform at their highest level when they operate in the immersive state of flow: when all their thoughts cease to exist and their selves completely merge with the object of their attention. When they are performing with such high concentration, awareness and action fuse together and their sense of time gets altered to focus on the present.

Mindfulness is like an untrained muscle: you can consciously develop it with the right exercise. Todd Pierce, former chief information officer of Genentech (and currently an executive vice president at salesforce.com), believes that leaders who consciously practice mindfulness can increase their self-awareness—and in doing so, they will be able to discover and tap into the best of themselves when leading others. Having personally experienced the benefits of mindfulness, Pierce was eager to introduce the company's IT staff to mindfulness development techniques and develop their own self-awareness to improve their performance. He realized that the best way to keep employees motivated and engaged is by contributing to their personal growth. To accomplish this at Genentech, he brought in Pam Weiss, a Buddhist meditation teacher, executive coach, and the founder of Appropriate Response, a company that trains leaders in mindfulness development.[27]

Pierce worked with Weiss to pilot the personal excellence program (PEP), a three-step personal development program based on mindfulness, for Genentech's IT staff. Each participant selects a skill or quality that they believe will contribute to long-term satisfaction in their life. Then the participant nonjudgmentally observes the factors that inhibit or support her personal development. In a third step, the employee practices the newly learned skill or quality until it becomes ingrained. Weiss points out that self-awareness, cultivated through nonjudgmental self-observation, isn't enough by itself to change behavior; you need to act on that self-awareness and practice the new behavior with diligence.[28] The whole purpose of the program that Weiss facilitated was to help Genentech's IT staff use self-awareness as a tool to remove their self-limitations and recognize and realize their true potential. Pierce believed that by participating in PEP, his staff would develop mindfulness and become more engaged in their professional role and cope better with work-related stress.

As Weiss pointed out, "Bringing your whole self to work—mind, heart, and body—helps you find the best response to a situation."[29]

Several years into the implementation of PEP, employee satisfaction in Genentech's IT department had dramatically improved. According to Pierce and Weiss, almost all PEP attendees (six hundred employees went through PEP in six years) reported increased engagement and productivity at work, and they said they had increased their ability to self-observe and self-correct. They also reported better listening and peer-coaching skills, and 80 percent said that they were better able to deal with change and ambiguity. Many employees were more confident in handling bigger and more challenging projects.

Overall, employee engagement in the IT department increased from the time when Pierce took over the department in 2002 to the second highest companywide in 2009, the year *ComputerWorld* magazine ranked Genentech as the second best employer for IT professionals. Pierce explains: "The capacity to deal with difficulties and the level of engagement—these things are very, very powerful. These are skills and qualities you need to cultivate and practice over time."[30]

You don't necessarily have to go to a meditation retreat to cultivate self-awareness. There are many ways to become mindful. Genentech employees have shown that they can cultivate self-awareness—and act mindfully—even in the midst of their busy work life, and Weiss's work with them was truly transformational. This success convinced Pierce, who joined saleforce.com in late 2011 as executive vice president of operations and mobility, to team up again with Weiss to launch a mindfulness-based PEP at salesforce.com as well.

You Are Part of a Whole

Many smart leaders might think of themselves as solo performers without realizing that they are part of a larger ensemble. They are like the lead violinist in a symphony orchestra: they could occasionally lead the orchestra but can't dominate the entire performance. They fail to understand or appreciate the complementary roles others have to play to put on a great performance. Wise leaders see interconnections among various roles all the team members play as one unified performance.

Back in 1993, Alan Mulally, Ford's current CEO, was a general manager at Boeing in charge of developing the 777 passenger aircraft. In his weekly project review meetings, he used to remind his functional heads—those in charge of R&D, manufacturing, and sales and marketing—that in their activities, they should strive to optimize the entire system, or plane, rather than overoptimize a subsystem such as the landing gear or engines. And yet he reminded his executives that every subsystem matters for the effectiveness of the whole system. He told them that a plane with great engines and seats and cockpit design couldn't take off unless all systems on the plane—from doors to engines, from toilets to wings—work together as one system optimized for excellence. It is common sense, isn't it? But when you get caught up with your role, common sense is the first thing that goes out the window. Most of us operate on a daily basis totally focused on the task at hand—as if we have a tunnel vision and miss out the big picture completely.

When leaders gain a broader perspective by seeing interconnections among various roles people play, they see the value of the synergy between the roles. They then are open to change the way they play their role, switch roles, or cast their staff in new roles to serve the higher purpose more effectively.

We consulted with a large technology consulting firm whose leaders were convinced that as long as they were giving their clients exactly what they specifically asked for, they were doing the right thing. They perceived their role as being order takers and so had invested in processes and skills that enabled them to execute their client orders faster, better, and cheaper. However, in interviews with this firm's clients, we discovered that although clients were happy with the firm's delivery capabilities, they expected more. They wanted the firm to anticipate their needs and proactively fulfill them rather than deliver what they explicitly wanted. In other words, the clients were more interested in the firm's innovation capabilities than its ability to deliver its services on time and on budget. We used this customer insight to broaden the perspective of the firm's leaders and help them shift their role from a service provider focused on meeting a client's explicit requirements to that of an innovator with more creative solutions to client needs. After investing in building new skills and capabilities to support this kind of role, the consulting firm has come to be recognized as a company that proactively serves its clients.

CULTIVATING A BEGINNER'S MIND

When we were studying in India, a story that passed around began with the professor asking his colleagues a question before his talk on aerodynamics: Why do bumblebees fly? Most of his colleagues had some smart answers and interesting propositions. Then the professor would say that bumblebees fly because they didn't know any aerodynamics; otherwise, they would simply stop flying. Why? Because according to known aerodynamics principles, bumblebees cannot fly.

The moral of the story is that when we are experts in a field, we see limited options, and because we think we know, we don't see many possibilities and it is difficult to be creative. A beginner's mind has more creativity and learning agility and growth potential, and yet we often operate from an expert mind-set.

Sam Palmisano, chairman of IBM until October 1, 2012, diligently cultivated a beginner's mind-set among his company's senior leaders. In the early 2000s, when he was IBM's CEO, Palmisano placed senior executives as general managers of new, emerging businesses with no resources: they had to build them up from scratch and learn everything all over again. Some of them resisted letting go of big company processes and approaches. Others realized that they had to unlearn and selectively forget some of the big business approaches before they could become entrepreneurs.[31] Over time, they began to develop humility in playing their new roles. They realized that their new position offered them a great opportunity for learning. This shift in mind-set helped them become effective in their new roles.[32]

We consulted for some of these general managers and experienced firsthand the way these wise leaders assumed their new role with great humility by demonstrating a willingness to learn from everyone on their team as well as from IBM's partners. Rather than reusing past success formulas, they willingly experimented with new business strategies, many of which proved to be successful.

LEARNING TO LET GO

Many organizations prefer to conduct all their R&D in-house and are afraid to share their innovation activities with outsiders. In 2000, Procter & Gamble (P&G) had seventy-five hundred engineers and scientists engaged in R&D. Despite its army of in-house inventors, it had difficulty keeping up with the rapid pace at which competitors were innovating and customer needs were changing. That's when its CEO at the time, A. G. Lafley, realized that innovation needn't be the sole responsibility of P&G. In order to innovate faster, better, and cheaper, P&G had to begin sharing the R&D process with inventors outside the company: customers, suppliers, universities, start-ups, and venture capitalists. Lafley estimated that "for every P&G researcher there were 200 scientists or engineers elsewhere in the world who were just as good—a total of 1.5 million people whose talents" P&G could use.[33]

As a result of these insights, Lafley implemented a strategy to shift the role of P&G from sole inventor to a shared inventor arrangement with outside partners. P&G would play the role of broker between external inventors and internal sales and marketing people. Today, more than 50 percent of the company's new product ideas come from outside the company.[34] As a result, the company is now able to innovate faster, better, and cheaper than it did in the past.

Business smart leaders suffer from the not-invented-here syndrome: they want to invent everything themselves and tend to hoard their ideas. Functional smart leaders care more about execution than about fresh ideas and are proud of making things happen with quality, speed, and customer satisfaction—even if those ideas belong to someone else. Wise leaders are open to everyone's ideas and also tap others to execute on those ideas. In this sense, these wise leaders are what Liz Wiseman, a management consultant and best-selling author, calls "multipliers."[35] Multipliers such as Lafley use their intelligence to amplify the smarts and capabilities of people around them to innovate faster and better and generate breakthrough growth.

Narayana Murthy of Infosys is also a multiplier. He dedicated much of his time as a leader to coaching, mentoring, and grooming other leaders in his organization, creating a multiplier culture at the company. "The best index of the longevity of a corporation is its ability to generate newer and newer leaders," he says. "If you are a leader, your task is to groom other leaders—not cling to your seat." Currently each senior executive at Infosys spends nine days a year as a faculty member at Infosys's corporate university, where they teach future leaders.[36]

Sharing a role with others isn't just about sharing responsibilities; it is also sharing both the risks and rewards associated with that role. A.P.J. Abdul Kalam, a former president of India, recalls working as a young scientist in the 1960s at ISRO, India's space agency. His boss was Vikram Sarabhai, a brilliant physicist and the father of India's space program, who was leading a team that was preparing to launch India's first satellite. When the first launch failed, Sarabhai took all the blame, believing that as leader, he bore full responsibility. Given his excellent reputation, the Indian government continued to support his program, and the second attempt to launch the satellite succeeded. At a press event afterward, the entire team was present except for Sarabhai. He chose not to attend because he felt that attention would center on him rather than the team.[37]

Many leaders do not act selflessly as Sarabhai did. He took full blame for the failure but gave full credit to the team for success. Rather than obsessing over their individual success, leaders need to create conditions for everyone in their organization and their ecosystem to share success by creating a "field of success" that allows a shared sense of ownership and reward.

CONCLUSION

Wise leaders are like skilled actors who have clarity about what role they want to play and how they should perform that role. They let their authentic selves shine through in every role they perform and bring humility, enthusiasm, and competence to that role. All of this is done with detached engagement—that is, they don't let themselves become attached emotionally to their role or to the outcome even as they engage with it fully and enthusiastically.

By gaining role clarity, you will recognize that you are far bigger than any specific role you play. When you know that you are neither the "doer" behind the role nor the ultimate "enjoyer" of its benefits, you have less difficulty in becoming a steward of your organization and acting as a servant leader. When you have a clear noble purpose—a North Star that acts as your guide—it becomes easier to transcend personal gain and ego and become a wise and effective leader (reread chapter 2 on how to discover and follow your North Star).

Leading from the front or leading from the back or letting others lead is not a one-time affair. It is a continuous process of developing oneself while developing others, a process that requires mindfulness to be effective and bear fruit.

When role clarity is developed properly and aligned with a broader perspective and authentic and appropriate action orientation—two capabilities addressed in the previous two chapters—it can provide a solid foundation for wise leadership. With this foundation in place, you can use the next chapters to learn to develop additional and complementary capabilities that will fortify your wise leadership.

For you to get the most out of this chapter, reflect on the following questions:

- Where do I get most caught up in my job? What bugs me the most about the role that I currently play?
- Which roles and responsibilities of my current job are my favorites? Which ones are my least favorites?
- How do I engage with my role at work? Do I tend to assume it as a red zone leader or a blue zone leader? How could I take my filters off and see the role from others' point of view?
- How good a follower am I? Do I always strive to be in the driver's seat? What do I need to learn about leading from behind and becoming a servant leader?
- What practices (e.g., meditation) will help me cultivate mindfulness so I can perform my role with detached engagement?
- Which competencies do I need to prioritize in my effort to become a wise leader: mindfulness, servant leadership, humility, empathy, compassion, or openness?

A shift in perspective will help set your direction, action orientation will give you forward motion, and role clarity will inform you when to accelerate, slow down, or take a break. You might come to a crossroads where you have to make decisions on which direction to take or even whether to continue. In those moments, having discernment—the ability to make right decisions using sound judgment and reflection—will allow you to make better decisions regarding the next steps on your journey. That is the topic of the next chapter.

CHAPTER FIVE

CLARIFY YOUR DECISION LOGIC
Decide with Discernment

When Steve Jobs informed Apple's board in 2000 that he would open the company's first retail stores, many of the directors were less than enthusiastic. "I'm scratching my head and thinking this is crazy," recalls Art Levinson, CEO of Genentech and an Apple board member at that time.[1] After all, the board members argued, computer makers like Gateway had ventured into retail and failed big time; others, including Dell, dominated the PC market without owning a single store. What's more, Jobs's retail adventure wasn't based on solid market research or customer feedback. Instead, Jobs asked the board to simply trust his intuition. His strategy was for Apple to manage the customer experience from start to finish, and that included a customer's first contact with an Apple product in a retail store. Jobs felt that big box retailers were unable to properly convey the brand value of Apple products to these buyers. In that sense, Apple stores would be brand ambassadors rather than a glorified point of sale.

Much to the dismay of the board—one member, Ed Woolard, resigned in protest—Jobs did not relent, believing that his intuition was right. The remaining members reluctantly approved a trial run of four Apple Stores, which, as we now know, have become a retail phenomenon with nearly 400 stores worldwide, over 370 million visitors in just one year, over $180 billion in sales in 2012, and nearly $5 billion in profits.[2] Apple Stores perform seventeen times better than average retail stores, generating more than six thousand dollars per square foot.[3] With their stunning design and open, minimalist spaces, along with a helpful staff and easy-to-use interfaces (like the Genius Bar help desk), Apple Stores have become one of the most potent symbols of the Apple brand, the company, and its products—just as Jobs predicted.

Opening Apple Stores was just one among many other intuitive decisions that Jobs made during his career. From buying the digital animation company Pixar to launching the iMac, through the iPod and iPhone and finally the iPad, Jobs routinely went against conventional wisdom, as well as the advice of analysts and shareholders and his own board and management team. Jobs was both the ultimate micromanager in his fussiness and an imperious decision maker and harbored a deep desire for perfection.

In late 2000, for example, two months prior to the launch of the first Apple Store, Ron Johnson, the vice president who was in charge of creating the stores, suggested to Jobs they organize the layout around customer activities (e.g., movie editing) rather than the products themselves. Jobs went ballistic, according to his biographer, Walter Isaacson, and apparently shouted at Johnson: "I've worked my ass off on this store for six months, and now you want to change everything!"[4] A few hours later, Jobs changed his mind, recognizing that Johnson was right to redesign the Apple Stores around customer experiences. Jobs was willing to reconsider his own decisions—and even adopt the decisions he once scoffed at—if he believed that such a course correction would help deliver a far better experience to the customer.

In many ways, Jobs was an unusual leader. Arrogant, intuitive, and impetuous, he antagonized many in the Apple organization yet at the same time built a remarkable company and inspired loyalty. He was also a wise leader in some ways because he made intuitive decisions while paying attention to the larger context; he usually paused for reflection before making a decision; and he was open to other opinions that went against his—if, that is, those opposing him could withstand his browbeating and argue back to convince him of the merits of their own decision logic. In India, they would say that Steve Jobs had the discernment and discrimination (*Viveka*) to distinguish not easily visible information and use it to make decisions that connected with the customers and differentiated from the competitors.

Leaders have always been under pressure to make swift decisions. But today that pace is faster than ever before. In such high-pressure settings, we find that most leaders end up doing the exact opposite of what Jobs did: they tend to rush into decisions without proper reflection, rely too heavily on data and analytics, and lack the ability to decide when to stick with their decisions and when to let go of them.[5] As a result, many leaders make poor choices for themselves in terms of the organization's values and their own, and they end up paying a high price for them. Complexity, information technology, and globalization are additional factors that affect leaders who are making important decisions. The majority of CEOs in a global CEO study felt they were unable to effectively address escalating complexity and leverage it for succeeding in the future.[6]

This chapter is not about decisions leaders make but what they pay attention to in making decisions: data, analytics, values, logic, and expectations. In this chapter, we show how you can learn to decide with discernment by integrating logic, instinct, intuition, and emotion in making decisions. Above all, ethical clarity will help you make better choices for yourself and your organization in an environment characterized by ambiguity and volatility.

THE NEUROBIOLOGY AND PSYCHOLOGY OF MAKING DECISIONS

Making decisions is one of the most important activities leaders engage in. While good decisions can yield productive outcome, bad decisions can potentially have major negative consequences. Decisions can be made rationally, nonrationally, or irrationally. They can be based on tacit or explicit assumptions that correlate with unconscious or conscious brain processing. And they can be emotional or analytical. On a day-to-day basis, we rarely think about how we make decisions; some happen unconsciously even though they could have a big impact on our lives.[7] For instance, while conducting his doctoral research, one of us (Prasad) made an unconscious decision one day not to go back to the physics laboratory to check whether the lights were turned off, and that led to a freak accident in the laboratory and eighteen months of extra work to complete his dissertation.

In our time, the idea that people make decisions primarily by using logic and reason has been in the ascendant. Alan Mulally, CEO of Ford, and Narayana Murthy, cofounder of Infosys, have said repeatedly in interviews that decisions have to be made based on data.[8] It is important to remember, though, that these leaders do not use just any data, but spend a lot of time and energy to make sure that their data are accurate, bias free, and current. Then they consciously choose to look at the context, their own and company values, and other factors before they make decisions for themselves and their organizations.

Recent research in psychology and neuropsychology shows that other factors such as emotions, biases, and discrimination capability, or *Viveka*—that is, the ability to see and make fine distinctions as well as notice and value quality—are equally involved in making decisions and can heavily influence the quality of decisions that are made.[9]

According to brain research, the dorsolateral prefrontal cortex (DLPFC), different regions of the frontal cortex (orbitofrontal, anterior prefrontal, and ventromedial frontal), and the anterior cingulate cortex (ACC) in our brain are all involved in decision making.[10] Previously the frontal lobe of the brain, the most recently evolved part of the brain, was thought to be hardwired for making logical decisions. However, recent studies have shown that many of these same regions (e.g., the ACC and DLPFC) that are involved in logical decisions are also involved in emotion perception, self-regulation, and decision making—parts of decision making that are called "hot executive functions." That is, emotion and thinking are not as separate as is commonly thought.[11] In fact, more recent studies have divided decision-making processes into components: the representation of value, response selection (including intertemporal choice and cognitive control), associative learning, and affective and social aspects.[12]

In addition, the amygdala also affects the quality of our decisions. This part of the brain is the seat of our emotional memory: it not only stores all our experiences but also assigns an emotional tone to each. That means that if we felt angry while making a particular decision, each time we execute that decision, we may feel angry. And because we then need to contend with the negative emotion of anger, we end up losing our commitment to executing that decision. Positive emotions like empathy, compassion, or even openness experienced when making a decision potentially increase the quality of our commitment to execution. Recent studies show that positive emotions do in fact increase motivation and creativity and that our overall well-being and happiness are enhanced when we are angry in appropriate situations (e.g., confrontations) instead of suppressing negative emotions.[13] These new insights into the neurobiology of emotion and decision making align with an age-old lesson: we have to watch out for our emotional attachments to a particular outcome because these can affect the quality of our decisions through (to use a phrase that borrows from neurobiology) "amygdala attacks."[14]

In addition to logic and emotions, our biases and our conditioning affect the quality of our decision making. When a leader makes decisions of high quality, with her own biases acknowledged and taken into account, one may say that she has good judgment or discernment. *Discernment* is defined as "the act or process of exhibiting keen insight and good judgment."[15] A discerning individual perceives and recognizes the underlying truth in the not-so-obvious and changing context and is thus considered to be wise.[16]

A fourth element involved in decision making is discrimination, that is, the ability to subtly differentiate or distinguish one set of data (or context) from a similar-seeming other set. Discrimination is a necessary precursor to discernment: it allows us to differentiate or distinguish accurately among stimuli; discernment allows us to judge the value of what we find.[17] Thus, in a decision-making context, discrimination refers to the cognitive process by which we differentiate among similar but different stimuli, leading to distinct decisions and actions.[18] It is important for leaders to develop a discriminating intellect in order to make good decisions and to learn to use their discriminating abilities properly (i.e., not in the service of prejudice or bias, another meaning for *discrimination*). When leaders decide with discernment after proper discrimination, they are exhibiting a quality of ethical clarity aligning with *swadharma*: their authentic and personal ethic and its noble purpose of being fair and just to one and all. Their decisions are aligned with what is ethical—in the context of the situation in which decisions are being made and also in a larger context—which in turn signals and ensures that these decisions are aligned with a noble purpose.

All of these factors—logic, emotion, bias and conditioning, discernment, and discrimination—collectively inform what we call *decision logic*, which we define as the system, process, and principles of reasoning used in making important decisions. Each leader possesses his own decision logic, and generally, the decision logic of leaders who usually operate in the blue zone is very different from that of leaders in the red zone.

SMART VERSUS WISE STYLES OF DECISION LOGIC

Smart leaders tend to make decisions without adequate recourse to discernment or discrimination. Leaders in the blue zone are usually cautious decision makers. They rely heavily on their experiences, beliefs, and instincts when making decisions. They excel at making low-risk decisions that can be executed in a predictable manner, such as those focused on the short term and bottom line. Unaware of the larger context, they sometimes struggle with decisions that affect the long term or those that need to be made by integrating other perspectives, which entail bigger risk and need to be carried out in uncertain conditions. Although they are open to comments and suggestions when making decisions, they tend to mainly look for validation rather than an intuitive point of view. They have great instincts, which are the collective sum of their experiences, but they often rely too heavily on them. As a result, they might repeat poor decisions they made in the past. Rather than relying on personal ethics, they may look at external best practices to guide their decisions. Being risk averse in general, they tend to procrastinate when they confront tough decisions or they may spend a lot of time collecting data to back up their big decisions. Finally, they do not use their discernment capability often.

Leaders in the red zone tend to favor decisions that carry high risks and high rewards and could personally benefit them. Quick thinkers and emotionally driven, they are prone to rushing into decisions in order to grab a fleeting opportunity. Overly confident, they trust their own discrimination and don't always consult others. In spite of having good discrimination, red zone leaders may sometimes decide against their own discernment and make decisions based on short-term benefits. As big picture thinkers, they may be perfectly aware of the larger context in which they make decisions, and yet their expeditious and somewhat self-centered approach to decision making could sometimes lead to ethical lapses that they might not have foreseen. Although they are great at helping others make important strategic decisions, they struggle to make important personal decisions due to their underdeveloped ethical clarity.

Wise leaders, by contrast, tend to make intuitive decisions based on both discernment and discrimination. They overcome

the limitations of smart leaders and exhibit a number of characteristics that differentiate their decision logic. They often make
decisions that seem to defy conventional wisdom and appear
counterintuitive to others, even illogical or irrational. That's
because they rely on a decision logic that is shaped by their intuition, discernment, and discrimination capability that takes the
larger context and personal values and ethics into account.

For example, Steve Jobs intuitively felt that Apple retail stores
would be the right channel not to sell products (which is what
stores are for) but to communicate the Apple brand values and
create a superior customer experience. He thought that if employees at Apple Stores were to delight customers by providing them
unforgettable experiences, sales would ensue automatically, But
if the store employees were to act as pushy salespeople, the customer experience—and sales—would suffer.

Apple Stores have been phenomenally successful, and they
have boosted not only Apple's profits but also its brand reputation. Interestingly, in summer 2012, John Browett, the new head
of Apple Stores, did not show the same discernment and discrimination capability and attempted to improve the bottom line—and
increase the profitability—of Apple Stores through layoffs and
salary cuts just before the holiday shopping season. The move
backfired: leaner Apple Stores couldn't keep up with escalating
demand. Customer experience suffered, and Apple had to issue
a press release apologizing for the "mistake" it made and in
October 2012 fired Browett.[19] This incident validated Jobs's discernment: as long as Apple Stores focus on delivering superior
customer service, the company's profitability will keep improving—but the inverse just won't happen.

Wise leaders also make decisions that exhibit both ethical
clarity and pragmatism. They have a strong sense of ethical clarity
that comes from their reliance on authentic and subjective ethics
(*swadharma* in Sanskrit), not on objective ethics that does not take
into account exceptions and the context. They are not driven
solely by ideology but rather tend to be pragmatists who have a

clear noble purpose and therefore a broader perspective on how to balance what the larger context demands with their inner values. Because they are context sensitive, wise leaders don't have a black-or-white view of the world: they see shades of gray in every situation in which they have to make a decision. Steve Jobs, for instance, demonstrated both ethical clarity and pragmatism when he decided in 1997 to partner with his archrival Bill Gates, then CEO of Microsoft. He allowed Microsoft's Internet Explorer Web browser to be shipped with every Apple computer; in return, Gates agreed to invest $150 million in Apple and support Microsoft's Office suite for at least five years for the Macintosh platform.[20] Jobs's intuitive decision to embrace Microsoft was predicated on his view that "[Apple] employees and users have to let go of the notion that for Apple to win, Microsoft has to lose."[21] Despite his reservations about Gates and Microsoft, Jobs made a practical and pragmatic decision that would help Apple in the long run.

In addition, wise leaders are level-headed when making decisions. They don't rush into decisions driven by strong emotions such as fear or greed. When they face a crisis, they don't try to outsmart the problem by devising a clever solution. They slow down their decision-making process and maintain their composure, exploring the best possible options before coming up with a simple and yet effective solution.

Wise leaders are likely to look at the big picture to reframe the situation. Then they gather all the information that is already available, explore different processes to make decisions, evaluate risks, and identify alternative scenarios instead of a single right decision. They bring ethical considerations and values to the table. Finally, they turn to their own instincts as well as intuition to think through trade-offs, risks, and execution issues. While all this may seem a time-consuming process, we have observed that wise leaders make these decisions quickly and many times unconsciously—as evidenced in the case of Captain Chesley "Sully" Sullenberger.

On January 15, 2009, shortly after taking off from New York's La Guardia airport, US Airways Flight 1549 was hit by a flock of birds. Both engines were disabled, and the plane began losing altitude at an alarming pace as it drifted over the densely populated city and its tall buildings. In the cockpit, Captain Sullenberger and his first officer were using all their skills to quickly figure out what to do. Sullenberger asked the first officer to focus on restarting the engines, while he focused on finding a way to land the plane safely. In that context, the logical option would have been to fly back to La Guardia, but there were issues with timing, distance, and traffic; other local airports, Kennedy and Newark, were also ruled out. The only option left was unorthodox: setting the plane down in the frigid waters of the Hudson River. Sullenberger later explained that his intuition told him that he could "improve chances of recovery" by landing in the river close to ferries and other maritime rescue services. And that's exactly what the level-headed Sullenberger did, saving the lives of all passengers and crew on board. It was the first time in fifty years of commercial flight that a jetliner landed safely on water in an emergency situation, the *Wall Street Journal* later reported.[22]

On that day, Sullenberger brought all his experience and intelligence to bear and made a wise decision by deciding to land his plane in the river. A smart decision would have been to try to get to any nearby airport at any cost, because that would have seemed a safer bet, but it potentially could have been fatal for all the passengers and crew on board.

In our research and experience, we also find that wise leaders decide with a view toward the long term. According to the Great Law of the Iroquois Confederacy, members of that Native American nation are trained to think seven generations ahead to ensure that the decisions they are making today will benefit their descendants seven generations into the future.[23] Business leaders today, making decisions in a fast-moving environment, don't think that they have the luxury of thinking seven generations ahead. Leaders making wise decisions differentiate themselves by displaying the courage to make choices that might not yield immediate gains but will reap long-term benefits for their organization as well as for society.

At the height of the dot-com bust in 2002, IBM's CEO at the time, Sam Palmisano, made two bold decisions: he acquired the consulting arm of the accounting firm PricewaterhouseCoopers and stepped up investments in R&D.[24] Investors weren't enthusiastic about Palmisano's decisions when most IBM competitors were slashing their costs to stay afloat. But Palmisano was focused on the company's prospects for long-term growth. He knew that when the recession was over, clients would be demanding innovative solutions.

Palmisano's strategy proved correct. By 2012 IBM had established itself as a leading business and technology consulting services provider and is now successfully commercializing solutions that are built on technologies—such as wireless sensors—that result from R&D projects IBM initiated in the early 2000s.[25] "A long-term view teaches you that your biggest challenge may not be surviving your failures, but your successes," Palmisano says.[26]

Wise leaders also tap into their discernment intuitively when they making decisions, especially critical ones. They know when to shape a decision and when to let a decision emerge. When they shape a decision, they use the data from the past to direct the outcome, whereas when they let the decision emerge, intuition plays a bigger role than logic, as Steve Jobs's decision making often demonstrated.

Finally, wise leaders strive to be open-minded when making decisions. They listen to the people around them, even those who challenge their assumptions and decisions. They believe that this inclusive process, which is known as dialectical decision making (or the Socratic method), generates creative tension that can lead to more robust decisions.

That's why leaders at Google and the pharmaceutical company Eli Lilly encourage the use of prediction markets, a way of forecasting the viability of a strategy based on input from frontline employees.[27] These employees can weigh in on strategic decisions that senior management is proposing and provide suggestions for improving them. Wise leaders are also willing to delegate decision-making power to people on the front line when appropriate. They practice a leadership style that INSEAD professor Herminia Ibarra refers to as "command and collaborate," which is the ability to both command or collaborate based on the necessity.[28]

Peter Grauer, the chairman of Bloomberg, is a wise leader who not only practices command and collaborate himself but is promoting this inclusive leadership style across his entire organization. Commenting on an internal Bloomberg study that sought to identify the most valued leadership competencies in his organization, Grauer noted that the top-performing executives at Bloomberg boasted contradictory attributes: "They had future vision but were tactically strong; they provided strong guidance but were open to challenge; they relied on extensive networks but were also capable of moving fast (i.e., unilaterally); they were hands-on but also empowering."[29] Bloomberg seems to be cultivating wise leaders capable of making decisions in a firm and yet inclusive manner.

DECIDING WITH DISCERNMENT

In this section, we identify some tools and techniques you can use to avoid decision traps that lead to poor choices and develop your decision logic. Because discernment is deeply connected with discrimination capability, you have to pay attention to subtle but important elements; you do that by bringing your emotions, body, and authentic spirit to the task in addition to your mind and intellect. Deciding with discernment involves cultivating an abundance mind-set; responding mindfully to events; balancing ethics and pragmatism; deciding with body, mind, and soul; thinking holistically and systematically; and demonstrating both flexibility and persistence.

Cultivate a Mind-Set of Abundance

Many smart leaders make decisions as if they were playing a zero-sum game: if you win, someone else loses. For them, it's all about beating the competition. Unlike smart leaders who operate with a mind-set of scarcity, wise leaders operate with a mind-set of abundance.

Wise leaders first appropriately frame the decision to be made and then are open to collaboration with the competition, if that is an appropriate choice to increase the size of the market.[30] When the goal is to create a larger market, the killer instinct is less central. Leaders don't collaborate out of pure altruism, of course, but out of enlightened self-interest, in the sense that serving the common good indirectly benefits everyone. "Profit as a singular goal is a fairly shallow aspiration, and it's not enduring," says Howard Schultz, CEO of Starbucks. "I've always said that you can't create long-term value for the shareholder unless you create long-term value for the employees and the communities you serve."[31]

To cultivate a mind-set of abundance, start identifying where you struggle with a scarcity mind-set. You can create your own logic—a rationale or process—and follow it with discipline for an extended period until that logic gets internalized and reduces your anxiety.

To begin, pick one resource—say, money or time—that you worry you might run out of. Expand the time frame from immediate to medium term or long term, and see whether you feel more relaxed about opportunities and abundance. Over the next thirty days, visualize that you actually do have a lot more of that resource—say, money—than what you may ever need. With that belief, for the next thirty days, donate some money—as little as two dollars every day. Each day, identify a charity or person for whom even two dollars a day would make a difference, and give it to that charity or person.

Remember that your job is to develop a new decision logic, so let go of short-term worries and concerns about scarcity just for that moment. Instead, consciously and appreciatively visualize what the people you are giving the money to could buy with your donation and, if they buy food, how they feel after eating that breakfast. You might even feel that you should increase your charity from two to five dollars sometimes and follow that instinct: your decision logic is slowly adjusting to a new abundance mind-set. Slowly your worry about scarcity will be eclipsed by an increased feeling of abundance. In October 2012, we met a shuttle driver named Norma working for Hotel VQ in Denver who has been practicing this exercise for twenty years. Every day, she prepares some sandwiches, buys some fruit, and keeps it all in a cooler next to her while she is driving the shuttle. She offers this food to homeless people she encounters throughout the day. In addition, she offers one dollar to every homeless person she encounters during the day. On average, each day, she gives away about ten dollars out of the tips she received that day. We were blown away by her generosity and her abundant mind-set.

After the thirty-day experiment, the chances are that you will become more committed to act out of an abundance mind-set. Discuss your experience with others, possibly sharing it on websites like HelpOthers.org. You will notice your changed mind-set based on the comments others will make of your abundance mind-set. Similarly, when you are working with lack of time, pay attention to consciously "stop" (rather than end) each activity before you "start" another activity, and pay special attention to how mindfully you "change" or transition from one to another.

Respond Mindfully to Events

Leaders are always forced to multitask and respond quickly to circumstances. Yet rather than responding creatively or thoughtfully, they sometimes react in a knee-jerk fashion out of fear or anger. We see many leaders make decisions in autopilot mode without contextual awareness, let alone self-awareness. By cultivating mindfulness, they can make decisions deliberately and consciously rather than reactively or emotionally. You will be able to choose the most appropriate response.

Brain research shows that when you are faced with adversity, your body releases chemicals that induce fear or anger. It takes your body ninety seconds to process these chemicals; in this interval, you have a choice of waiting or reacting.[32] If you wait and the chemicals recede, you will be more grounded. If you don't wait, you will go into firefighting mode and make rash decisions.

Brain researchers have also found that if people develop anticipatory anxiety—that is, they worry about confronting something in the future that scared them in the past—that anxiety disrupts their prefrontal cortex and can create bias in their decision making by increasing amygdala activation, which induces fear.[33] Hence it's critical for leaders to be mindful of their feelings and respond appropriately when those feelings arise.

In 2011 Carlos Ghosn, the CEO of the Renault-Nissan Alliance, a strategic partnership between French carmaker Renault and Japanese automaker Nissan, had to confront five crises simultaneously, including the devastating earthquake and tsunami in Japan (which caused the meltdown of a nuclear power plant in Fukushima) and flooding in Thailand, all of which hit the company's supply chain hard. Ghosn responded swiftly but mindfully to these events—in particular, by giving increased authority and decision-making powers to people in factories that suffered the worst damage.[34] Ghosn also gave more autonomy to R&D engineers and product experts to make hundreds of small changes to numerous car models in order to use parts that were readily available and circumvent supply chain problems. The plant with the most damage was the engine plant in Iwaki, Japan, where Nissan had been producing more than one thousand engines per day. The plant sustained large cracks in the foundation, its roofing was ripped apart, and other major structural problems. The plant was immediately closed, and many people feared that it would remain so permanently. However, Ghosn traveled to the plant, which was perilously close to the Fuku-shima radiation zone, and insisted that the team in Iwaki had "fighting spirit." Within several months, the plant had not only reopened but had returned to full production. The catastrophe also had unintended opportunities. In particular, Ghosn's decision to empower people in the field ended up helping the company identify next-generation star performers who rose to the occasion of leadership. Even as he dealt with multiple crises, Ghosn always acted with equanimity, a quality that denotes total openness to all experiences without judgment.[35]

Decide with Ethical Clarity

When making decisions, smart leaders, especially those operating in the red zone, tend to exhibit ideological rigidity. They ensure that all their decisions are always aligned with their ideological principles regardless of the context in which they make decisions. That's why their decisions can be clouded by a polarized viewpoint.

Wise leaders aren't likely to be attached to any ideology. Rather, they base their decisions on values they believe in, which inform their evaluation of right and wrong. Yet this ethical clarity doesn't make wise leaders rigid: they are pragmatic enough to adapt their decisions when the external context changes. They demonstrate what is called *ethical pragmatism*, in that they start with the assumption that their moral criteria used to conduct an inquiry into the future are valid for now and might be improved on in the future. Ethical pragmatism is different from moral relativism, in that it aims toward a moral objective and converges toward it in time.

In a rapidly changing environment, ethical pragmatism can be a huge asset for decision makers. Adam Werbach is a leader who eschewed ideological rigidity in favor of ethical pragmatism. Werbach was always a committed environmentalist. At age thirteen, he convinced his parents to let him open a checking account so he could join Greenpeace. At twenty-three, he was president of the Sierra Club and wrote a book, *Act Now, Apologize Later,* in which he described Walmart as a "new breed of toxin that could wreak havoc on a town." But in 2006, Werbach did something that many thought was unimaginable: he agreed to be a consultant to Walmart to help transform the company into a corporate role model of sustainability. Werbach's decision was motivated by a shift in his perspective: he realized that he could be more effective in changing the system from inside rather than fighting it from outside. "Our goal is to have Wall Street look at Wal-Mart's green performance, and say, 'Wow, do more of that," he explained.[36] This attitude didn't go down well with Werbach's friends and colleagues, who thought he had sold out his green credentials and principles.

Werbach's change of heart was rooted in the recognition that Walmart's interest in sustainability was genuine and that the organization truly wanted to integrate sustainable practices into its business model. He also saw this as an opportunity to take environmentalism mainstream, in this case, with the world's largest retailer and its 127 million weekly customers.

Over several years, Werbach worked closely with Walmart to roll out the Personal Sustainability Project (PSP), a voluntary program aimed at making sustainability personal for the company's 1.3 million employees. Each PSP participant developed a plan for making an aspect of his or her life sustainable by either changing small habits, like signing up for electronic bank statements, or making radical lifestyle changes, such as stopping smoking. The underlying concept of PSP is to make participants feel that they are personally gaining something with their actions. "For too long, environmentalists have been telling people they need to sacrifice. But the great modern challenge is how to be happy. This is the missing link," Werbach figures.[37] If the 1.3 million Walmart employees feel happier by embracing sustainability in their daily lives, then they are more inclined to spread the message to customers.

PSP has been quite successful: over 40 percent of the participants are staying committed to it. In this case, we see that Werbach
has eschewed ideological rigidity in favor of pragmatism, but he
has not abandoned his personal ethics and beliefs. While working
with Walmart within the system, he continues to be an active
campaigner for sustainability and corporate responsibility when
it comes to the environment. He didn't sell himself out; he shifted
his perspective and demonstrated ethical pragmatism, or doing
the right thing for the greater good.

Use Logic, Instinct, Intuition, and Emotion to Decide

Many smart leaders make decisions by relying heavily on externally derived logic (not the unique decision logic that they have
evolved over time). They might not, for example, approve a new
R&D project unless marketing can demonstrate enough commercial value for the potential product. Or they may decide to
acquire a company because analysts recommend it and the
potential synergies appear convincing on paper. But when uncertainty is present, wise leaders bring their entire being—their
body, mind, and soul—into the decision-making process by integrating logic with three other qualities: instinct, intuition, and
emotion.

Instinct

We once coached Philip, the CEO of a multibillion-dollar U.S.
manufacturing company that was interested in a $100 million
acquisition. On paper this deal made sense. Yet Philip felt uncomfortable about the acquisition for a reason he could not explain.
He had an instinct but didn't have evidence to support it.

In a coaching session, we helped him figure out what to do
by using a tool called the Mithya Wheel, which displays words and
colors that people are asked to choose based on their emotional
state.[38] We asked Philip to pick words that represented his state
of mind. He landed on the word *resisting*. He said that was the

perfect word because although nothing appears to be wrong with the acquisition, he was resisting going ahead. Then we tried to find out more by getting him to verbalize his feelings. With the help of the Mithya Wheel and our guidance, he managed to put his finger on the source of his discomfort: he thought that the numbers for this company looked too good to be true. Heeding his instinct, he investigated further and found that some numbers were indeed inflated and didn't match reality. He then made a sound decision: he rejected the deal.

It's worth noting here that sometimes leaders mistake their instinct for their intuition. Your instinct is conditioned by your past experiences. For instance, your instinct may tell you not to make a particular decision because you paid a heavy price the last time you made a similar decision. Your instinct is very useful when you are making decisions in a relatively stable environment for the near term. According to our framework, your intuition is like a movie that includes your past and the future.

Intuition

Kip Tindell, chairman and CEO of the Container Store, a leading U.S. housewares chain, uses his intuition extensively to make his business decisions.[39] In a highly volatile environment like retail, Tindell believes that a manual can't teach everything you need to know about customer service. Instead, he has made intuition one of his company's founding principles. Employees are encouraged to use their intuition to make decisions that best serve customer needs. As Tindell explains: "We just beg and plead and try to get employees to believe that intuition does have a place in the work force. After all, intuition is only the sum total of your life experience. So why would you want to leave it at home when you come to work in the morning?"[40] Tindell says employees who rely more on their intuition feel empowered, and they learn to trust their own judgment to solve a problem without having to consult their supervisor. He says this has in part led to higher productivity and lower attrition rates at this company (The Container Store has less than 10 percent turnover, extraordinary in the retail industry where 100 percent turnover is common).[41]

It is important to note that however much you trust your intuition, you have to validate it with data and information (even Steve Jobs, famous for always heeding his intuition, used data to validate that his intuition was right). Therefore, the best way to minimize the risks of investing in the wrong products and services is to test your intuitive ideas early on in the marketplace and use customer feedback to iterate design or drop the offering altogether if customer interest is tepid. Both Google and Facebook encourage employees to validate the intuitive product ideas by beta-testing them with users and then adopting concepts that achieve significant customer uptake into their mainstream product line.[42]

Emotion

While it is true that making decisions in a highly emotional state triggered by anger or fear can often be detrimental, some positive emotions—such as passion, empathy, and compassion—can help wise leaders develop better decision logic when they are channeled properly.

Passion is an important emotion that leaders often tap into when they face critical decisions. Without an emotional connection, it is difficult for leaders to communicate effectively and rally support for their decisions. For example, Steve Jobs had a highly emotional personality that he channeled to create what people called a reality distortion field—his ability to believe and convince others that the impossible was possible.[43] When venture capitalists in Silicon Valley make investment decisions, they look at the so-called 3Ps—passion, people, and plan—in a start-up. Even if a start-up has the right people (talent) and an excellent strategic plan, without passion the people can't execute the plan successfully.

Empathy and compassion are two other positive emotions that leaders can tap into to make wise decisions. Customers, employees, and partners are attracted to organizations whose culture is infused with empathy and compassion—as reflected in their leaders' decisions. We were asked by a CEO of a pharmaceutical company to coach a vice president whose performance had dropped significantly in the previous two quarters. The CEO empathized with the vice president and felt that she should be given a chance to improve before she was let go. The vice president was not receptive to coaching at first and told us that she did not have any time for coaching after dealing with her work and health issues in her family. Further gentle probing led us to believe that somebody close to her was going through addiction issues, and she did not know where to seek help confidentially in her community. We made some discreet inquiries about a treatment center far from her city and sent her the information. We then promptly forgot about this encounter. We met her accidentally in an airport a year later, and she told us how thankful she was for our support and was interested in our coaching. It seems that her high performance in the past several months had secured her a promotion and she wanted our help in becoming successful in the new job.

Factor in the Larger Context

The world is an interconnected place, and therefore decisions must be connected to a context beyond the immediate and obvious business context. "Our world has become a global system of systems," notes IBM's former CEO, Sam Palmisano.[44] Most leaders, however, do not think holistically and inclusively. They have been trained to make decisions that optimize a subsystem or one whole system at best. Now they increasingly need to demonstrate systems thinking and make decisions in a more holistic and integrated manner.

Alan Mulally is a wise leader who consistently has encouraged members of his organization to cultivate and practice systems thinking. As we have noted, he served as general manager in charge of developing Boeing's 777 passenger plane. Given the immensity of the 777 project, the development of the plane was divided in smaller chunks, with dedicated teams put in charge of designing and building various parts and subsystems (e.g., wings, engines, entertainment system). Mulally's job was to coordinate these multiple teams and integrate their efforts.

Traditionally Boeing teams had tended to operate in silos and collaborated little, which had led to project delays and higher costs, and Mulally sought to change that. In every project review meeting, he began by reminding all teams that they had to factor in the larger context when making decisions. Mulally used to say that building the best plane means it is optimized at the system level as well as at the customer level. You cannot have the best engines on the plane and put together a great entertainment system and seats but not pay sufficient attention to the doors of the plane which would make the plane unusable. Similarly, building the best plane for one airline might not be a very different experience from building it for another one. Your product decisions will be optimal only when you simultaneously pay attention to customer, competition, cost, quality, and design, Mulally told his team managers at Boeing. He took the same decision logic into Ford and led Ford back to profitability and success.[45]

A key advantage of thinking holistically is the ability to anticipate competition from unexpected sources and make preemptive decisions. For example, Canon and Nikon did not anticipate that cell phone makers Apple and Nokia would move into their territory with camera-equipped cell phones. Even a few years ago, Apple and Nokia didn't appear to be potential competitors for Canon and Nikon. The leaders of these companies failed to think holistically and inclusively and did not anticipate that new competitors from nontraditional industries would enter their market and attract what they had viewed as their customers.

As a wise leader, Sam Palmisano anticipated big shifts in the marketplace and decided to shift his company's business model before competition disrupted it. In 2004, he boldly decided to sell

IBM's PC business to Chinese computer manufacturer Lenovo even though IBM's PC unit was performing relatively well at that point. Palmisano's decision was based on his holistic thinking: he could foresee that the PC business was rapidly becoming commoditized and that the real profits were to be made in the software and services businesses.[46] Nearly a decade later, Palmisano's foresight seems to have proven right: IBM has established a stronghold in the software and services business. In contrast, HP, IBM's rival, is struggling, burdened by a hardware business that is rapidly getting commoditized and one that HP's successive leaders have been unwilling to let go of.[47]

CONCLUSION

In today's fast-paced and hyperconnected global economy, leaders are pressured to make multiple decisions and do so quickly. In such a volatile environment, leaders tend not to take the time to reflect and use sound judgment; the result is hurried decisions that lead to poor outcomes for themselves and their organization. In particular, leaders who operate in the blue zone tend to decide instinctively based primarily on their own experience, without paying enough attention to the changes in the larger context. Risk averse, they may either procrastinate when faced with difficult decisions or make decisions that may yield tactical benefits but be unviable in the long term. Leaders in the red zone are more willing to make bold decisions that could generate strategic long-term benefits. But given their self-centered and emotional personality, they tend to rush into decisions without heeding their intuition, let alone getting input from others—an oversight that could lead to ethical or even legal lapses that may have a high cost.

Wise leaders are more effective decision makers due to their unique decision logic—that is, the set of systems, processes, and reasoning principles they use in decision making—developed over time and tested in different scenarios. Context awareness and ethical clarity altogether form the cornerstone of a wise leader's decision logic. Indeed, wise leaders decide with ethical clarity—that is, they rely on an ethical compass that tells them what is right or wrong not only in a particular situation but also in a larger context that is connected to a noble purpose. This clarity gives wise leaders discernment—the ability to judge well in crises and make ethically sound and yet pragmatic decisions using a combination of logic, instinct, intuition, and emotion.

A wise decision logic anchored by ethical clarity will enable you to avoid the decision-making traps that smart leaders often fall into, such as overreliance on data, rushing into decisions without enough contextual awareness, or favoring short-term gains at the expense of long-term rewards.

Here are some ways you can learn to infuse wisdom into your own decision logic and access it consciously to make highly productive decisions. You can use these points to assess past decisions and get a clearer picture of what your traps, flaws, and automatic tendencies tend to be (and where they are operating). You can also use them more dynamically as touchstones when you are engaged in decision making:

- In addition to relying on your experiences and instinct when making decisions, pay closer attention to the broader context and explore various options that resonate well with your own values and ethics.
- Rather than evaluating options based purely on their tangible benefits, assess them based on their ability to serve a larger purpose—and then decide which among these options will get you closer to your North Star.
- Don't let tactical execution issues or emotions sway your discrimination and discernment when making strategic decisions that will affect your own or your organization's long-term future.
- Avoid justifying your own unique decision logic to yourself or others, even when you have an inkling that it is flawed. Rather,

become mindful of your decision traps—such as an emphasis on short-term benefits or overreliance on experience—and work to consciously avoid them so you don't get blindsided by them.

- Pay attention to three components of good decision making. First, take the time to gather complete, appropriate, and unbiased data. Second, be mindful of the context in which the decision is to be made. Third, focus on making prudent and intuitive judgments with ethical clarity. Don't compromise on any of the three components.
- If you get stuck while trying to make a tough decision, take into account whatever data are readily available to evaluate the external context and then ultimately trust your intuition in making the final decision.
- Focus on pragmatic and ethical approaches instead of idealistic and impractical ones.

Making a decision with discernment is the first step of wise decision making. Knowing when to stick with it and when to let it go is the second step. And that requires flexible fortitude, that is, the ability to know when to hold on and when to fold, which we explore in chapter 6.

CHAPTER SIX

DEVELOP FLEXIBLE FORTITUDE
Know When to Hold and When to Fold

Leaders must apply discernment and discrimination when making decisions: they must be perceptive of the data and the context in which the decision is being made, and they must bring logic, emotion, intuition, and instinct to bear on the final decision. Once they come to a decision, leaders need to demonstrate fortitude—the courage to stay the course and see the decision through and yet be flexible enough to change direction or even abort the project when needed. In her tenure as founder and leader of Teach For America, Wendy Kopp has demonstrated an ability to hold and to fold at the appropriate times.

Kopp wasn't a star student when she started at the Highland Park High School in Dallas, Texas.[1] She was shy and awkward, and behind many of her peers academically when she entered middle school, but she worked hard and gained ground and thrived in high school. By the time she finished high school, she was accepted at Princeton University, having graduated at the top of her class.

At Princeton, Kopp realized that too many low-income communities in the United States lacked qualified teachers, and she came up with the idea of creating a national teacher corps modeled after the Peace Corps. For her senior thesis, she outlined the business model of what would become Teach For

America (TFA), now a $300 million social enterprise. At the time, Kopp's academic advisor thought her idea was unrealistic and that she was "deranged" and tried to dissuade her from pursuing it.[2] "I was completely torn by the decision to start TFA," she says. "There was a voice in my head telling me not to do it—to take a more normal path. I did have one thing going for me, which was that I had been rejected from all the other jobs I'd applied to."[3] Kopp then sent a proposal to thirty CEOs to enlist their support. None took her up on the offer. Finally, just before her graduation in 1989, oil giant Exxon Mobil offered her a twenty-six-thousand-dollar grant, and TFA was born.

In its first year, TFA operated as a nimble start-up with a lean staff of twenty-five members. The team recruited and placed the first group of five hundred teachers from a pool of twenty-five hundred applicants. There were challenging issues surrounding funding and managing growth. Among them, the overworked staff couldn't keep up with the escalating number of applications, resulting in serious delays in recruiting and placing new teachers. Employees also complained about Kopp's tendency to micromanage, which was due to her lack of experience leading a rapidly expanding organization. Some help came from Nick Glover, an organization development expert who helped the team develop an effective organizational structure. "Teach For America made it, not only through its launch but [also] through many dark years when we were constantly on the brink of collapse," she explains.[4]

This experience taught Kopp that sheer grit could take her only so far; she also had to be flexible in the way she ran her organization. As a start-up, TFA was fighting for survival, and she had to begin leading the organization as an enterprise built for scale. That shift in perspective led her to completely reorganize TFA in 1999.[5] She brought in people with proven experience to head strategic planning, program development, and fundraising, and they managed to put TFA on a solid footing that enabled it to grow and expand its reach.

In 2012 TFA received more than forty-eight thousand applications—12 percent of them from Ivy League students—to fill slots for fifty-eight hundred hundred new corps members. Since 1990, over thirty-three thousand corps members have taught some 3 million students in underresourced areas nationwide.[6] Although many education groups continue to challenge TFA's model, the overall academic achievement of students being taught in the program gets good reviews, and Teach For America remains a bold idea in the movement to improve America's failing schools. And it is certainly a major accomplishment for Kopp, who displayed flexible fortitude during the struggle to establish the organization.

Kopp told us that what sustained her perseverance over the years were her core values and the eagerness to serve a noble purpose: give low-income kids a fighting chance in life through better education. Kopp's purposeful tenacity is widely shared by her TFA members. "It is always hard to challenge the traditional notions about the profession of teaching and how teachers should be trained," she said. "For a lot of Teach For America teachers, staff, and alumni, the key to success is perseverance. And what sustains their perseverance is their deep belief in this mission."[7]

In our analysis, Kopp tapped into her willpower to let go of her "smart" way of micromanaging Teach For America and embraced a wise leadership approach based on delegation. There are still many question marks about TFA. Critics are continuing to challenge its approach, but Kopp is continuing to learn, grow, and transform TFA to make it more effective.

SMART LEADERS GET STUCK

We find that smart leaders interpret and act on their fortitude differently and uniquely depending on whether they operate predominantly from a blue or red zone. Functional smart leaders—those who generally operate in the blue zone—tend to create tight boundaries for their work and operate strictly within those limits. Their working style is slow and methodical as they focus on execution until completion. But there is no constancy of purpose or flexibility in leaders' fortitude when operating in the blue zone. They can get caught up with dreams or irrational fears and give up their projects easily. It is difficult for them to change their mind once it is made up. Stubbornness is one of the issues that leaders who consistently operate in the blue zone have to watch out for. They also take time to evaluate their fit with a project before they take it on. While others might complain about their slow start, functional smart people, who are known for operational excellence, generally cross the finish line and produce high-quality work.

Business smart leaders (in the red zone) are also a tenacious bunch: they can persist in their decisions, defend them against critics, and see their projects through. But they typically demonstrate such persistence only as long as they have something personal to gain—since business smart leaders tend to value rewards and recognition too much. They love to compete with others and like challenging and exciting projects, and they strive to complete them ahead of schedule. They have a tendency to get anxious often and take everything as a challenge. Business smart leaders can be moody and love to multitask, prioritizing what they take on based on what is in it for them personally. For instance, they might drop one project that they had decided earlier to invest time and energy into and jump to another project if it holds the potential to elevate their power and status more quickly. They constantly worry about and plan for their legacy, and that self-centered obsession can often become their Achilles' heel. Since they want to succeed at any cost, they are able to bounce back from failures with resilience—but they may not necessarily learn lessons from their failures.

Given these personalities (broadly sketched as they are), smart leaders tend to demonstrate faulty fortitude in two distinct ways: they will decide either to put up a good fight to defend and stick to their decision at any cost (this is the case with functional smart leaders), or they will give up too easily and abandon their decision when better opportunities present themselves (as in the case of business smart leaders).

In our consulting work and research, we've found that many smart leaders—business types and functional types—tend to stick to what they think are the right decisions, even when they should be regularly reevaluating their decisions to ensure they are in alignment with a rapidly changing external context. They maintain this attitude even when presented with evidence that their decision is wrong. This perseverance, which in one particular context can serve as their core competence or signature strength, can become part of their core incompetence in another context.[8]

Former Intel chairman Craig Barrett is a smart leader whose legendary resoluteness served him and his organization as he swiftly identified emerging business opportunities and decided to invest in them. But that same tenacity became his Achilles' heel when he persevered in his decision to invest in the ill-fated Itanium computer chip. In the 1990s, under Barrett's leadership, Intel invested billions of dollars in developing the Itanium chip, which was initially touted as a superchip that would turbocharge Intel's high-end server business. But the chip never delivered on its promise. At the time, Intel's customers were reasonably satisfied with Intel's good-old x86 chips that delivered all the performance they wanted, so they didn't see the need to upgrade their IT systems to Itanium. With this recognition, Intel's key partners like Microsoft and Oracle backed away from their initial support of Itanium. Despite the clear writing on the wall and the tepid customer interest, Barrett pushed ahead with investing in Itanium, which later earned the industry moniker "Intel's Titanic." When Intel announced Itanium processors in 1997, IDC estimated Itanium sales to be around $38 billion by 2001 though by 2004, they were merely $1.4 billion, and by 2012, the processors were kept alive only because HP had paid $690 million to keep Itanium processors alive until 2017.[9] Barrett's fortitude—his courage under fire—is admirable if sticking to his decision pays off for Intel. Otherwise, it is just stubbornness.

Conversely, many smart leaders tend to give up too quickly on productive decisions, either their own or those made by predecessors. The problem is that they are too impatient to wait for their decisions to mature and yield results, so they quickly shut down their own initiatives or those they inherited when they fail to meet even initial expectations.

In March 2010 the CEO of Hewlett Packard at the time, Mark Hurd, made the decision to acquire smart-phone maker Palm for $1.2 billion as a way to enter the mobile devices sector. He set up a three-year program to develop a suite of mobile consumer devices that would be built around WebOS, Palm's operating system. A year later, HP introduced TouchPad, a tablet built on WebOS. The product received decent customer reviews but fared poorly during the first three weeks on the market. A few weeks later, as unsold inventory of TouchPads began piling up, HP's new CEO, Léo Apotheker, decided to pull the plug, saying: "Our TouchPad has not been gaining enough traction in the marketplace. We have made the difficult but necessary decision to shut down the WebOS hardware operations."[10] Apotheker had run out of patience with the new product's slow progress. Unfortunately, this left HP without a product in a growing tablet market. By the end of 2011, it was clear that PC sales were dropping while tablets like iPad had sold over 55 million since it was introduced in 2010 and HP does not have a product in that segment. It reflects poorly on the kind of fortitude Apotheker demonstrated as CEO.

Business smart leaders sometimes have a tendency to roll back a predecessor's decisions, even if they were sound, so that they can put their own stamp on the organization by taking it in a new, and perhaps radically different, direction. For example, many public sector organizations hire a CEO from outside with a limited tenure of a few years. During that brief period, the CEO enjoys total power and control and uses it to build a legacy as quickly as possible. Yet every time a new CEO comes in, existing programs are rolled back or replaced with new ones, which shifts the organization into a different orbit. We have seen this dynamic through our work with several large public sector organizations in India. However, this isn't limited to India or the public sector: leaders in many political, nonprofit, and private organizations worldwide tend to discard older decisions without applying discernment.

In our view, lack of the right kind of fortitude can damage an organization. New leaders must take the time to objectively assess programs and strategies that are already in place to determine which ones need to be kept as is, altered, or possibly abandoned. Sometimes staying on a course charted by a predecessor may be a wiser decision than shifting course just because you have the power to change the status quo.

WISE LEADERS DISPLAY FLEXIBLE FORTITUDE

Wise leaders eschew the two behavioral extremes of smart leaders—sticking to decisions at any cost or giving up too quickly—and exhibit what we call flexible fortitude. *Flexible fortitude* means using one's discernment to gauge when it's appropriate to hold on to things and when it's appropriate to let them go.

Rather than operating in fight-or-flight mode like many smart leaders tend to do, wise leaders choose a third path: they surrender to the context. In Western cultures, the word *surrender* implies passivity or giving up, but in Eastern traditions, especially in Hindu and Buddhist philosophy, surrendering requires both will and grace.[11] Indeed, it takes strength and courage to surrender one's ego to a noble purpose. It takes willpower to overcome your pride and acknowledge with humility that even as a leader, you can't totally control the outcome of your decisions. And it requires poise to embrace the larger forces in play that influence how your decision will play out. This ability to surrender to the constantly evolving context constitutes a wise leader's flexible fortitude.

Wise leaders demonstrate their flexible fortitude in the following ways: they stick to decisions when appropriate, they inspire others to support their decisions and see them through, they revise or reverse decisions willingly when the context shifts, and they draw on the collective willpower to push through transformational decisions.

Stick to Decisions When Appropriate

Wise leaders have a constancy of purpose: they stick with their critical decisions until those decisions produce the desired results. Their perseverance doesn't come from a sense of ego but the belief they are defending an important decision that serves a noble purpose. For her part, Wendy Kopp never regretted her decision to launch TFA in spite of the enormous challenges and criticism she faced during the first years of its existence. She firmly believed in her vision to improve the quality of education for all students and was firmly committed to serving that noble purpose. In this context, her fortitude and perseverance were appropriate, as they were in service of her noble purpose.

Inspire Others to Support Decisions

We have observed that wise leaders generally don't make decisions based on popularity or try to convince others of the merits of their decisions. Rather, they believe in the power of the pull approach— of letting the merits of a decision speak for themselves. Instead of convincing other people to support their decision, they inspire them to do so. In 1997, Oprah Winfrey, host of the popular *The Oprah Winfrey Show* and CEO of OWN Network, launched Oprah Angel Network, a public charity with a vision of inspiring "individuals to create opportunities that enable underserved women and children to rise to their potential."[12] On her TV show, she requested millions of viewers to send in their spare change to help those in need. That initial request raised $3.5 million and was contributed to 150 deserving students in the form of twenty-five-thousand-dollar scholarships. In about thirteen years, Oprah Angel Network raised over $80 million from over 150,000 donors whose funds support hundreds of inspirational projects in thirty countries that empower women and children.[13]

Like Winfrey, TFA's Kopp relied on her "power of attraction"—rather than her persuasion skills—to encourage others to join her in the noble mission to educate underprivileged students. When seeking funding for TFA, Kopp didn't try to convince potential investors with compelling PowerPoint presentations and Excel spreadsheets. Rather, she articulated the critical relevance and importance of TFA's mission and shared inspiring stories from TFA participants that won over prospective investors.

Revise Decisions When the Context Shifts

Wise leaders are open to revising or adapting their decisions—or even reversing them—if they feel that is the right thing to do. They can let go of past decisions—even their own. They are respectful of the past but are not nostalgic for it. They are more focused on building a future that will be better than the present.

Ursula Burns, the current CEO of Xerox, has demonstrated this ability. She retained some decisions made by her predecessor, Ann Mulcahy, but rolled back others, including some strategic decisions that had shaped Xerox's core identity throughout the twentieth century. Having worked for Xerox for more than three decades, Burns is proud of Xerox's rich heritage and famous products. And yet she is not nostalgic about the past because she wants to build a new future for Xerox. That includes outsourcing manufacturing and cutting back or even eliminating marquee products. She is moving into new areas, such as business process management, and in the process reinventing Xerox as a high-tech solution provider for the digital era.[14] Taking a cue from Kodak's misstep in this regard, Burns is disrupting Xerox's analog business before its digital competitors do.

Draw on Collective Willpower for Transformational Change

The concept of willpower has become popular as the theme of personal leadership and self-help books.[15] Willpower is viewed generally as the inner strength a leader needs to steadfastly see a decision through to completion. The emphasis is on individual willpower and individual ownership of decisions. This focus may be applicable when it comes to personal transformation and may also explain why leaders operating in the red zone, who are so driven by personal goals of success, demonstrate amazing will-power to carry through their vision and decisions.

However, when it comes to big decisions about transforming an entire organization, wise leaders, who often believe in shared leadership, tend to draw on the collective willpower of multiple stakeholders to see these transformational decisions through to completion.[16] Wise leaders perceive organizations and societies as complex nonlinear systems in which change can't be enabled by any individual agent but instead requires the interaction of multiple agents. Rather than relying on their individual will-power to drive transformational changes in their company—or in their society—wise leaders form coalitions of stakeholders who share ownership of the decision and facilitate systemic changes.

For instance, when Sam Palmisano took over as CEO of IBM in 2002, he recognized the need to revamp the company's century-old culture to make it more relevant and effective in the new century. "The core responsibility of leadership is to understand when it's time to change—the organization and yourself—and what not to change, what must endure," he told us in an interview.[17]

For over a century, IBM's culture had been built on three core beliefs outlined by founder Thomas Watson Sr.: respect for the individual, the best customer service, and the pursuit of excellence. These three principles, which informed leaders' decisions and actions, had long served the company well, and Palmisano wanted to use them as the foundation for a new set of corporate values that would guide IBM's success in the future. Given IBM's democratic culture, he knew he couldn't impose these values from the top down; instead, he wanted the new value system to emerge from the grassroots to ensure that they would be more than just words handed down from on high.[18]

To do this, Palmisano organized a three-day online brain-storming session in 2003, Values-Jam, where over 300,000 IBM employees from around the world were invited to jointly identify and define the best company values for the twenty-first century.[19] During this exercise, employees debated what IBM truly stands for and what it wants to be known for in the coming decades. One thing they agreed on is that IBM should no longer measure innovation merely by the number of patents coming out of its famous R&D labs. Instead, innovation should be measured by the impact of IBM's technology on society.

That insight led to the formation of a new core value: "Innovation that matters—for our company and for the world."[20] Employees also came up with the values of "dedication to every client's success" and "trust and personal responsibility in all relationships." By tapping in to the collective wisdom of all IBM employees, Palmisano facilitated the cocreation of a new set of corporate values that have shaped all major decisions that IBM leaders have made since 2003.

CULTIVATING FLEXIBLE FORTITUDE

The good news is that you can learn to cultivate flexible fortitude even if you are deeply rooted in your habits. We have seen many leaders build flexible fortitude by harnessing the strength of their noble purpose, managing their energy selectively, using flexibility to combat complexity, and demonstrating fortitude as a team effort.

Harness Your Noble Purpose
In a significant study published in 1998, psychologist Roy Baumeister and his research partners reported that willpower is like

a muscle and can be easily fatigued.[21] In their book *Willpower: Rediscovering the Greatest Human Strength*, Baumeister and John Tierney explain how willpower is not only a nonrenewable resource but also a limited resource that can easily be depleted.[22]

We have consulted many leaders who demonstrate fortitude by sticking to decisions but whose willpower is fueled by desire ("I need to complete this project at any cost so I get my bonus") or fear ("If I don't see through this company reorganization, the board will kick me out"). But neither the desire to win nor the fear of losing, both driven by ego, can sustain willpower for very long. As we explain in chapter 7, you need to have the right motivation—one that transcends self-gratification or self-preservation—to see your decisions through. By striving to serve a noble purpose, you can find that right motivation needed to fuel your willpower and provide the courage, passion, and determination to carry on.

Manage Your Energy Selectively

Tony Schwartz, a best-selling author, leadership consultant, and founder of the Energy Project, believes it is time for leaders who are constantly interrupted by distractions, a common problem among multitasking managers in our hyperconnected world, to "take back their attention."[23] Instead of squandering their limited energy with too many projects, they need to channel their energy by investing in one strategic initiative at a time and stay with this project as long as is required.

Before Alan Mulally took over as CEO at Ford Motor Company, the carmaker routinely put together multiple strategic plans every year. But Mulally had a different idea: he believed in the concept of One Ford and having a single plan or strategy to stay with until it achieved the desired results. The plan was based on four critical elements: coming together as a team, leveraging the company's global assets, building vehicles that customers wanted and valued, and arranging the financing to pay for it all.[24] Mulally hammered home these four points at every opportunity—every town hall meeting, interview, and press conference. By managing your energy selectively, just as Mulally has done, you will avoid overinvesting emotionally in multiple projects.

Foster Flexibility Through Ethical Clarity

Being resolute is important, but this must be balanced with pragmatism. You need to be flexible and continually adapt your decisions and strategies in response to a rapidly changing external context. Otherwise your fortitude will become your Achilles' heel, as in the case of Intel's Craig Barrett.

The simplest way to cultivate flexibility is to remain aware of context changes and shift decisions and strategies rapidly so they retain their relevance in the new context. But you need to demonstrate the right flexibility: flexibility that is informed more by ethical than contextual clarity. Contextual clarity, your awareness of what's happening around you, helps you take the appropriate steps to deal in a dynamic situation without worrying about long-term consequences. Ethical clarity is shaped by values and your noble purpose and can help you make sound decisions with a view to the long term and that serve a larger cause.

Demonstrate Fortitude as a Team Effort

Many smart leaders erroneously mistake bravado for fortitude and prefer going it alone. They rely on persuasion to enlist support from others in the organization to back their decision and see it through, or they use outright coercion to impose an unpopular decision on their organization. But such approaches usually backfire because team members or employees either won't accept the decision or, if it is adopted, will try to sabotage the decision—and even remove their leader. Hence, it's vital for leaders to recognize that demonstrating fortitude is a team effort, not a solo act: you need to garner your team members' commitment to see your

decisions through, and you need their support to let go of unfruit-
ful decisions.

For instance, when Ursula Burns took over as CEO of Xerox
in 2009, the company was in deep financial trouble. In an attempt
to save costs, Burns, who once headed Xerox's supply chain operations, made the tough decision to outsource Xerox's manufacturing to Flextronics, a global contract manufacturer. Under this
deal, Xerox was expected to transfer half of its office equipment
manufacturing operations to Flextronics, a move that could save
Xerox $1 billion in costs.[25] Burns took time to convince union
leaders, who opposed the outsourcing deal, that by helping her
see her decision through, they would have fewer jobs but better
ones, but if they didn't work together, there would be no jobs left
in the manufacturing unit if Xerox's financial woes were to get
worse. Anne Mulcahy, Xerox's former CEO and Burns's mentor,
recalls: "She literally convinced the union that it was going to be
either some jobs or no jobs. For anyone. It was survival. There was
no other way."[26] The union ended up supporting Burns's decision.
Under the outsourcing deal, forty-nine hundred Xerox factory
workers were transferred to Flextronics and kept their jobs. Burns
won the support of Xerox's unionized factory workers for implementing her outsourcing decision because she made them feel
that they were part of the solution rather than the problem.

CONCLUSION

Fortitude is courage under fire. You need the right kind of fortitude to make ongoing determinations about decisions you have
already made so you know when to stick to a decision and when
to revise or reverse it. When the environment is stable, smart
leaders demonstrate fortitude in successfully executing on any
decision that has been made before. But when the context
becomes more complex and the decision itself has to be revisited
often, functional smart leaders generally struggle to take respon-

sibility for making a change. Business smart leaders are more willing to revisit prior decisions during their execution as long as they believe such a change would yield personal rewards or recognition.

Wise leaders demonstrate flexible fortitude: they know when to hold and when to fold—and they do so for the larger benefit. They stick to decisions when appropriate but revise or even reverse them willingly when a shift in the context requires it. They know how to inspire others within a team or organization to support their decisions—and foster and tap into the collective willpower to push through transformational decisions.

Here are some ways you can build up your flexible fortitude when you are dealing with previously made decisions as well as when you are engaged in projects in a shifting context:

- *Stretch yourself.* When you are given a challenging project, don't balk or panic. Rather, stretch yourself to do the best job you can in that project and see what you can learn from it.
- *Let your North Star guide you.* When you get stuck in a project or struggle to see through a decision you made before, avoid giving up too easily or using "brute force" to complete your project or see through a decision. Rather, pay attention to any shift in its external context. If a shift did occur that requires you to discontinue a project or roll back a decision, consider whether doing so would best serve your North Star—and only then decide whether to hold on or to fold.
- *Reframe failure.* Fortitude isn't about avoiding failures at all cost and being successful at all times. Rather, it is the ability to "fail successfully." Indeed, Winston Churchill famously said, "Success is the ability to go from one failure to another with no loss of enthusiasm." Hence, if you were to abandon a project or revise a decision for the right reason, step back and reflect on what you could learn from that setback.
- *Cultivate psychological capital.* According to Fred Luthans, an expert in organizational behavior, leaders can learn to

demonstrate fortitude in the face of adversity by cultivating what he calls "psychological capital." It is built on four attributes known as HERO:[27]

H: Hope   Don't lose it even if the situation looks gloomy.

E: Efficacy   It is about operating with self-confidence.

R: Resilience   Failure is always a stepping stone to future success; hence, try to learn from your past failures.

O: Optimism   Expect to succeed while others might have failed.

Motivation, the fuel for fortitude, helps answer the question: "Why I am I doing what I am doing? What gives me the staying power?" Motivation is therefore the focus of the next chapter.

CHAPTER SEVEN

DISCOVER DRIVERS OF YOUR MOTIVATION
Act with Enlightened Self-Interest

On a rainy day in the monsoon season in 2002, Ratan Tata, then CEO of Tata Group, India's biggest industrial conglomerate, was on his way to the airport in India's high-tech capital Bangalore when a scooter suddenly zipped by, lost control, and skidded while trying to make a turn on the slippery road. Nobody was injured, although the scooter driver, as well as his wife and two children, who were all on the vehicle, were not wearing helmets.

Witnessing that potentially fatal accident and recalling scenes of families riding around in such vehicles in precarious situations triggered a radical thought in Tata's mind: "It led me to wonder whether one could conceive of a safe, affordable, all-weather form of transport for such a family."[1] That random thought led Tata Motors, the automotive arm of Tata Group, to design a two-thousand-dollar car that would be the world's cheapest. Launched in India in 2009 and called the Nano, the compact car provides access to affordable transportation to the emerging middle class in India.[2]

Developing the Nano wasn't easy. There was criticism and disbelief that anyone would want to develop such a car, because no one believed there was a market for such low-cost vehicles.[3]

Tata's motivation behind the Nano, however, was to create an entirely new market, one that could benefit not only his company but rival carmakers as well. "People in the industry said it wasn't possible to build such a car, but now they feel they have to do it themselves [because we showed that it can be done]," he explained. "[Our success] proves there's a large market at the bottom of the pyramid, a market big enough for others as well as for us. If we have started a trend, that will be satisfying to all of us."[4]

Tata has described the Nano as a "people's car" because it brings affordable, fuel-efficient, and safe personal mobility to many families who could never afford a car before.[5] In many ways, the Nano is an embodiment of how a wise leader practices enlightened self-interest, an ethical philosophy that postulates that people who endeavor to serve others' interests eventually end up serving their own self-interest.[6] In other words, leaders who act and lead out of enlightened self-interest attempt to tread a middle path between two extremes in the motivation spectrum: total self-interest and selfless altruism. Tata, for instance, was deeply moved by the scooter accident he saw, as well the needs of a large portion of India's population for better and safer transportation. Yet he wasn't entirely selfless in coming up with Nano. He also knew that the small car market held the potential for huge sales because many people sought to enter the market and buy a car but could not afford expensive models. Indeed, the middle class in India is expected to expand from 5 percent of the population in 2007 to 40 percent over the next two decades, creating the world's fifth-largest consumer market by 2025.[7] India is poised to become the world's fourth largest auto market by 2015.[8]

Tata's philosophy was modeled on that of his great-grandfather, Jamsetji Tata, the founder of Tata Group, who said in 1868, "We do not claim to be more unselfish, more generous or more philanthropic than other people. But we think we started on sound and straightforward business principles, considering the interests of the shareholders our own, and the health and welfare of the employees, the sure foundation of our success."[9] In fact, a philanthropic organization, Tata Sons, holds the majority of shares in Tata Group, a diversified conglomerate made up of for-profit companies engaged in everything from information technology to chemicals and car manufacturing. More than 65 percent of Tata Sons is owned by charitable organizations created by Tata Group, a structure that allows a large portion of the company's profits to flow back into the community for investment in social development projects. The Tata Group states that all its companies believe in "returning wealth to the society they serve."[10] Ratan Tata embodies this selfless spirit and fits the definition of a wise leader—one who "leverages smartness for the greater good." For a corporate chief, he leads a relatively simple life, residing in a modest house with his dogs. He is also actively involved as head of charitable initiatives like Dorobji Tata Trust and Sir Ratan Tata Trust.

While both kinds of smart leaders tend to decide and act motivated primarily by benefits they can accrue for themselves, wise leaders like Ratan Tata make decisions and actions driven by something far beyond personal gains: enlightened self-interest and serving a noble purpose.

ENLIGHTENED SELF-INTEREST: THE NEW BUSINESS IMPERATIVE

Acting and leading with enlightened self-interest is becoming a business imperative in the twenty-first century for two key reasons.

First, the world has become so complex that a leader no longer has all the capabilities or the resources to create all the products and services that customers want. To be effective, leaders need to find partners. In a survey conducted by IBM in 2012 with seventeen hundred CEOs, 70 percent of them indicated that extensive partnerships are critical for the long-term success of their organization.[11] Yet to orchestrate these partner networks effectively, leaders need to rein in some of their own self-interest. Indulging in competitive zero-sum games doesn't work in an interdependent partner relationship: leaders must devise win-win strategies that create value to all of their partners as well.

Second, the values and expectations of a growing number of customers and employees are shifting: they prefer to buy products from and work for companies that are motivated by a purpose beyond financial gain. For instance, 70 percent of the consumers surveyed by the public relations company Burson-Marsteller indicated their willingness to pay a premium for products and services provided by socially responsible companies that invest, among other things, in environmental protection initiatives.[12] Such socially responsible companies include the Tata Group, Whole Foods Market, Panera Bread, and Better World Books (featured in chapter 8), along with several hundred B Corporations (a new type of corporation that uses the power of business to create public benefit) and thousands of social enterprises, all of them using a noble purpose as their North Star to guide their businesses. Jim Collins and Jerry Porras, the best-selling coauthors of *Built to Last,* found that organizations that are driven by a noble purpose outperformed the general market by fifteen to one and outperformed their industry peers by six to one.[13] Collins believes that a noble purpose has "the power to ignite the passion and commitment" of a company's employees, customers, and partners alike.[14] In this chapter, we explore how smart leaders can shift their motivation beyond self-interest to serve this larger purpose.

SMART LEADERS AND SELF-INTEREST

The motivation of leaders depends on whether they operate predominantly from the blue or the red zone.

Leaders in the red zone tend to be driven by the strong desire to achieve fame and success in life. Adventurous by nature, they eschew routine projects and find greater motivation in challenging initiatives. They seem to value external validation more than inner satisfaction and tend to measure their happiness by tangible indicators of success: a big bank account, a large house, and perhaps media recognition. They could easily lose their motivation when they are not properly rewarded or recognized for their efforts. As a result, their energy level is highly variable: they feel elated when they are at the top of their game but deflated when they are bored, overwhelmed, or criticized. Competitive by nature, they get a thrill from winning new clients or gaining market share from their rivals. As leaders driven by high self-interest, they generally struggle to motivate others on their teams other than by traditional means such as financial rewards like bonuses.

In our research and experience, we often find that the biggest difficulty business smart leaders face in their journey toward wise leadership is in shifting their motivation from primarily self-interest to enlightened self-interest. Rajat Gupta is one such business smart leader who, having made great strides in becoming a wise leader, paid a heavy price when in one instance, his self-interest seemingly got the better of him and pulled him down.

Rajat Gupta was born in India in 1948 and grew up in modest circumstances. He quickly showed his intelligence and eventually studied for an M.B.A. at Harvard. After graduating, he worked for McKinsey & Company, where he facilitated multibillion-dollar mergers. At age forty-five, he became the firm's first foreign-born managing director and stayed in that role for nine years; during that time, McKinsey opened offices in twenty countries and doubled its consultant base (from thirty-three hundred to seventy-seven hundred) and more than doubled its revenues (from $1.5 billion to $3.4 billion).[15] Gupta was invited to join the boards of blue chip companies like Goldman Sachs and Procter & Gamble and influential foundations.

Throughout his career, Gupta leveraged his legendary smartness and large network of contacts to improve the well-being of others, especially in developing nations. He listened to others without interrupting for hours, and as *BusinessWeek* wrote, he appeared "egoless" in his responses. *BusinessWeek* quoted Joel Bleeke, Gupta's former McKinsey colleague, in an article that his style had a "very Eastern orientation," emphasizing "wisdom rather than pure intellect." Alan G. Lafley, the former CEO of Procter & Gamble, was quoted in the press comparing Gupta to the thirteenth-century philosopher Saint Thomas Aquinas.[16] So it came as a surprise to everyone when Gupta was convicted in 2012 and sentenced to serve two years in prison for divulging confidential information he gained from the boards of two Fortune 500 companies to the Galleon hedge fund. Gupta's fall from grace was quick and complete when enlightened self-interest was overtaken by not-so-enlightened self-interest.

Blue zone leaders are generally risk averse and primarily motivated by operational excellence and high-quality execution. Getting a job done—whatever job that may be—efficiently with quality motivates them more than name and fame or financial gains. They are motivated by basic needs: taking care of their families, earning enough income to sustain a decent life, and having a stable job. When deciding on new projects or initiatives, they are motivated to pick ones that leverage their existing skill set rather than stretching and expanding their competencies. Once they pick a project, they are mainly interested in getting it done and moving on rather than going beyond the call of duty and outperforming themselves to meet new goals. When it comes to motivating others in their organization, leaders in the blue zone use the traditional followership model and show others how to bring about operational excellence to whatever they do. Benjamin Disraeli, the nineteenth-century British prime minister, summarized followership well: "I must follow the people. Am I not their leader?"[17]

WISE LEADERS ARE DRIVEN TO SERVE OTHERS

While smart leaders can be self-centered—driven by either the basic need for safety and security (blue zone) or the desire for fame and money (red zone), wise leaders are other-centered: they are purposefully driven to mainly serve others.

Wise leaders are not motivated by personal wealth, recognition, and success, though they are comfortable with them. So what really motivates them? They derive a great deal of satisfaction from serving their noble purpose, which often has a strong ethical basis. Intrinsically motivated, they can exercise great self-discipline in staying with an issue and resolving it without seeking any external reward or recognition. Even when asked to lead a routine project, they can look at it from a systemic or holistic perspective and find ways to make the project more engaging and effective—for both themselves and others on their teams—and try to learn the most from that experience. Wise leaders thrive on happiness and effectiveness around them and find joy in bringing the best out of others. They are driven by high aspirations, such as peace and well-being for all; translate those noble aspirations into actionable steps; and work on them for the rest of their lives, as we saw in the case of Dr. V, founder of Aravind Eye Hospital (profiled in chapter 2), which has delivered affordable eye care to millions of people. Highly self-disciplined, wise leaders keep their body, mind, and spirit fit by engaging in activities like exercise, yoga, meditation, or gardening.

Most important, rather than competing with others in an organization, wise leaders engage everyone inside and outside their organization in win-win scenarios in an attempt to cocreate sustainable value for all stakeholders. They motivate others in their organization or ecosystem to follow them in serving a higher purpose. Whereas smart leaders use financial incentives like bonuses to motivate their employees and partners, wise leaders leverage their personal authenticity and deep commitment to the larger purpose to set an example. Consider Om Prakash Bhatt, who, as chairman of the State Bank of India (SBI), transformed the bank's culture by instilling a sense of pride in all its employees.

In 2006, Bhatt became the chairman of SBI, the country's largest bank in terms of assets, branches, and customers, with about 200,000 employees and a storied history dating back more than two hundred years. At the time, though, the bank had been steadily losing market share for two decades. Customers were unhappy, and staff were demoralized and lacked a common set of objectives, goals, and vision.[18]

In September 2006, Bhatt convened the first strategy meeting with his senior management team as the chairman. He kicked it off with segments of *The Legend of Bagger Vance*, a movie about a great golfer who fell on hard times after World War I and eventually rediscovered his swing as well as his pride. Bhatt then told his senior managers: "India is on a growth burst. The banking sector is on a roll. But, sadly this growth is largely bypassing us. What has gone wrong? Have we hit a midlife crisis? We have become like Bagger Vance: we have lost our 'swing'. How do we regain it?" Bhatt hoped to rekindle SBI's *swabhiman* (Sanskrit for self-respect) and encourage his senior managers to find ways restore SBI to its prior glory.[19]

We know of many organizations that bring in a turnaround expert as CEO to revive their sagging fortunes. They link the CEO's compensation (with big bonuses) to improvements in the organization's bottom line. In this case, the CEO's motivation to drive major transformation in the organization is primarily self-interest: the hope of getting a fat bonus check at the end. But at SBI, Bhatt's salary was less than one thousand dollars a month. His motivation to transform SBI wasn't about financial reward but enlightened self-interest to put the bank on a sustainable growth path—something he could derive satisfaction from even after retiring.

In a similar way, recognizing that he couldn't motivate SBI employees through financial rewards, Bhatt leveraged his core asset, authentic communication, to rally his demoralized troops, starting at the senior management meeting in September 2006. The effect was immediate: most of the senior leaders in that meeting who were initially skeptical were energized by Bhatt's wakeup call and, with Bhatt, devised an action plan for reinvigorating SBI's performance. This plan of action included transformational initiatives in various critical areas such as customer service, employee engagement, and technology infrastructure.

Having enlisted senior management support for transforming SBI and having cocreated with them a plan for that transformation, Bhatt set out to secure the buy-in for that plan from middle management. Over three months, he personally met with two thousand middle managers and shared with them his inspirational vision for the future of SBI: an agile and customer-centric organization run by a highly motivated and innovative workforce. With both passion and humility, he requested these managers to join him in realizing that vision. Bhatt's gift for authentic communication stoked the passion in his unmotivated middle managers: no senior leaders had engaged them in this genuine fashion before. As one middle manager who interacted with Bhatt explained, "We were almost resigned to the inevitable demise of a bank we had grown up with and the only option for us to grow seemed to be to leave the bank and join our competition to contribute anything significantly. [Bhatt's message was like] music to our ears."[20]

As staff enthusiasm grew for the transformation agenda, two powerful unions of bank employees came to believe that such a process could boost low employee morale. And so they added their voices and contributed to the transformation process too.

In mid-2007 SBI rolled out Parivartan (Sanskrit for *transformation*), a change management program, across all fourteen regions in the country simultaneously. Parivartan was a massive communication and training program that was executed in thirty-eight hundred (two-day) workshops held in over one hundred venues across India over one hundred days. Over 130,000 employees attended these workshops.

In the wake of this program, employees at different levels began demonstrating more creative leadership and cultivating closer bonds with customers. For example, Shiva Kumar, at the time the chief general manager of SBI's operations in Hyderabad (currently he is the managing director of State Bank of Bikaner and Jaipur), set up a mobile text-messaging service for customer complaints, which addressed seven thousand complaints within five months.

By unleashing and harnessing the ingenuity within all employees, Bhatt was able to expand SBI's market share to 19 percent from 16.5 percent in a highly competitive industry during his tenure. At the same time, SBI's stock value doubled, and customer satisfaction climbed.[21]

Bhatt retired in 2011 after thirty-nine years of service to SBI. Looking back, he told us that the transformation agenda evolved through conversations as he engaged leaders from all levels in his ecosystem, including all employee unions and customers, in addition to regulators. "It was like building a bridge while walking on it," he said.[22]

How did Bhatt lead SBI wisely? First, he was guided by a noble purpose—to restore the past glory of an illustrious establishment—and aligned his decisions and actions with that purpose. Furthermore, he acted as a servant leader by allowing his employees to lead the bottom-up transformation of SBI. In addition, he demonstrated fortitude by seeing through his decision to make SBI more innovative and customer-centric. Ultimately, however, it was his wise motivation—his enlightened self-interest to restore the sense of pride within SBI's workforce—that gave him credibility and inspired the 200,000 SBI employees to support and help implement this transformational change.

COCREATING SUSTAINABLE VALUE WITH ALL STAKEHOLDERS

In keeping with their competitive nature (the red zone) and fixed mind-set (the blue zone), smart leaders believe that the size of the market is fixed. They aim to grab as big a piece of pie as possible, or, in the case of leaders operating out of the blue zone, to hold on to every piece of pie they already have. This selfish attitude stems from their belief in business being a zero-sum game.

Wise leaders recognize that the world is becoming more interdependent and therefore seek to cocreate value with others. They reach out to others and invite them to collectively create a bigger pie so everyone can get a bigger slice. Outdoor clothing and apparel company Patagonia, for example, encourages its customers to consume less by offering them an exchange and recycling program that allows them to share or trade their used Patagonia products with others.[23] Through this initiative, Patagonia is catalyzing the growth of a grassroots movement called collaborative consumption—a socioeconomic system that enables the sharing and exchange, on a large scale, among consumers of all kinds of goods and services, ranging from clothes to cars to skills to spaces.[24]

In a similar way, Facebook CEO Mark Zuckerberg regularly reminds his staff how the social networking platform that the company has built can make a difference in the world.[25] He actively encourages employees as well as Facebook users to be socially involved. Given the site's vast reach, this can be extremely effective: in 2012 more than 100,000 Facebook users signed up to be organ donors, thanks to a new feature on the social networking site that made registering for organ donation easy.[26]

Gitanjali Group is a $900 million company that pioneered the concept of affordable branded diamond-studded jewelry in India. It is a vertically integrated jewelry manufacturer and retailer with a wide range of activities ranging from diamond sourcing to manufacturing and retail. When Gitanjali Gems set up a facility for cutting and polishing diamonds and making jewelry on a 176-acre campus outside Hyderabad, a South Indian city, it faced a major human resource challenge: there were no skilled workers available in Hyderabad, unlike traditional hubs of diamond polishing like Surat, Gujarat, in western India, where diamond-polishing skills are passed down through generations. The cost of training diamond workers is high, and the work is intricate and detailed, which means a high dropout rate that adds to production costs. The question facing Gitanjali's leaders was how to hire, train, develop, and retain productive employees and make the new unit cost-effective.

Mehul Choksi, the chairman of the Gitanjali Group, is a leader committed to developing society around the workplace and was therefore open to the concept of hiring disabled rural youth as a corporate social responsibility (CSR) initiative in 2005.[27] The plan was put into effect, and today more than 11 percent of Gitanjali's twenty-five hundred employees are disabled youth. The company found that the attrition rate among this disabled employee group is much lower—and its productivity level much higher—when compared to the rest of the workforce. This convinced Gitanjali's leaders to change the disabled youth initiative from a CSR project to a core element of the company's talent management strategy. As the company expands, it envisions hiring up to five thousand more people in 2013 and 2014, with at least one thousand of them disabled youth.[28]

We analyzed the factors that made hiring disabled youth a good business case for the Gitanjali Group. First, it helped the company tap into a large labor resource pool (India has a population of 20 million disabled; barely 0.1 percent of them are employed). Second, the training it offered to these young people quickly paid for itself, because disabled youth have a greater sense of loyalty, as the attrition rate suggests. Third, productivity among these disabled workers is also higher because they have more motivation to prove that their disability is not a deterrent to performance. Fourth, it leads to a more diverse workforce. It's worth noting here that these disabled youth often earn more money than the company's able-bodied workers because they are more productive and therefore receive performance bonuses. Enlightened self-interest is the prime motivation for Gitanjali's leaders to hire disabled youth in an initiative that not only supports local communities but also garners a highly motivated and productive workforce for the company.

CULTIVATING ENLIGHTENED SELF-INTEREST

We have found that the best way for smart leaders to make the transition from pure self-interest to the enlightened self-interest of wise leadership is to experience it. You can do this by reading about other wise leaders in this book or coming in contact with someone who exhibits it—and this might inspire you to take a similar path.

ServiceSpace (introduced in chapter 2), an initiative that leverages social networking tools (such as its website servicespace .org) to build compassionate and service-oriented communities worldwide, takes this principle seriously and has experimented with ways to generate compassion and enlightened self-interest in others for years. In 2003, CharityFocus (the organization's original name) came up with the concept of smile cards, which it describes this way: "[Smile cards] are markers of a newfangled game of tag, where 'you're it' because someone has done something nice for you. Then it's your turn to do something nice for someone else and, in the process, pass the card along. This is a game of pay-it-forward: anonymously make someone smile, leave behind a card asking them to keep the ripple going."[29]

We came across smile cards (you can print your own cards or order them on online at helpothers.org and get them shipped to anywhere in the world) several years ago when our colleague Ragunath Padmanabhan was buying a large pack of chewing gum for a family who was visiting from Singapore, where gum was prohibited. We were amazed at the childlike joy Padmanabhan displayed while wrapping up the chewing gum carefully and sticking a smile card inside, then anonymously leaving it with the family. Padmanabhan had met the family only the day before and overheard them say, in a ServiceSpace meeting, that they wanted to buy a pack of gum.

As leaders' perspectives consciously evolve, their engagement with others in their organization and in the community evolves as well from an antagonistic winner-takes-all relationship to a collaborative approach with the belief that helping others in the long run will help them. This transition—or evolution—typically occurs in four phases during which a leader's aspiration evolves from fear-driven survival to a compassionate desire to make society better.[30]

Level 0: Zero-Sum Game (1 + 1 = 0)

Without inspiration from outside or deeper introspection from inside, leaders keep doing what they have done before and rarely change their actions. When they are in a smart state of mind, they can be fiercely competitive. Proving that they are smarter than their competitors sometimes dominates all other concerns. When focused on the short term, they may perceive opportunity as a zero-sum game and want to grab and hold on to as much as they can—market share, profits, or something else. Hence their motivation is primarily shaped by their black-and-white thinking, and it results in scorched-earth situations where one or even both sides sustain heavy losses; the larger market or society may lose too.

A grim example of such thinking is the many "vaporware" introductions in Silicon Valley where competing companies announce products that never ship but in the meantime discourage potential customers from buying them from the competition.[31] In marketing, creating a "FUD factor" (fear, uncertainty, and doubt) in the minds of competition and sometimes customers is a well-known strategy that actually risks frustrating customers, who then lose interest in products from both parties.[32]

Level 1: Give and Take (1 + 1 = 2)

Smart leaders shift their perspective when they see that they have more to gain by partnering with others than by competing with them. Role modeling by others and experiencing some empathy is key to softening smart leaders' competitive stance. At this stage, they are more willing to share knowledge or resources with others as long as their actions are reciprocated and they can benefit from the give-and-take transaction.

For instance, in 1997, Steve Jobs returned to Apple as CEO and convinced Bill Gates to invest $150 million and commit to developing Microsoft Office for the Mac for another five years. Gates saw an opportunity for presenting this investment in Apple as evidence of a noble act—helping a competitor—to the Department of Justice, which had filed an antitrust lawsuit against Microsoft for its aggressive promotion of Internet Explorer. Microsoft would also be able to generate additional revenues for its Office product by selling it to the vast Apple customer base. For Jobs, support by Microsoft would convince Apple customers and developers of the long-term viability of Apple and its platform. In exchange for receiving the investment from Microsoft, Apple dropped a long-standing lawsuit against Microsoft for allegedly copying the look and feel of the Mac operating system for Windows. This deal between Apple and Microsoft is a transactional version of enlightened self-interest or win-win: both parties get what they put in as long as both trust each other and stay in the game.[33]

Level 2: Making the Pie Bigger (1 + 1 = 3)

Successful engagement with level 2 of enlightened self-interest means leaders are more open to experiment and more curious about exploring opportunities together, making synergistic partnerships possible. At this level, leaders begin to recognize the unique value of others and seek to amplify them for their collective good. They may begin to cocreate new offerings with others by combining and synergizing their individual capabilities in a way that brings greater value to both of them.

For instance, under Alan Mulally, the 777 program managers shifted the way Boeing collaborated with suppliers: rather than engaging suppliers on a transactional level by telling them what to do, program managers began engaging them as innovation partners and seeking their creative input. An example of how this worked was the Dreamliner or 787 project: over 60 percent of the plane was designed or built by suppliers and also financed by suppliers, so they had a stake in the game (this is the shared-risk/shared-reward model).[34] Boeing clearly saw that the Asian countries and airlines are going to be big customers in the future. They found that to receive the orders from China Airlines, Air India, and other such companies from Asia and emerging economies, they had to create jobs and cocreate technology that benefits the local industry in those countries as well. That means that Boeing cocreates the planes and sells them to the customers in countries with reduced trade barriers. It was synergistic, because companies in both countries benefited from this cocreation, and it enlarged the market for Boeing.

In the early 2000s, we consulted with leaders at a large enterprise software vendor—let's call it BIGSOFT—who were operating in the blue zone. The company leaders, most of them engineers by training, were content developing high-quality software that automated companies' manufacturing processes. Despite having a high-quality product, BIGSOFT was struggling to make a big dent in that software market because aggressive competitors run by leaders operating in the red zone were investing far more in sales and marketing than BIGSOFT was.

We advised the software vendor to take the higher road: rather than continuing to butt heads with its aggressive rivals in existing niche markets, it needed to create a new market for end-to-end supply chain solutions and paint a larger vision for their corporate clients on how they can benefit from these new solutions. In other words, rather than competing for tiny pieces of an existing small pie, BIGSOFT had to create a much larger pie, of which it can command a bigger slice.

BIGSOFT leaders recognized the need for partners to create a bigger pie and followed our advice. Over three years, BIGSOFT patiently built an ecosystem of software and services partners and cocreated with them a comprehensive solution that optimized the end-to-end supply chains of large manufacturing firms. BIGSOFT kept its partners motivated by forging win-win contractual agreements, such as revenue-sharing deals. This synergistic win-win partnering strategy became a big commercial success and established BIGSOFT as a market leader.

Level 3: The Rising Tide Lifts All Boats (1 + 1 = 11)

When leaders successfully engage with level 3 of enlightened self-interest, they begin to operate from a much broader and wiser perspective. This is the level at which outperformers succeed in partnering with others to do radical innovation, according to the 2012 IBM Global CEO report.[35] Instead of being limited by a compartmentalized worldview, these leaders have a systemic view of the world: they recognize that everything is interconnected. They are driven by an urge to tackle big challenges and issues that affect entire industries and even entire societies worldwide. Intrinsically motivated and possessed of a noble purpose that they strive to serve, they don't worry unduly as to how financial analysts will judge their decisions and actions.

At this level, business leaders make socially conscious decisions and contribute to local communities—no longer as part of a CSR initiative but as a core element of their corporate strategy. Ron Shaich, the cofounder and executive chairman of Panera Bread, a chain of bakery-cafés with over fifteen hundred outlets nationwide, is a wise leader who clearly believes that the rising tide can lift all boats. For him, socially responsible policies make business sense. He is driven by enlightened self-interest in its noblest form. "Corporate America will both serve its shareholders and strengthen its reputation when it finds ways to use its expertise and core competencies, as well as its scale, to be truly conscious citizens," he says. "Imagine if more large corporations were more active in trying to address social needs locally. Imagine if Wal-Mart ran distribution for food shelters. Or if Gap opened thrift shops. Or if Home Depot rehabilitated housing in under-privileged neighborhoods."[36]

Under Shaich's leadership, Panera has been experimenting with various initiatives that embody the spirit of enlightened self-interest. In 2010, Shaich launched Panera Cares to combat food insecurity in America: nearly 50 million Americans struggle at some time during the year to provide adequate food for all their members due to a lack of money and other resources. According to the U.S. Department of Agriculture, one in seven U.S. households in 2011 was food insecure.[37]

Panera Cares are cafés that address America's food insecurity by serving nutritious food without a fixed price: guests pay what-ever they can afford.[38] After opening its first "pay what you can café" in St. Louis, Missouri, Panera has since added three more; overall it served more than 500,000 people in the first year and 1 million the next year. It's not about money, Shaich says: "We didn't launch Panera Cares to improve our balance sheet. And that's why it's succeeding. Whatever tangible and intangible benefits accrue to the business, they're simply by-products of committing to a purpose that goes above and beyond profit and next quarter's earnings per share."[39]

Indra Nooyi, chairman and CEO of PepsiCo, is another leader who believes that the rising tide can indeed lift all boats. Deeply convinced that businesses can do well while doing good Nooyi has fostered a culture of "Performance with Purpose" within her orga-nization. Under her wise leadership, PepsiCo has proactively engaged multiple stakeholders to cocreate value for all stakehold-ers in a manner that is financially, socially, and environmentally sustainable. (In chapter 3 we discussed how PepsiCo has imple-mented Performance with Purpose.)

CONCLUSION

Motivation is the intent and the driving force behind our actions. It can be intrinsic, such as the pleasure we find in certain activities, or extrinsic, that is, goal directed. Blue zone leaders, who excel at execution and operations, tend to be motivated by getting things done on time and under budget with high quality; they excel at increasing short-term productivity and profitability within an organization. Red zone leaders, who excel at seeing and seizing new opportunities that will bring top-line growth, fame, and success to their organizations and themselves, tend to be driven primarily by self-interest.

Unlike smart leaders, who tend to be self-centered, wise leaders are other-centered. They are mainly motivated by enlightened self-interest. They are driven by the belief that what is in the public interest is eventually in the interest of all individuals and groups, including themselves and their organizations. Wise leaders do care about bottom-line productivity and top-line growth, but they pursue these business objectives in a collaborative way by forging partner ecosystems that collectively strive to serve a noble purpose while simultaneously cocreating value for all members in an ecosystem.

As a leader in today's increasing complex and interdependent world, you can no longer afford to do everything yourself or think that your organization can or should operate on its own. You need to reach out to partners and cocreate value with them. When you undertake any new project or venture that involves other people or organizations, instead of asking, "What's in it for me?" focus on the question, "What's in it for others?" The answers you discover may surprise you.

In addition to reading about other leaders and organizations operating from a place of enlightened self-interest and cocreation of value, here are some ways you can cultivate enlightened self-interest. Use these points as touchstones or ways to focus your reflection about the purpose and meaning of your initiatives:

- When identifying your long-term priorities, choose to invest in projects that are aligned with your North Star. These will be meaningful to you and fulfill your deepest aspirations.

- Learn to differentiate short-term motivation from long-term motivation. You may need to forgo immediate gratification for the sake of achieving bigger and longer-term gains for you, your organization, and the larger society.
- If you are competitive by nature, recognize that business is not a zero-sum game. Eschew win-lose strategies and start working to cocreate win-win scenarios with partners—ideally, scenarios that both serve a noble purpose and deliver sustainable value to everyone in your ecosystem, though even give-and-take and synergistic scenarios are an improvement over a zero-sum stance.
- Engage in every project with a learning attitude. If it is boring and you get demotivated, find ways to make the project more engaging and meaningful. Can you reframe the project in a way that adds interest and value to it? Can you help others on the project team complete their tasks and learn more about their job?
- See whether your happiness can multiply by bringing happiness to others. In other words, see whether you can bring energy, enthusiasm, and happiness to your colleagues and partners and help fulfill their goals and increase their motivation. What is the result for your own happiness and motivation?

As you begin to cultivate enlightened self-interest, strive to align it with the other five capabilities discussed in previous chapters: all of them are interlinked and synergistic. Each chapter contains one or more lists of questions and suggestions to understand and build a version of the capability that reflects wise leadership.

Begin by reconnecting with your noble purpose:

- Do the opportunities you see for enlightened self-interest get you closer to fulfilling it (chapter 2)?
- Take appropriate actions that are also authentic for you. These will bring you great satisfaction and lead to increasing trust

and respect for your leadership within your organization's ecosystem (chapter 3).

- Reflect on whether the role you are playing is allowing you and others to lead effectively. If it is not, you may need to switch to another role that you will find more fulfilling or recalibrate your commitment to the role you are in—that is, exercise role clarity (chapter 4).

- Examine whether your decision logic is leveraging your intuition and instincts effectively and whether it is based on wise discernment (chapter 5).

- Reflect on episodes that show your fortitude. Are you flexible and resilient or rigid and unpredictable (chapter 6)?

Based on your assessment, how does your vision for enlightened self-interest support the other five capabilities?

Aligning your motivation with the other five capabilities optimizes your wise leadership. It has to be done consciously and iteratively, until you are comfortable that all six capabilities are synergized and are allowing you to be the best leader you can be. We call this process *developing your own wisdom logic*. As you evolve as a wise leader, you can accelerate your own transformation by partnering with other leaders and creating a field of wise leadership. When you start leveraging collective wisdom to develop wise leadership in others around you—on your team, in your organization, and beyond—you truly act and lead with wisdom. Finding your wisdom logic and creating a field of leadership are the focus of the next and final chapter.

CHAPTER EIGHT

COCREATE A FIELD OF WISE LEADERSHIP
Find Your Wisdom Logic

It is our belief, based on experience, that you can become an effective and wise leader by developing the six leadership capabilities we have identified and discussed: perspective, action orientation, role clarity, decision logic, fortitude, and motivation. These capabilities are separate but also interdependent elements: if you develop them together, each leveraging the power of the others, you can accelerate your wise leadership journey. When you integrate some or all of these capabilities into a larger whole, you will have created your own wisdom logic—that is, your unique, authentic path to wise leadership.

Many leaders grow into one or two capabilities (usually those that are most appealing to them or that they pick up easily) and then, as inclination and necessity dictate, integrate other capabilities in an ongoing process. The process is one of trial and error, and many of the wise leaders we have studied and consulted with are what we might call work in progress—wise in some ways but not so wise in others.

In chapters 2 through 7, we laid out a sequence for developing and integrating the six capabilities, starting with broadening your perspective and ending with making enlightened self-interest your main source of motivation. We find this sequence has a logical flow and momentum. But the path you choose to take toward wise leadership—whether you start from the blue zone or the red zone—will be unique to you. It has to be based on the context in which you live and work, your noble purpose, and who is part of your field of leadership (more on this concept below). What is important is that you stay on the path, developing and clarifying your own wisdom logic throughout your life and career. It's not a linear process, and you will need patience and courage, but there is no path more rewarding for you to embark on.

Although many leaders travel on their wise leadership journey alone, you don't have to. Especially in today's interconnected and interdependent world, it's possible to create a field of leadership around yourself by connecting to other leaders and working together to develop wise teams, organizations, communities, and nations. In this way, you turn your individual journey to wise leadership into a shared journey—a collective pursuit involving mentoring, coaching, and shared insight that will be highly rewarding for all of you.[1]

ONE JOURNEY TO WISE LEADERSHIP: STEVE JOBS

Steve Jobs was a smart leader who created his own wisdom logic through trial and error. He discovered his noble purpose—to "put a dent in the universe"—early in life, but he limited himself to applying that purpose to Apple and his own family rather than the greater good of society. He had a somewhat rigid perspective and didn't often value—or even tolerate well—the views of others. His role clarity—his understanding of his role in the world— seems to have improved as he went along: he picked the right people for the right roles. Many of his decisions were deeply intuitive, though they seemed counterintuitive to everyone else, like opening Apple retail stores. And he knew when to lead (as when he stuck to his decision to launch iPad despite significant skepticism) and when to let others lead (when, for example, he opened up the iPhone's operating system to third-party application developers by creating App Store).

We do regard Jobs as a wise leader, though with some weaknesses. In our analysis, he was for most of his career unable to keep his identity separate from his role, a combination that turned him into both an egotistical manager and a great inventor. In other words, through most of his professional life, Jobs struggled to gain and demonstrate role clarity. And yet because he was so comfortable in playing the role of a customer himself—"I create products to please myself," as he put it—his ego-centered approach to developing new products ended up also meeting the interests and needs of customers. Toward the end of his career, however, Jobs seems to have made huge progress in gaining role clarity. Aware of his mortality, he came to realize that he was a mere steward of the company he cofounded, and he gradually let go of the reins of Apple, gracefully passing the baton to a capable executive team that included Tim Cook and design chief Jonathan Ive. Hence, in Steve Jobs's case, his six leadership capabilities were tightly integrated and worked in harmony, providing the foundation for his wisdom logic.

We surmise that Jobs discovered a great deal of his wisdom logic while running Pixar, where he learned to lead from behind and let others shine. When he returned to Apple in 1997 after his twelve years of exile, he had completed a "hero's journey"—to use the term coined by the mythologist Joseph Campbell—bringing home (to Apple) a precious gift: his wisdom logic.[2] Not only did he apply his wisdom logic to create amazingly fine products, but he also cultivated a field of wise leadership within Apple. For instance, Jobs was known for his ability to shift other leaders' perspectives at Apple and encourage them to make intuitive decisions and stick to them with fortitude no matter how unpopular they might be among Apple investors. As a result of this expanding field of wise leadership, Apple became highly successful.

In the last years of his life, Jobs began expanding the field of wise leadership beyond Apple by selectively (sometimes reluctantly) mentoring young leaders like Facebook CEO Mark Zuckerberg and Google cofounder Larry Page.[3] Even after his untimely death, Jobs continues to inspire scores of leaders across industries to act and lead authentically with a laser focus on innovation.

WISDOM LOGIC: YOUR AUTHENTIC PATHWAY TO WISE LEADERSHIP

Wisdom logic is like the balance that you discover when learning to ride a bicycle: you achieve balance only after mastering all the individual elements of riding a bike. Discovering and then maintaining that balance is an iterative process, just as cultivating wisdom is. You cannot become a wise leader simply by reading a book—including this book—in the same way that you can't learn to ride a bicycle just by reading a book on it. Discovering and honing one's wisdom logic is an iterative process. It is also a highly subjective one because one has to take time to discover one's North Star (noble purpose) and learn to act authentically in alignment with it. Moreover, one needs to choose one's roles with discernment and assume these roles with high integrity. Furthermore, one has to discover one's own decision logic—that is, knowing when to let go of power and control and when to hold on to them. Finally, serving others and developing other leaders with enlightened self-interest is a significant transformation for one to go through.

No two leaders share the same wisdom logic: each possesses his own and each developed it in his own way. For instance, the wisdom logic of Bill Gates—both the process by which he developed that logic and the way he is manifesting it now—is very different from the approach that Steve Jobs cultivated to develop his own wisdom logic, which he also expressed distinctively. Whereas Jobs applied his wisdom logic mainly in the technology field,

Gates slowly left the tech industry in the mid-2000s—once he experienced a perspective shift—and has since focused completely on serving his noble purpose: improving the lives of millions of people around the world. Once Gates's perspective shifted, he began cultivating his own wisdom logic by gradually aligning and integrating his actions, role clarity, decisions, fortitude, and motivation with his noble purpose. As the cohead of the Bill & Melinda Gates Foundation, Gates is now using his wisdom logic not to build a great company but to build a better world.

To prepare yourself for a discovery of your own wisdom logic, first clarify your intent—that is, why you want to be a wise leader. You can do so by first discovering your North Star and then connecting your intent to it, which will give you a new and clear sense of direction in life (chapter 2 examined how to find your North Star). Second, pay attention to the leadership zone (blue or red) in which you currently operate and create a plan to bridge the gaps between where you are and where you want to be. Third, be clear and aware that there will be bumps and detours along the journey to wise leadership: remain humble and resilient to learn from your missteps, just as Jobs and Gates did, and enjoy the journey, which is a gift to yourself.

An effective way to speed up the discovery of your wisdom logic is to partner with others who are in the process of discovering their own. This collaboration becomes a kind of learning laboratory where you can experiment and practice what you have learned, share your experiences, and see what others are doing and learn from their experiences. Collaborating with others also involves developing your wise leadership in a wider scope of engagement with social systems, such as teams, organizations, and communities. We call this engagement across many levels of social organization the *field of wise leadership*.

As depicted in Figure 8.1, a spiral of development forms when leaders evolve and facilitate the growth of others at different levels, outward from the personal through the team, organization,

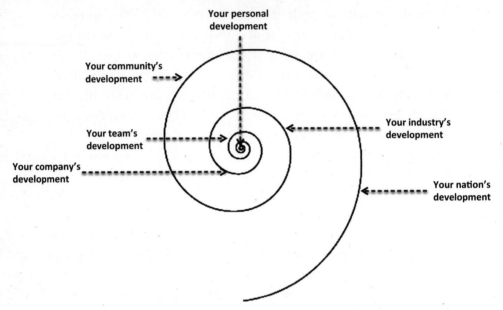

Figure 8.1 A "Field of Leadership" Tends to Expand Spirally.

industry, community, and nation levels. When you are developing along such a spiral, you recognize the opportunity to shift the perspectives of others around you so they can embark on their own journey to wise leadership. Depending on the circle of your influence, you might opt to focus on your team, your organization, your community, or even your nation—and keep expanding your field of wise leadership.

Once you start operating as a wise leader—without any filters—you will begin to see others who operate in the red or the blue zones more clearly. Through role modeling, mentoring, and coaching, lead them toward wise leadership. When you do this in the context of a team—be it your family or a work team—you help shift the culture of that team. In a similar way, you can focus on the organization or a community, whether a parent teacher association or a spiritual community. You can even create a book club or a dialogue group to read and discuss this book with others and help each other grow. And you can join the online communities on fromsmarttowise.com where you can share your learning with others on the wise leadership journey and benefit from their own insights.

CULTIVATING LEADERSHIP WISDOM ACROSS SOCIAL SYSTEMS

As your focus shifts to cultivating wisdom in yourself and others in a wider sphere, you will recognize that each level of a social system can operate as smart or wise. When you are by yourself, your own actions and your interactions with others are based primarily on your personal thoughts and feelings. But when you are part of a larger social system—a team, organization, or community—your own intentions (expectations), behaviors, and culture (shared values and assumptions) tend to shift based on the social system that you are part of. We elaborate on the evolution of these three aspects of social systems, based on a framework of Kaipa, Newham, and Volckmann, in the next paragraphs.[4]

A social system can be a group, team, organization, or community. Each social system has its own intention, behavior, and culture. Let's begin with intention. We generally choose to join a group with a deep desire to belong to it, and that desire shapes our intent. On a team, we stretch and grow to accommodate the shared intent of the team, whereas in a group we might not stretch beyond our comfort zone. In an organization, we focus not on the process of stretching and growing as individuals but on collectively producing results by generating competitive products and services. In a social system like a community—be it a neighborhood community or a large trade association—the focus of all members shifts toward fulfilling the promise of that community.

In correspondence with the intention, behavior also evolves across social systems. In a group, members are primarily focused on supporting each other as long as they don't have to go outside their comfort zone. A team is more active and goal oriented; hence, its members collaborate and co-create what needs to get done. In an organization, such co-creation takes place over an extended period in a developmental fashion to achieve the desired results. And when one is part of a community, one operates with a higher purpose and one's actions are geared toward serving others in the community.

Finally, cultural attributes also vary across social systems. A group usually fosters a transactional give-and-take culture. When a group evolves into a team, members become more appreciative of each other and develop deeper relationships beyond one-off transactions. In an organization, people tend to work together synergistically to make the company successful. And in a community setting, the success depends on the care that we take to include each other and serve each other. Of course just like individual leaders, groups, teams, organizations, and communities also tend to operate in the red or the blue zones.

The next sections discuss how groups, teams, organizations, and communities can become wise—and how you can accelerate your own wise leadership development by creating and expanding a field of leadership that extends across these systems.

Wise Groups

The smallest unit among social systems is a group, an ad hoc collection of individuals who get together based on their need to belong. Groups tend to emerge organically, and while the members cooperate and support each other, their interactions tend to be transactional in nature. In the initial stages, some groups tend to operate in the blue zone when everyone in a group could be narrowly focused on addressing their own tactical needs rather than contributing to the group's collective long-term interest. Entrepreneurial groups helmed by red zone leaders may collectively pursue strategic opportunities for the benefit of all—but such group cohesion tends to be short-lived since the leaders' own self-interest eventually takes over. The group continues to exist only as long as its members can get what they want from each other. They break up if there is no longer any transactional value. Groups by themselves rarely demonstrate wisdom, and when they evolve into the next level of social systems—a team—they begin to have deeper relationships that lead to deep knowledge and begin to exhibit wisdom from within.

Wise Teams

Just like individuals and groups, teams also tend to operate in red or blue zones. Team leaders and team members, based on their own level of wisdom, can tilt the balance and steer teams toward wise leadership. When the majority of the team operates wisely, its members are more likely to stretch beyond their comfort zone, co-create value for themselves and others, and appreciate contributions from other participants.

A wise team spirit is the cornerstone of Taj Hotels, the largest hotel chain in India, and part of Tata Group. Taj Hotels operates with the core belief that "happy employees lead to happy customers." Its leaders invest heavily in the personal development of every employee, training them extensively to understand the concepts of integrity, teamwork, initiative, and of course customer satisfaction, to the point where they internalize the Taj Hotels' noble purpose: "The Guest is God."

The degree to which Taj employees internalize this noble purpose was poignantly demonstrated in November 2008 when a group of Islamic terrorists carried out coordinated attacks on five well-known sites in Mumbai, resulting in the deaths of 174 people. One of the sites the terrorists targeted was the Taj Mahal Hotel, a flagship property of Taj Hotels. The hotel siege lasted sixty hours. Through it all, many Taj employees demonstrated wise leadership characteristics—discernment, role clarity, fortitude, and selflessness—and managed to save the lives of hundreds of hotel guests and others nearby. Some of them died while helping others escape through secret exits or remained trapped with them in hotel rooms (the hotel had caught fire during the terrorist siege). In one case, a twenty-four-year-old banquet manager named Mallika Jagad single-handedly coordinated the evacuation of executives from the global consumer goods company Unilever, including the outgoing global CEO and the incoming CEO who were attending a private party that night in the hotel.[5]

The hotel's general manager, Karambir Singh Kang, lost his wife and two young children, who were trapped in their residence on the top floor of the hotel. When we spoke to Kang, now the head of Taj Hotels in the United States, he told us that he believed the Taj Mahal Hotel team acted as one and stretched beyond the call of duty because the organization had inculcated a strong team spirit. The staff was putting into action what managers had taught them, which focused on doing whatever it takes to keep the customer happy and improvising solutions without having to consult a supervisor.[6]

H. N. Shrinivas, the senior vice president of human resources at Taj Hotels, echoed this idea when discussing his company's approach to team training. He told us that Taj Hotels recruits managers from second-tier business schools rather than top-ranking ones because, he says, these managers will be more humble and open to learning.[7] New employees are evaluated on their character as well as their smarts, and character building continues as long as they work for Taj Hotels. They receive specific skills training as well as soft skills training in creativity, empathy, and teamwork. Taj Hotels has set up a Special Thanks and Recognition System (STARS) that rewards employees as much for their performance as for their character. It is based on how well they demonstrate integrity, respect for customers, initiative, courage, kindness, and teamwork. Since the implementation of STARS in March 2001, employee engagement has significantly improved, and it has led to a dramatic increase in customer satisfaction. Shrinivas told us that thanks to STARS, his company's employee satisfaction has shot up above 80 percent—the highest in the Indian hospitality industry. In 2011, Taj Hotels received the Gallup Best Places to Work award—which recognizes the twenty top employers worldwide—becoming the only company in the world to receive this award for three consecutive years.

In our experience, wise teams like those at Taj Hotels are the exception rather than the rule. In most companies where we have provided consultation, employees form teams that tend to operate mostly in either the blue or the red zone, which can lead to poor performance. The Taj teams show that this needn't be the case.

Building Wise Cross-Functional Teams

We recently had an opportunity to develop a wise team in a large communications company, Comco (not the real name). Comco had bought a start-up for $400 million and had invested another $100 million to develop a new product called HELLO that was based on the start-up's technology. But Comco had failed to attract interest for HELLO from its channel partners, which traditionally sell and service its products to end users, mostly corporate buyers. These channel partners were not convinced that Comco had the right competencies or the right culture to commercialize HELLO successfully. And they were right.

Indeed, HELLO was more than just a product: it was an end-to-end solution that had to be personalized to meet the unique needs of individual end customers. To be successful, HELLO needed a business model called relational selling, which would require a collaborative approach between Comco and its channels to attract, market, and sell a solution to the end client. This approach is very different from Comco's traditional business model, which was based on transactional selling, an arm's-length approach to engaging channel partners by which Comco would first develop an off-the-shelf product, and its partners would later sell it. Not a great deal of collaboration was needed. Knowing that

Comco's culture was steeped in transactional selling, its channel partners doubted the company would ever be able to adopt a relational-selling model.

Comco was on the verge of losing its $500 million dollar investment in HELLO when we were invited to work with the cross-functional team that was attempting to develop and commercialize this product. We quickly realized that the team was operating in the blue zone: every member of the team—R&D, manufacturing, sales, marketing—was primarily focused on executing its specific task without interest in or consideration for how their task was connected to other functions along the value chain. There was minimal collaboration among various functions that made up HELLO's go-to-market team. The R&D unit, for example, was used to developing products without any input from manufacturing, sales, marketing, or customer service. Once it developed a product, R&D would throw the product over the wall to manufacturing, which would then throw it over to marketing, which would eventually engage the sales force, including channel partners. That might have worked for Comco in the past, but this linear product development and commercialization process wasn't suited for HELLO, which required that all Comco's internal functions as well as external partners collaborate intimately and constantly throughout the product's life cycle.

To understand the root of the problem, we interviewed various team members, including directors and vice presidents, both individually and collectively, across various functions. We realized that they lacked a shared purpose, a collaborative culture, or a system of rewards and recognition that individuals in the team considered fair. They did not operate like a synergistic project team. They supported each other but did not cooperate or collaborate on making decisions and taking actions. There was no willingness to compromise. Nobody wanted to stretch to meet each other's needs and schedules. In fact, there was a transactional quality to their relationships: they were functioning, in short, as a group rather than as a team, let alone a wise team.

While the team as a whole predominantly operated in the blue zone, its individual members were actually a mix of business smart (red zone) and functional smart leaders (blue zone): sales and marketing members operated in the red zone, whereas manufacturing and IT members functioned in the blue zone. To elevate the entire team into a wise leadership state, we helped develop a shared purpose and a collaborative team culture that supported the relational selling model required for successfully commercializing HELLO. Although the team consisted of managers at the director and vice president levels, they were all focusing just on operations and looked up to the senior executive team to give them strategic direction. We encouraged these managers to think entrepreneurially and identify a clear and strategic intent for the HELLO project. They soon gained enough confidence to develop the business model and strategy that was needed to sell HELLO without active input from the senior executives. Over time, the team evolved into a dynamic start-up inside a large company. They began to take risks and started appreciating each other's contribution. Eventually HELLO became a big success instead of a huge loss.

We worked with the team to shift their perspective from treating HELLO as an extension of their existing products to embracing it as an entirely new business model that was better suited to commercialize HELLO. Rather than thinking insularly as leaders in the blue zone, some of the key managers began to think and act as wise leaders who were serving a higher purpose that benefited the entire ecosystem.

The evolution from a smart team to a wise team occurs when there is a major shift in the team's intention, behavior, and culture. When operating in a wise state, team members grow as one unit; they exhibit collaborative behavior as they attempt to co-create value with others, and they appreciate each other's strengths. They relate to each other rather than look for quid pro quo in their relationship. While it's relatively easy for a team to learn to operate wisely, it's much more challenging for an organization to transform itself into a wise organization.

Wise Organizations

What makes a wise organization different from a wise team? Part of it is that an organization can have multiple teams and projects going on simultaneously. Some of the teams could be operating in a wise leadership mode, but others could be operating in the red or the blue zones. The structure, culture, strategy, and purpose of an organization are generally more complex than those of a team. To get at the differences, we can compare and contrast wise teams and wise organizations using the three parameters of intention, behavior, and culture.

In terms of intention, wise team members help each other stretch beyond their comfort zone and learn what they need to learn. Their behavior is focused on collaborating to get a specific project done in a culture in which each person's contribution is valued and appreciated by others. Wise organizations, however, operate at a higher order, with all members driven by a desire to produce results in alignment with a noble purpose—that is, to manifest the noble purpose. In terms of behavior, they focus not just tactically on the project at hand but rather on developing other people so they can collectively take on bigger projects. The culture of wise organizations is more synergistic, and the outcome is much more than a culmination of individual outcomes.

Given these differences, cultivating a wise organization is generally more difficult and time-consuming than building a wise team. The culture of an organization is more likely to be entrenched; it can take years for many organizations to change their culture. But it is possible, as demonstrated by two companies we have interacted with: Better World Books and a Fortune 500 company we'll call XCo.

Promoting Literacy: Better World Books

Better World Books is an online bookseller with about $70 million in annual revenue. It was established a decade ago as a for-profit social enterprise by three University of Notre Dame students: Xavier Helgesen, Chris Fuchs, and Jeff Kurtzman. Their vision was to build "a global bookstore that harnesses the power of capitalism to bring literacy and opportunity to people around the world." Their business model was to collect and sell unwanted books and use a share of the profits to support global literacy projects like Room to Read, Books for Africa, Worldfund, and the National Center for Family Literacy. So far, Better World Books has reused or recycled over 87 million books and raised over $12 million for literacy projects. Under an original initiative called Book for Book, Better World Books matches every book purchase on its website with a book donation to someone in need. So far, it has donated over 6 million books to partner programs around the world.

In order to scale up the company, the founders started looking for an experienced CEO and eventually picked David Murphy, who had been their mentor and a judge in a social venture business competition they had won at the university. Because their company was based on a noble purpose—to encourage and spread literacy—Murphy and the founders decided to register it as a B Corporation (Benefit Corporation or B Corp, for short), a new kind of company that must meet the requirements and goals related to the triple bottom line (planet, profit, and people) and is committed to solving social and environmental problems.[8] Hence, from the very beginning, the business model and strategy of Better World Books were firmly in the wise zone, and Murphy helped create structures and processes consistent with the company's noble purpose.

Based on our personal interview with Murphy, as well as our analysis of the company, we discovered that Better World Books's culture is built on synergies among its leaders who complement each other but are all driven by a shared desire to serve a noble purpose.[9] Murphy brought experience, business savvy, and passion for building a social enterprise, and the young cofounders brought their tech knowledge and commitment to work effectively with each other and Murphy to build the company. The noble purpose helped attract high-quality staff. In addition, most of the employees were given shares of the company.

Beyond its noble purpose, what makes Better World Books a wise organization is the trust-based developmental relationship (rather than transactional relationship) between the cofounders and Murphy during the initial phase of the company, as well as the role clarity of its leaders. Although Murphy was a seasoned business veteran, he held the young cofounders in high respect and saw himself as a trustee of this organization and an equal partner with the cofounders. By the time Better World Books had its best year in 2011, Murphy, satisfied that his work was done, stepped down from his position and helped recruit and mentor a new CEO. In our consulting experience, it's rare to find the kind of synergistic culture and great role clarity that is found at Better World Books.

The Better World Books story is unique, and isn't likely to happen in larger and well-established companies that already have structures and operational strategies in place. But it does prove that it is possible to build a wise organization from the ground up if the structure (in this case, a B Corp) and corporate governance model are aligned with a noble purpose.

How do you help large organizations to become wise? Changing structures and governance models is one approach. Culture change is another. Changing the mission, vision and values along with strategy to get to the new vision is the third approach. How each of these can be accomplished is beyond the scope of this book. You can read about them elsewhere, but in this chapter we focus on one approach to culture change: employee engagement.

Culture Change at XCo

XCo (not the real name) is a large organization that wanted to initiate a culture change in its global manufacturing division to increase employee motivation. It hired big consultancies to help drive this change, but these consultancies' traditional cultural change approaches tended to be process driven and top down. They didn't work well at XCo, which had a relatively decentralized culture. After two such failed interventions, XCo turned to us for our experience and success in driving change in a bottom-up fashion.

We brought together thirty-six managers from eighteen factories and began talking about what motivated them and when they believed they did their best work. From this feedback, we identified the ten most common elements from their experiences, which reflected what is most important to them in terms of self-motivation and mutual empowerment. These were archetypal— or patterns typical in a larger population—because the assembled managers were from different countries, had different backgrounds, were different ages, and had different job roles.

The four cornerstones of motivation they spoke of were communication from the heart, trust, information to get the job done, and knowing the resource and ethical boundaries. The six key enablers of motivation they identified were openness, learning, responsibility, respect, good communication, and balance. The group also identified four broad metrics for measuring increased motivation: self-esteem, ownership, shared meaning, and a shared vision. We asked this group of managers to identify the next steps needed to convert their insights into an action plan to increase motivation.

One insight was that they were so busy focusing on widgets that they forgot about the people making them. Another insight was that by overemphasizing processes and quality management, the managers ended up focusing on "getting things done" rather than nurturing human relationships with their subordinates. Their rapport with the workforce lacked empathy and compassion. A third insight was that they genuinely cared about their workforce but didn't know how to engage and communicate with them in an open and transparent manner.

Their action plans included sharing their experiences at the meeting with the workforce and encouraging their teams to engage in similar exercises and openly share and discuss specific moments when they felt most motivated. Then they wanted to have conversations on a regular basis with their workforce about what was working and wasn't in their day-to-day job. They also formulated action plans for their individual factories, with the workforce involved in figuring out how to improve working conditions. By implementing all these changes, XCo experienced a 15 percent improvement in employee motivation levels and about an 8 percent increase in productivity over the following two years.

The key message here is that the culture of any organization can be positively affected when their leaders take authentic and appropriate actions.

Our research into wise organizations is ongoing, of course, but so far we have found a few that are well advanced on their path toward becoming wise. Tata Group, owner of Taj Hotels, is one of them—it is infused with wise culture. The Tata Group's structures, reward systems, and talent management are all aligned with its noble purpose. Two-thirds of the shares of Tata Sons, the holding company of the group, are held by philanthropic trusts. Its leaders decide and act with ethical clarity: they do not engage in lobbying and won't do business in places where ethics are not valued.[10]

(We are interested in learning about and studying more wise organizations around the world. Please visit fromsmarttowise .com to contribute case studies and learn about other wise organizations.)

Wise Communities

Individual leaders, teams, and organizations all focus on specific outcomes to measure their effectiveness, but for communities this can be difficult. Organizations have a beginning, middle, and an end in their life cycle while communities have beginnings but the end is unknown. We might not experience that end in our lifetime, which makes the effort to develop wise communities even more crucial. Nevertheless, some enlightened individuals are bravely attempting to build wise communities. Oprah Winfrey is one of them. She has been building wise communities through her foundation and multiple nonprofit initiatives such as the Angel Network. Another is Peter Senge, author of the best-selling *The Fifth Discipline*, who has catalyzed interest in building learning communities around the world.[11] Similarly, over many decades, Rick Smyre, founder of Communities of the Future, has been actively involved in efforts to transform neighborhood communities into wise communities worldwide.[12]

We focus now on the efforts led by three remarkable individuals to build wise communities: Peter Block, Nipun Mehta, and Raj Sisodia. Peter Block, an organizational development expert, is striving to build "abundant" communities (those infused with a sense of abundance rather than scarcity) around the world; Nipun Mehta is a technologist who is trying to leverage the power of social networking technologies to build global communities infused with compassion and a sense of service; and Raj Sisodia is an academic building a community of wise businesses following the principles of conscious capitalism.

Peter Block: Developing Abundant Communities

For over thirty years, Peter Block has helped build wise communities worldwide as a community builder and a consultant. He has written eight books in the areas of organizational development, civic engagement, and community development. Many of his ideas and concepts—such as giftmindedness (focusing on what is possible to achieve with gifts we already have rather than striving to fill in our deficiencies), stewardship, responsibility, and abundant community—are considered seminal in reframing how we think about service, trusteeship, accountability, connectedness, and authenticity in the context of a community.[13] For instance, Block's idea of "abundant community" calls for citizens to stop looking for external sources of happiness and discover an abundance of resources within their local community.

We have personally experienced and witnessed the impact of Block's ideas in real communities. In India, as early as in 1994, he worked on leadership development with Amul, a large nation-wide milk producer cooperative, and the National Dairy Development Board that markets the milk collected by Amul. He has also worked in Ireland, where he cofacilitated peace and reconciliation in communities torn by religious conflict.[14] In the United States, he has been working on implementing abundant communities in states like Ohio and Mississippi.

Through his vast experience, Block learned that when it comes to building wise communities, results and outcomes are much less important than invitation, connection, passion, and engagement. Communities today are less engaged directly with each other and more engaged online. If you want to increase engagement in your community and you are passionate about it, you have to take initiative, share your noble purpose, and invite others in the community to engage and create a shared vision for the community instead of waiting for formal leaders (if there are any) to propose it. There are no onlookers, only activists who take responsibility in community building.

Many of Block's concepts and frameworks are aligned with the wise leadership model in that they help people in communities think and act wisely. Many of the perspectives, principles, and practices that he suggests are conditions under which community wisdom emerges in a bottom-up fashion without any one individual or team taking leadership responsibility. Block believes it's critical for communities to build an "abundant mentality"—that is, a focus on future possibilities—and when a few people take positive steps in a community toward sufficiency, responsibility, and ownership for themselves, others begin to follow them. That is how organically, a wise community evolves.[15]

Nipun Mehta: Scaling Up Service and Compassion

Nipun Mehta, founder of ServiceSpace, is in his early thirties, but he has already become known as one of the leading wise community builders of our times. Mehta is building wise communities by focusing on young people (Generation Y and younger) and using social networking tools to reach them. The programs he helped initiate, such as a daily positive news service (dailygood.org), an acts-of-kindness portal (helpothers.org), and Karma Kitchen, a gift economy restaurant, are run entirely by young volunteers.[16]

Karma Kitchen is a collection of half a dozen restaurants around the world that serve as a real-life laboratory for experimenting with generosity. If you go to any Karma Kitchen restaurant, volunteers will serve you healthy and delicious food prepared with organic ingredients cooked by volunteers (book in advance: the waiting list is several weeks long). The food you have that day is paid for by people who came to the restaurant before you. You can choose to do the same, paying for the food others will be having later if you feel generous—and you are free to contribute any amount you want to.

We have eaten and volunteered at Karma Kitchen several times, and the experience has been memorable. The testimonials posted by volunteers and guests or on karmakitchen.org attest to why this concept built on anonymous generosity is spreading fast across America. Karma Kitchen embodies all the characteristics of a wise community: people come to Karma Kitchen to serve others (their intention) as guests willing to pay for others after them or volunteers who cook in the kitchen or serve guests (their behavior), enriching a culture of caring and love, and creating a sense of fulfillment and inclusivity.

Karma Kitchen is one of the experiments that you can personally experience in community building activities organized by ServiceSpace. The ServiceSpace platform has inspired volunteerism worldwide by allowing young people to stay connected with others interested in service and identify and participate in volunteering projects. The ServiceSpace network boasts over 400,000 members globally.[17]

Raj Sisodia: Building Conscious Communities

In contrast to Peter Block and Nipun Mehta, community builders with business and technology backgrounds, Raj Sisodia is an academic who is in the initial stages of building another kind of community: a community of business organizations committed to the principles of conscious capitalism.[18]

Conscious capitalism is a term popularized by Muhammad Yunus, the Nobel Prize–winning economist who pioneered the concepts of microfinance and microcredit.[19] It has been defined as "a philosophy based on the belief that a more complex form of capitalism is emerging that holds the potential for enhancing corporate performance while simultaneously continuing to advance the quality of life for billions of people."[20] In spirit, conscious capitalism is philosophically aligned with other notions like creative capitalism and compassionate capitalism, and initiatives like B Corporations, all of which look at reinventing capitalism to be more inclusive and caring.

Sisodia, a marketing professor at Bentley University in Waltham, Massachusetts, believes that the time is ripe for conscious capitalism. Capitalism today, he says, especially in the West, is focused primarily on maximizing shareholder value and promoting extreme competition, which he believes has led to unsustainable economies—reeling under growing income inequality (for instance, the top 5 percent income earners in the United States currently account for 37 percent of the country's spending) and environmental degradation.

The genesis of conscious capitalism is an academic research project that Sisodia undertook in the early 2000s about marketing excellence. After studying hundreds of companies, Sisodia noted that customer satisfaction, loyalty, and trust were falling steadily while marketing spending was up. Sisodia also identified twenty-eight companies—eighteen of them publicly traded and ten private—that had lower marketing expenses but higher customer loyalty and trust. He found that customers, employees, and suppliers all trusted these companies. The leaders of these companies had a number of things in common: they led through mentoring instead of controlling, paid themselves modest salaries, and acted as servant leaders.[21]

What's more, Sisodia's financial analysis showed that these companies invest in environmental sustainability and in the well-being of their employees and engage suppliers in win-win partnerships. And it seems to pay off. These companies financially outperformed other companies in their industry by a factor of 9 to 1 over a ten-year period. Having seen the performance data, Sisodia wanted to create an institute that could study this phenomenon in more detail, but it was too large an undertaking at that time. Rather, he captured his thinking in a book, *Firms of Endearment,* that got the attention of John Mackey, co-CEO of Whole Foods Market. Mackay reached out to Sisodia and they jointly initiated the conscious capitalism movement in 2008. They invited a select group of business leaders and academics and consultants and the Conscious Capitalism organization was born.[22] Conscious Capitalism Inc., which is run by Doug Rausch, the former president of Trader Joe's, is helping to form communities of companies that are run as responsible organizations with conscious leadership, higher purpose, and conscious culture with a stakeholder (not stockholder) orientation.

Again, we have personally experienced and can vouch for the unique approaches and cultures that member companies, including Whole Foods, The Container Store, Trader Joe's, Panera Bread, and Southwest Airlines, operate and bring to the conscious capitalism community. The community is growing rapidly in the United States, Europe, Australia, and India. Although it is still in its infancy, the potential impact of this community is huge because it is being developed as a wise community from the beginning.

Wise Nations

Nations are far more complex than organizations and communities. They are comprised of highly diverse societies with well-developed cultures and conflicting interests and viewpoints. At a national level, it's more challenging to achieve consensus on major decisions and to act cohesively. Yet as with individuals, organizations, and communities, it is possible to influence a nation to move toward wisdom by fostering interest in a larger purpose.

Bhutan is a small, landlocked nation set in the towering mountains of the Himalayas. In 1972 it was one of the poorest countries in the world. At the time, Bhutan's Oxford-educated king, Jigme Singye Wangchuck, developed a concept called gross national happiness (GNH) and suggested that gross domestic product be replaced with GNH as an indicator of national progress.[23] The king believed that his impoverished land needed to embrace a holistic approach to socioeconomic development that balances economic growth with cultural and religious preservation, universal access to health care and education, and environmental protection. Western educated and yet steeped in Bhutan's Buddhist traditions, the king wanted to modernize his country in a way so that material and spiritual development take place together.

In 1999 the king created the Centre for Bhutan Studies in Thimphu, Bhutan, which developed the gross national happiness index (GNHI), a multidimensional set of thirty-three indicators that measure the overall well-being of the Bhutanese population. These indicators range from psychological factors to community vitality and guide the formulation of public policy.[24]

Under the king's leadership, the Bhutanese government has relied on GNHI to make wise socioeconomic decisions—for example, laws regulating mining and logging protect 70 percent of Bhutan's forested land. While Bhutan is gradually opening up to foreign investors, tourism remains highly restricted (limited to two thousand tourists annually). There is universal health care, with an emphasis on preventive care, and free education for all.

Not surprisingly, in 2006 Bhutan was ranked by *BusinessWeek* as the "happiest" nation in Asia and the eighth happiest in the world.[25]

The king invested time and energy to try to spread his ideas outside his small nation and change the perspective of the global community. He advocated GNH at international forums, noting that "there must be some convergence among nations on the idea of what the end objective of development and progress should be."[26]

Inspired by Bhutan's success, several Western leaders have sought to incorporate elements of GNH into their own economies. For example, in 2008, former French president Nicholas Sarkozy commissioned a study by Joseph Stiglitz and Amartya Sen, Nobel laureates in economics, to identify indicators other than GDP to measure societies. Based on the recommendations of the report, the official French statistics agency has begun incorporating indicators of the happiness and well-being of its citizens—such as health, status, social connections, and leisure time—as part of the economic assessment of the country.[27]

The king's son, Jigme Khesar Namgyel, succeeded him in 2008. He shares his father's noble purpose to create a veritable shift in the development paradigm. Recognized by the World Economic Forum as a Young Global Leader in 2008, he is striving to incorporate happiness into the agenda of global institutions such as the United Nations. In July 2011, the U.N. General Assembly unanimously adopted a resolution calling for a "holistic approach to development" that can drive sustainable happiness and well-being. "Conscious that the pursuit of happiness is a fundamental human goal," the resolution recognized "that the gross domestic product [GDP] does not adequately reflect the happiness and well-being of people."[28]

You don't need to be a king to move a nation toward wise leadership. Mahatma Gandhi, Dr. Martin Luther King Jr., Nelson Mandela, and Lech Walesa have proven that the power of ideas can be strong enough to shift the direction of a country and raise its level of consciousness. These men rallied their people around a noble purpose and led by example. They were historic wise leaders, as is Aung San Suu Kyi.

Myanmar, formerly known as Burma, has faced an ongoing political struggle since the 1960s when a military dictatorship under General Ne Win was established, followed by counter coups and efforts to oust the regime by protestors. A key figure among the protesters was Aung San Suu Kyi, daughter of Aung San, who fought for Myanmar's freedom from the British colonial rule (Aung San was assassinated six months before his country gained independence in January 1948).

After spending several decades abroad (she was married to an Oxford academic, Michael Aris), Suu Kyi returned to Myanmar in 1988 for family reasons. At the time, she witnessed the brutal repression of student protesters and decided to take action. In an inspiring speech that started her political career, she told protesters, "I could not, as my father's daughter, remain indifferent to all that is going on." In 1989, the military regime placed Suu Kyi under house arrest, and she spent the next two decades confined to her residence in austere conditions without a telephone, television, or Internet. She received few visitors and spent her time meditating, reading, and writing.[29] In 1997 Suu Kyi demonstrated her iron will and adherence to principle by refusing to travel to England to see her terminally ill husband, fearing that the military rulers wouldn't allow her to return. Given her tenacity and unwavering commitment to democracy Suu Kyi was unwilling to make any compromise with the military regime. When she won the Nobel Peace Prize in 1992, the military refused to let her go to Norway to accept it.

Her resilience and capacity for patience were finally rewarded in 2010 when, under pressure from the international community, the junta released Suu Kyi from house arrest and agreed to hold parliamentary elections in 2012 in which Suu Kyi won a seat.

Many wondered why Suu Kyi decided to participate in elections that were run by the same junta that had imprisoned her and kept democracy at bay in the country for decades. Her admirers worried that Suu Kyi, respected for her unwavering adherence to principle, had finally relented and softened her stance. In fact, we believe that Suu Kyi was acting as a wise leader. Taking part in elections run by an illegitimate government was opportune, not opportunistic. She realized that the political system was changing, due in part to pressure from the Obama administration, and that she could do this better from the inside, as a freely elected member of parliament, rather than continuing the struggle from outside as a persecuted political activist.[30] In 2011, U.S. Secretary of State Hillary Clinton paid a historic visit to Myanmar, paving the way for full restoration of diplomatic ties with Washington a year later, and Suu Kyi went to Oslo in June 2012 to belatedly pick up her Nobel Peace Prize. In November 2012, President Obama visited Myanmar to extend his support to the process of democratization.

From our point of view, Suu Kyi recognized this changing geopolitical context and demonstrated flexible fortitude. While remaining committed to her noble purpose—leading Myanmar to democracy—she pragmatically decided to shift her role from a protest figure to a reformer of the system. In her Nobel acceptance speech, Suu Kyi said: "It is in human nature to contain both the positive and the negative. However, it is also within human capability to work to reinforce the positive and to minimize or neutralize the negative. Absolute peace in our world is an unattainable goal. But it is one towards which we must continue to journey."[31]

WISE LEADERSHIP IN A COMPLEX WORLD

Aung San Suu Kyi's words about the journey toward peace have some resonance with what we know and have tried to convey about the path to wise leadership. It is a lifelong, ever expanding, and unending journey. It requires much from us: discipline and humility, reflection and action, a commitment to continuing growth and change. For a smart leader busy dealing with a complex and changeable business environment, the question may be,

"Why?" Leadership is a challenging endeavor in itself. Why must we also strive for wisdom?

We touched on this question in the Preface, but it bears revisiting. It's true that the quest for wisdom in leadership yields many gifts on many levels, from personal to organizational. But on the most pragmatic level, wise leadership is the strongest position we know of from which to meet the demands and challenges posed by a rapidly changing globalized world. In particular, five contextual variables—diversity, interconnectivity, velocity, ambiguity, and scarcity—are increasingly shaping how people respond to problems and how organizations function. These variables aren't new within organizations or social systems, but we see them becoming more intense and widespread in the twenty-first century, and we are not alone in this assessment. In a survey conducted by IBM in 2010 with over fifteen hundred chief executives worldwide, eight in ten CEOs anticipated greater complexity in the future, but fewer than half of them said they feel confident about coping with complexity and being able to innovate and drive higher revenues in these circumstances.[32]

For smart leaders, complexity tends to trigger the fight-or-flee reflex: functional smart leaders hunker down, and business smart leaders tend to tackle complexity head-on, often reusing outdated formulas that served well in the past. But wise leaders are not overwhelmed by complexity: rather, they see the potential benefits in complexity and seek to turn it into an opportunity to bring value to their organization and the larger community. And since wise leaders are both grounded in a noble purpose and at ease accepting the idea of change as a constant, they are much more likely than smart leaders to turn the key drivers of complexity (diversity, interconnectivity, velocity, ambiguity, scarcity) to their organizations' advantage.

While smart leaders might feel challenged by the growing diversity among employees and in the customer base, wise leaders have the capacity to welcome this diversity and turn it into a competitive advantage—for example, by leveraging the creativity of their diverse workforce to address the needs of their more heterogeneous customer base.

Smart leaders who are generally used to command-and-control management style can feel threatened by the world's pervasive interconnectivity, which disrupts the top-down leadership model they prefer in favor of an open, bottom-up, participative approach.[33] Wise leaders can more readily see social media–enabled interconnectivity as an asset because it allows more stakeholders to interact and collaboratively solve problems in a way that is faster, better, and cheaper.

Change is now the only constant in business, which means that ambiguity and velocity are the rule. The velocity of change continues to accelerate, drastically shortening product life cycles and forcing firms to rapidly adapt or reinvent existing business models. When confronted with such high velocity, smart leaders tend to either refuse to adapt or to attempt tepid changes when bigger and bolder transformation is required. And many smart leaders, accustomed to basing decisions on past patterns, fail to leverage ambiguity, which, by its nature, provides conflicting signals and breaks down traditional patterns. Wise leaders, who are able to integrate logic, emotion, instinct, and intuition into their decision making, can more readily improvise innovative solutions that factor in the nuances of the rapidly changing context, or situation.[34]

And finally, smart leaders attached to a more-is-better growth model (which produces more output by consuming more resources) are ill equipped for the resource scarcity ahead. Wise leaders, whose worldview does not depend on zero-sum or tit-for-tat thinking and action, are freer to devise sustainable business strategies that make more efficient use of limited resources and yet generate higher value to consumers and the society at large.[35]

This is why, all other benefits of wisdom aside, we believe that only by tapping into their inner wisdom will leaders be able to cope with the escalating complexity in the global business environment.

CONCLUSION

Smartness is indeed vital for success in today's knowledge age, though it appears increasingly insufficient in itself. Yet for many leaders, the unrelenting and single-minded pursuit of smartness has a shadow side on a personal level: they risk losing their ethical clarity, authenticity, and sense of meaning, purpose, and happiness. Smartness is like a double-edged sword: with discrimination, you can wield it to cut through mountains of data to find nuggets of knowledge and insights; without discernment, you risk falling on your own sword. Intelligence, when combined with discrimination and discernment, leads to wisdom.

Traditionally there are two approaches to finding wisdom: a spiritual path and a practical one. Spiritual wisdom is typically transmitted through mystical religious traditions, such as Vedanta in Hinduism, Kabbalah in Judaism, or Sufi in Islam. The other kind of wisdom, generally known as practical wisdom, is developed through personal experiences, with action and reflection feeding one another.[36]

These two approaches to gaining wisdom are not mutually exclusive; they are actually complementary.[37] Practical wisdom begins subjectively, with personal benefit as the driving force, whereas spiritual wisdom begins objectively with common good as the driving force. It is principles—what in this book we call capabilities—that serve as the bridge between the spiritual wisdom and practical wisdom. The six foundational principles presented here as the six leadership capabilities are derived from both spiritual and philosophical texts from both Eastern and Western traditions and from our decades of working with leaders on their journey from smart to wise leadership.[38]

The journey to wise leadership can start anywhere. You can begin by reading this book and adopting the best practices of wise leaders we have profiled here. Or you can try to develop the six capabilities outlined in chapters 2 through 7 one at a time. But mastery comes only when you develop your own wisdom logic—

your unique path to wise leadership. Along the way you will discover your North Star (your noble purpose), begin to act authentically and appropriately, gain greater role clarity, learn to make decisions with discernment, develop flexible fortitude, and cultivate enlightened self-interest—all of them critical elements of acting and leading with wisdom. Once you have developed your own wisdom logic, you will be able, as a wise leader, to leverage your smartness in an ethical manner for the larger good by balancing smarts with reflection and introspection.

Becoming a wise leader is not an individual act performed in isolation. Part of your journey involves helping others on your team or in your organization to find their authentic selves, creating a field of wise leadership to help unleash collective wisdom for the greater good. Nipun Mehta did this with ServiceSpace, establishing compassionate communities using the power of social networking tools. King Wangchuck of Bhutan did this by attempting to increase the level of happiness in his community (a nation, in this case), finding ways to enhance the well-being of its members.

We hope you will use this book to accelerate your own transformation into a wise leader and infuse wisdom into your teams, organizations, communities, and country and that you'll share your experiences on fromsmarttowise.com, contributing to a global virtual field of wise leadership.

NOTES

Chapter One

1. Russolillo, S. "Apple's Market Value: To Infinity and Beyond!" *Wall Street Journal,* August 20, 2012. http://blogs.wsj.com/marketbeat /2012/08/20/apples-market-value-to-infinity-and-beyond/

2. Cooper, S. "Jack Mezirow, Transformational Learning." N.d. http:// www.lifecircles-inc.com/Learningtheories/humanist/mezirow .html

3. Lashinsky, A. "How Tim Cook Is Changing Apple," *Fortune,* June 11, 2012, 110; "Seven Things Tim Cook'ed in Apple," *Daily Bhaskar,* September 4, 2012. http://daily.bhaskar.com/article/SCT-FTR-7 -things-tim-cooked-in-apple-3707804-NOR.html

4. Binet, A. "New Methods for the Diagnosis of the Intellectual Level of Subnormals." In *The Development of Intelligence in Children: The Binet-Simon Scale.* E. S. Kite (Trans.). Baltimore: Williams & Wilkins, 1916, 37–90; Feuerstein, R., S. Feuerstein, L. Falik, and Y. Rand. *Dynamic Assessments of Cognitive Modifiability.* Jerusalem: ICELP Press, 2002; Feuerstein, R. "The Theory of Structural Modifiability. In B. Presseisen, ed. *Learning and Thinking Styles: Classroom Interaction.* Washington, DC: National Education Association, 1990. H. Gardner, *Frames of Mind: The Theory of Multiple Intelligences.* New York: Basic Books, 1993.

5. Sternberg, R. J. *Successful Intelligence.* New York: Plume, 1997.

6. "Jack Welch." *Wikipedia.* http://en.wikipedia.org/wiki/Jack _Welch

7. "Ken Wilber Online." http://wilber.shambhala.com/html/books /kosmos/excerptC/part2–4.cfm/

8. Schwartz, B., and K. Sharpe. *Practical Wisdom.* New York: Riverhead Books, 2010.

9. Ibid.; Aristotle. *Nicomachean Ethics.* Trans. Martin Oswald. Indianapolis, IN: Bobbs-Merrill, 1962.

10. Bhagavad Gita, chap. 2. The meaning is loosely translated from Sanskrit text by the authors.

11. These capabilities are independently identified in both wisdom traditions—Bhagavad Gita, chap. 18—and empirical research: Adams, J. "Building a Sustainable World: A Challenging OD Opportunity." In B. Jones and M. Brazzel (Eds.), *The NTL Handbook of Organization Development and Change.* San Francisco: Jossey-Bass/ Pfeiffer, 2006.

Chapter Two

1. Desh Deshpande, interview with Prasad Kaipa and Navi Radjou, September 24, 2011.

2. "What Is Logotherapy and Existential Analysis?" http://www .viktorfrankl.org/e/logotherapy.html

3. Frankl, V. *Man's Search for Meaning.* Boston: Beacon Press, 1959.

4. Collins, J., and J. Porras. *Built to Last: Successful Habits of Visionary Companies.* New York: HarperBusiness, 2002.

5. Collins, J. Interview with Marcia Stepanek, March 20, 2008. http:// www.msnbc.msn.com/id/23715656/ns/us_news-giving/t/what -makes-good-charity-great-one/#.UJywmY7IpU5

6. *Noble purpose* and *North Star* are synonymous, and we use them interchangeably in this book. We have used *North Star* in most of our consulting and writing since 1990.

7. Kaipa, P. "What Wise Leaders Always Follow." *Harvard Business Review Blog,* January 18, 2012, and "Four Questions: An Approach to Ignite Your Natural Genius." 2005. http://kaipagroup.com /articles/four_questions/fourquestions.pdf

8. Nipun Mehta, conversation with Prasad Kaipa, February 2012.

9. Mehta, N. "When Generosity Meets Venture Capital." *DailyGood .com,* November 14, 2011. http://www.dailygood.org/view.php ?sid=117

10. Ibid.

11. For information on the Giving Pledge, go to http://givingpledge.org

12. Allianz Group. "HR Development of the Future." March 29, 2011. https://www.allianz.com/en/press/news/company_news/human_resources/news_2011–03–29.html

13. Allianz Group. "Change of Perspective: Employees Learn in the Dark and in Silence." April 17, 2012. https://www.allianz.com/en/press/news/company_news/human_resources/news_2012–04–16.html

14. Steven Milovich, interview with Prasad Kaipa, May 20, 2012.

15. Mehta, P. K., and S. Shenoy. *Infinite Vision: How Aravind Became the World's Greatest Business Case for Compassion.* San Francisco: Berrett-Koehler, 2011.

16. Pavithra K. Mehta, coauthor of *Infinite Vision* and grand niece of renowned ophthalmologist G. Venkataswamy, interview with Prasad Kaipa, July 15, 2012.

17. P. K. Mehta, S. Shenoy, R. D. Thulasiraj, and D. Krishnan, conversations with Prasad Kaipa, 2006–2012.

18. Kris Gopalakrishnan, interview with Prasad Kaipa, October 7, 2012.

19. Radjou, N., J. Prabhu, P. Kaipa, and S. Ahuja. "How Reframers Unleash Innovation in Their Companies (and Beyond)." *Harvard Business Review* (blog), July 13, 2010.

20. Carol Dweck, interview with Prasad Kaipa and Navi Radjou, February 9, 2012.

21. Dweck, C. *Mindset: The New Psychology of Success.* New York: Random House, 2006.

22. Shaw, J. M., and M. J. Cliatt. "A Model for Training Teachers to Encourage Divergent Thinking in Young Children." *Journal of Creative Behavior* 20, no. 2 (1986): 81–88.

23. Alan Mulally, interview with Prasad Kaipa, December 2005, and phone and e-mail conversations, November 2010 and June 2011.

24. Mulally, A. Presentation to Stanford Business School, February 7, 2011, http://www.youtube.com/watch?v=ZIwz1KlKXP4&feature=player_embedded#!

25. Kaipa, P. "Steve Jobs and Mental Model Innovation." *Ivey Business Journal* (May–June 2012), http://www.iveybusinessjournal.com /topics/leadership/steve-jobs-and-the-art-of-mental-model -innovation

26. Niedermeyer, P. "Mulally: Ford to Reduce Lineup from 97 to as Few as 20 Models." *Truth About Cars*, September 27, 2010. http://www .thetruthaboutcars.com/2010/09/mulally-ford-to-reduce-lineup -from-97-to-as-few-as-20-models/

27. Alan Mulally, interview with Prasad Kaipa, December 2005, and phone and e-mail conversations, November 2010, June 2011.

Chapter Three

1. V. R. Ferose, interview with Prasad Kaipa and Navi Radjou, January 27, 2012.

2. "SAP Labs India Named Among the Top IT Employers in India." September 28, 2011. http://www.sap.com/india/press.epx?pressid =17567

3. *American Heritage Dictionary of the English Language*, 4th ed. Boston: Houghton Mifflin, 2001.

4. Ibid.

5. Isaacson, W. *Steve Jobs*. New York: Simon & Schuster, 2011.

6. Satyam bruyat priyam bruyat na bruyat satyam apriyam/Priyam cha nanrutam bruyat esha dharmah sanatanah. This Sanskrit verse (Manusmriti, chap. 4, verse 138) is translated as, "There is a two way restriction to share the truth. Never tell an unpleasant truth (without first creating a context for people who receive it) and also never tell a lie for pleasing others. Otherwise, always speak the truth and always speak pleasing words. That is a hard acid test to follow to tell only pleasing truth, in that truth always need not be a pleasant one. This is the path of timeless ethics."

7. George, B. *Authentic Leadership: Rediscovering the Secrets to Creating Lasting Value*. San Francisco: Jossey-Bass, 2003.

8. Trivers, R. "The Elements of a Scientific Theory of Self-Deception." *Annals of the New York Academy of Sciences* 907 (2000): 114–131; Arbinger Institute, *Leadership and Self Deception*, 2nd ed. San Francisco: Berrett-Koehler, 2010.

9. Kim, P. *Consumers Love to Hate Advertising.* Cambridge, MA: Forrester Research. November 26, 2006.

10. Roberts, K. "Why Lovemarks Are More Valid Than Ever, or Welcome to the Age of Now." *Ad Age,* February 14, 2011. http://adage.com/article/agency-news/kevin-roberts-lovemarks-valid/148831/

11. Charlene Li, interview with Prasad Kaipa and Navi Radjou, January 26, 2012.

12. "Pop Quiz: Can Indra Nooyi Revive PepsiCo?" *Knowledge@Wharton,* March 28, 2012. http://knowledge.wharton.upenn.edu/article.cfm?articleid=2966

13. Mainwaring, S. *We First: How Brands and Consumers Use Social Media to Build a Better World.* New York: Palgrave Macmillan, 2011.

14. Parker, J. F. *Do the Right Thing: How Dedicated Employees Create Loyal Customers and Large Profits.* Philadelphia: Wharton School Publishing, 2008; Stansberry, G. "Ten Examples of Tremendous Business Leadership." *Open Forum,* February 24, 2010. http://www.openforum.com/articles/10-examples-of-tremendous-business-leadership-1

15. Ramón Mendiola Sánchez, interview with Navi Radjou, December 19, 2011.

16. "Triple Bottom Line." *Economist,* November 17, 2009. http://www.economist.com/node/14301663

17. The concept of water neutrality is discussed in Gerbens-Leenes, W., et al. "Water Neutrality," November 20, 2007. http://www.indiaresource.org/campaigns/coke/2008/Waterneutrality.pdf

18. Mendiola interview.

19. Kaipa, P., and M. Kriger. "Empowerment, Vision and Positive Leadership: An Interview with Alan Mulally, Former CEO—Boeing Commercial, Current CEO—Ford Motors," *Journal of Management Inquiry* 19 (2010): 110–115. For an interview with Mulally, go to http://kaipagroup.com/interviews/alan_mulally_full.html

20. Mulally, A. Presentation to Stanford Business School, February 7, 2011. http://www.youtube.com/watch?v=ZIwz1KlKXP4&feature=player_embedded#!

21. Paul, A. M. "The Science of Intuition: An Eye-Opening Guide to Your Sixth Sense." http://www.oprah.com/spirit/Scientific

-Facts-About-Intuition-Developing-Intuition#ixzz26x9RHjgW; Srinivasan, C. P. "What is the Difference Between 'Instinct' and 'Intuition'"? *Hindu,* March 12, 2002. http://www.hindu.com /thehindu/edu/2002/03/12/stories/2002031200160203.htm

22. Gelles, D. "The Mind Business." *Financial Times,* August 24, 2012. http://www.ft.com/cms/s/2/d9cb7940-ebea-11e1–985a-00144 feab49a.html#axzz2BbQIbGyh

23. Kaipa, P. "Integrity and Personal Leadership." *Kaipa Group Newsletter* (January 2010). http://kaipagroup.com/newsletter /happynewyear2010.html

24. Ibid.; Kaipa, P. "Recovering Your Credibility." *Harvard Business Review* (blog), July 2, 2012. http://blogs.hbr.org/cs/2012/07 /recover_your_credibility.html

25. Doug Conant, interview with Prasad Kaipa and Navi Radjou, February 23, 2012.

26. John Mackey, interview with Prasad Kaipa and Navi Radjou, February 10, 2012.

Chapter Four

1. Greenleaf, R. K., and C. S. Larry. *Servant Leadership: A Journey into the Nature of Legitimate Power and Greatness.* 25th anniversary ed. Mahwah, NJ: Paulist Press; Block, P. *Stewardship: Choosing Service over Self Interest.* San Francisco: Berrett-Kohler, 1993.

2. "Servant Leadership." *Wikipedia.* http://en.wikipedia.org/wiki /Servant_leadership

3. Vaughan, L., and A. Choudhury. "Barclays CEO Quits After Record Libor-Rigging Fine." *BusinessWeek,* July 3, 2012. http://www .businessweek.com/articles/2012–07–03/barclays-ceo-quits-after -record-libor-rigging-fine

4. "Leaders Clash over Barclays Rate-Rigging Inquiry." *BBC News,* July 4, 2012. http://www.bbc.co.uk/news/uk-politics-18702653

5. "Barclays Boss Diamond Quits After Apology." *Express Tribune,* July 3, 2012. http://tribune.com.pk/story/402967/barclays-boss -diamond-quits-after-apology/

6. "Letter from Bob Diamond." *Barclays,* June 28, 2012. http://group .barclays.com/news/news-article/1329925904937/navigation -1330349038798

7. "Barclays Ex-Boss Diamond Slams 'Reprehensible' Action." *BBC News*, July 4, 2012; "UK's Barclays Looks to Move on from LIBOR Scandal," *Chicago Tribune*, October 30, 2012. http://www.bbc.co .uk/news/business-18708226, http://articles.chicagotribune.com /2012–10–30/business/sns-rt-us-barclays-earningsbre89u000 –20121030_1_libor-manipulation-uk-s-barclays-matt-scuffham

8. Heffernan, M. "Why Barclays Ex-CEO Bob Diamond Is Clueless." *Moneywatch*, July 12, 2012. http://www.cbsnews.com/8301–505125 _162–57470868/why-barclays-ex-ceo-bob-diamond-is-clueless/

9. Treanor, J. "Bob Diamond's Resignation: The Late Exchanges That Led to His Demise." *Guardian*, July 3, 2012. http://www.guardian .co.uk/business/2012/jul/03/bob-diamond-resignation-barclay; Perkins, T., and P. Waldie. "Jerry del Missier: A Sudden Halt to a Stellar Career." *Globe and Mail*, July 3, 2012. http://www .theglobeandmail.com/report-on-business/jerry-del-missier-a -sudden-halt-to-a-stellar-career/article4385606/

10. Treanor, J. "Former Barclays Executive Insists Bob Diamond Instructed Him to Cut Libor." *Guardian*, July 16, 2012. http://www .guardian.co.uk/business/2012/jul/16/barclays-del-missier-bob -diamond-libor?newsfeed=true

11. Perkins, T., and Waldie, P. "Jerry del Missier: A Sudden Halt to a Stellar Career." *Globe and Mail*, July 3, 2012. http://www .theglobeandmail.com/report-on-business/jerry-del-missier-a -sudden-halt-to-a-stellar-career/article4385606/

12. N. R. Narayana Murthy, interview with Prasad Kaipa and Navi Radjou, February 8, 2012.

13. Patel, V. "Capitalism Mind, Socialist Heart." *Hindu*, July 30, 2006. http://www.hindu.com/mag/2006/07/30/stories/2006073000 110200.htm; Gates, B., and N.R.N. Murthy. "NDTV: Changing India." December 7, 2005. http://www.infosys.com/newsroom /infosys-in-the-news/Documents/NRN-Billgates-NDTV-transcript .pdf

14. " 'Compassionate Capitalism' Urged for India." *BBC News*, June 1, 2004. http://news.bbc.co.uk/2/hi/south_asia/3757843.stm.

15. N. R. Narayana Murthy, interview with Prasad Kaipa and Navi Radjou, February 8, 2012.

16. Kris Gopalakrishnan, interview with Prasad Kaipa, November 15, 2010.

17. "Libor Scandal: Bob Diamond to Receive £2m Payout." *BBC News*, July 10, 2012. http://www.bbc.co.uk/news/business-18779089

18. "Many Wall Street Executives Say Wrongdoing Is Necessary: Survey." *Reuters*, July 10, 2012. http://www.reuters.com/article /2012/07/10/us-wallstreet-survey-idUSBRE86906G20120710

19. Christensen, C. "How Will You Measure Your Life?" *Harvard Business Review* (July 2010). http://hbr.org/2010/07/how-will-you -measure-your-life/ar/1

20. Kiran Mazumdar Shaw, interview with Prasad Kaipa, March 4, 2012.

21. Conversation with Peter Block, Dinesh Chandra, and Prasad Kaipa, August 12, 2009.

22. Kearns, D. *Team of Rivals: The Political Genius of Abraham Lincoln.* New York: Simon & Schuster, 2005.

23. "Robert De Niro." *Answers.* http://www.answers.com/topic/robert -deniro

24. Mark Milani, interview with Prasad Kaipa, February 2, 2012.

25. Kabat-Zinn, J. *Wherever You Go, There You Are: Mindfulness Meditation in Everyday Life*, 10th anniversary ed. New York: Hyperion, 2005.

26. Csikszentmihalyi, M. *Flow: The Psychology of Optimal Experience.* New York: Harper, 2008.

27. Pam Weiss, interview with Prasad Kaipa and Navi Radjou, January 25, 2012.

28. Weiss, P. "Growing People: The Heart of the Organizational Transformation." *ManagementExchange.com*, October 17, 2012. http:// www.managementexchange.com/story/growing-people

29. Martin, C. "Four Ways to Increase Your Workplace Well-Being." *O, The Oprah Magazine* (January 2012). http://www.oprah.com/spirit /How-to-Be-Calmer-at-Work-Well-Being-in-the-Workplace

30. LaBarre, P. "Developing Mindful Leaders." *Harvard Business Review* (blog), December 30, 2011.

31. "Emerging Business Opportunities at IBM." Case No. 9–304–075. Boston: Harvard Business School, 2005.

32. Deutschman, A. "Building a Better Skunk Works." *Fast Company* (March 2005). http://www.fastcompany.com/magazine/92/march-2005

33. Huston, L., and Sakkab, N. "Connect and Develop: Inside Procter & Gamble's New Model for Innovation." *Harvard Business Review* 84, no. 3 (2006): 12.

34. Radjou, N. *Innovation Networks: A New Market Structure Will Revitalize Invention-to-Innovation Cycles.* Cambridge, MA: Forrester Research, June 17, 2004.

35. Liz Wiseman, interview with Prasad Kaipa and Navi Radjou, January 26, 2012.

36. Kris Gopalakrishnan, interview with Prasad Kaipa, November 15, 2010.

37. Kalam, A.P.G. "Creative Leadership in the Global Knowledge Economy." Presentation at the Centre for India and Global Business, University of Cambridge, June 9, 2009. http://www.india.jbs.cam.ac.uk/news/events/2009/090603_abdul_kalam.html

Chapter Five

1. Isaacson, W. *Steve Jobs.* New York: Simon & Schuster, 2011.

2. Poeter, D. "300 Million Store Visitors Since October." *PC Magazine*, August 21, 2012. http://www.pcmag.com/article2/0,2817,2408757,00.asp; Blodget, H. "Seventeen Facts About the Apple Store Profit Machine." *Business Insider*, June 25, 2012. http://www.businessinsider.com/apple-store-facts-2012–6?op=1

3. Dediu, H. "Apple Stores Have Seventeen Times Better Performance Than the Average Retailer." *ASYMCO*, April 18, 2012. http://www.asymco.com/2012/04/18/apple-stores-have-seventeen-times-better-performance-than-the-average-retailer/

4. Isaacson, *Steve Jobs*, p. 373.

5. "In a Fast World, Think Slowly." *HBR IdeaCast*, August 16, 2012. http://blogs.hbr.org/ideacast/2012/08/in-a-fast-world-think-slowly.html

6. "Capitalizing on Complexity: Insights from the 2010 IBM Global CEO Study." IBM. http://www-935.ibm.com/services/us/ceo/ceostudy2010/?sa_campaign=message/leaf1/gbs/study/CEO

7. Brooks, D. *The Social Animal.* New York: Random House, 2011.

8. Kiely, D. A. "Mulally: The Outsider at Ford." *Business Week*, March 4, 2009. http://www.businessweek.com/stories/2009–03–04/alan -mulally-the-outsider-at-ford. "In God we trust, but rest of you need to bring data" is considered to be a favorite statement of N. R. Narayana Murthy. He repeated it in his interview on February 8, 2012.

9. We use the definition of discrimination in thefreedictionary .com (http://thefreedictionary.com/discrimination) and *Oxford Dictionary* (http://oxforddictionaries.com/definition/english /discrimination).

10. Camille, N., A. Tsuchida, and L. K. Fellows. "Double Dissociation of Stimulus-Value and Action-Value Learning in Humans with Orbi-tofrontal or Anterior Cingulate Cortex Damage." *Journal of Neuroscience* 31 (2011): 15048; Kovach, C. K., et al. "Anterior Prefrontal Cortex Contributes to Action Selection Through Tracking of Recent Reward Trends." *Journal of Neuroscience* 32 (2012): 8434–8442; Damasio, A. R. *Descartes' Error: Emotion, Reason and the Human Brain.* New York: Picador, 1994; Kennerley, S. W., et al. "Optimal Decision Making and the Anterior Cingulate Cortex." *Nature Neuroscience* 9 (2006): 940–947.

11. Moreno-Lopez, L., et al. "Neural Correlates of Hot and Cold Execu-tive Functions in Polysubstance Addiction: Association Between Neuropsychological Performance and Resting Brain Metabolism as Measured by Positron Emission Tomography." *Psychiatry Research*, September 5, 2012, 214–221.

12. Blakemore, S. J., and T. W. Robbins. "Decision-Making in the Ado-lescent Brain." *Nature Neuroscience* 15 (2012): 1184–1191.

13. Tamir, M., and B. Q. Ford. "When Feeling Bad Is Expected to Be Good: Emotion Regulation and Outcome Expectancies in Social Conflicts." *Emotion* 12 (2012): 807–816; Ford, B. Q., and M. Tamir, "When Getting Angry Is Smart: Emotional Preferences and Emotional Intelligence." *Emotion* 12 (2012): 685–689; Tamir, M., and B. Q. Ford. "Should People Pursue Feelings That Feel Good or Feelings That Do Good? Emotional Preferences and Well-Being." *Emotion*, February 6, 2012, 1061–1070. doi:10.1037 /a0027223.

14. Pillay, S. *Life Unlocked: Seven Revolutionary Lessons to Overcome Fear.* New York: Rodale, 2010.

15. *The American Heritage Dictionary of the English Language,* 4th ed. Boston: Houghton Mifflin, 2009.

16. Tychonievich, L. "Discernment and Discrimination." http://www.cs.virginia.edu/~lat7h/blog/posts/213.html

17. Blavatsky, H. *Theosophical Quarterly Magazine, 1932 to 1933.* La Vergne, TN: Lightning Source, 2003.

18. Marshall, G. "Stimulus Discrimination." *A Dictionary of Sociology Encyclopedia.com,* September 4, 2012. http://www.encyclopedia.com/doc/1O88-stimulusdiscrimination.html.

19. Foresman, C. "Apple Store May Be Shifting from Customer Experience to Profit Machine." *Ars Technica,* August 28, 2012. http://arstechnica.com/staff/2012/08/op-ed-apple-store-may-be-shifting-from-customer-experience-to-profit-machine/; Elmer-DeWitt, P. "Report Traces Apple Store Turmoil All the Way to Tim Cook." CNNMoney, August 29, 2012. http://tech.fortune.cnn.com/tag/apple-stores/

20. Kawamoto, D., B. Heskett, and M. Ricciuti. "Microsoft to Invest $150 million in Apple." *CNET,* August 6, 1997. http://news.cnet.com/2100–1001–202143.html

21. "Photos: Microsoft-Apple Collaboration, the 10 Greatest Moments." http://www.techrepublic.com/photos/photos-microsoft-apple-collaboration-the-10-greatest-moments/479462?seq=8

22. Lunsford, L. "Praise Heaped on Veteran Airman for Pulling Off Rare Feat." *Wall Street Journal,* January 16, 2009. http://online.wsj.com/article/SB123205611103787217.html

23. "Seven Generation Sustainability." *eAlmanac.* http://www.ealmanac.com/1891/numbers/seven-generation-sustainability/

24. Hemp, P., and T. A. Stewart. "Leading Change When Business Is Good: An Interview with Samuel J. Palmisano." *Harvard Business Review* (December 2004): 60–71.

25. LaMonica, M. "IBM Vows to Make Computing Pervasive." *CNET,* September 23, 2003. http://news.cnet.com/IBM-vows-to-make-computing-pervasive/2100–1012_3–5080866.html; and "Smarter Cities." *IBM Journal of Research and Development* 55, nos. 1&2 (2011).

26. "Speeches: Samuel J. Palmisano." *IBM,* November 9, 2011. http://www.ibm.com/ibm/sjp/11_09_2011.html

27. Thompson, D. *How Prediction Markets Turn Employees Into Visionaries.* Boston: Harvard Business Press, 2012.

28. Ibarra, H. "Is 'Command and Collaborate' the New Leadership Model?" *Harvard Business Review* (blog), February 3, 2012.

29. Ibid.

30. Radjou, N., J. Prabhu, P. Kaipa, and S. Ahuja. "The New Arithmetic of Collaboration." *Harvard Business Review* (blog), November 4, 2010.

31. Fast Company Staff. "Letter from the Editor: The Lessons of Innovation." *Fast Company,* February 14, 2012. http://www.fastcompany.com/magazine/163/the-lessons-of-innovation

32. "Your Personal Best: Jill Bolte Taylor." *Success.* http://www.success.com/articles/936-your-personal-best-jill-bolte-taylor

33. Suszynski, M. "What Is Anticipatory Anxiety?" *Everyday Health,* April 28, 2010. http://www.everydayhealth.com/emotional-health/anxiety/what-is-anticipatory-anxiety.aspx; Pillay, S. S. *Your Brain and Business: The Neuroscience of Great Leaders.* Upper Saddle River, NJ: FT Press, 2011; Lieberman, M. D., T. K. Inagaki, G. Tabibnia, and M. J. Crockett. "Subjective Responses to Emotional Stimuli During Labeling, Reappraisal, and Distraction." *Emotion* 11 (2011): 468–480; Kanske, P., et al. "How to Regulate Emotion? Neural Networks for Reappraisal and Distraction." *Cerebral Cortex* 21 (2011): 1379–1388.

34. "Crisis Is the New Normal, Says Carlos Ghosn." *Renault Nissan,* November 21, 2011. http://blog.alliance-renault-nissan.com/blog/crisis-new-normal-says-carlos-ghosn

35. "Leading in the 21st Century." *McKinsey Quarterly,* June 2012.

36. Sacks, D. "Working with the Enemy." *Fast Company,* September 1, 2007. http://www.fastcompany.com/magazine/118/working-with-the-enemy.html

37. Ibid.

38. For an explanation of the Mithya Wheel, go to http://mithya.prasadkaipa.com/pyramids/mithyawheel.html

39. Kip Tindell, interview with Prasad Kaipa and Navi Radjou, January 25, 2012.

40. "Three Good Hires? He'll Pay More for One Who's Great." *New York Times*, March 13, 2010.

41. "Putting Our Employees First." *Container Store*, http://standfor .containerstore.com/putting-our-employees-first/

42. Personal interviews with seven Google and Facebook employees, September 2012.

43. Madrigal, A. C. "The Steve Jobs 'Reality Distortion Field' Even Makes It into His FBI File." *Atlantic*, February 9, 2012. http://www .statmyweb.com/s/reality-distortion-field

44. Palmisano, S. "Thoughts on the Future of Leadership." *IBM*, September 11, 2011. http://www.ibm.com/ibm/sjp/09_20_2011 .html

45. Prasad Kaipa served as a consultant to various projects at Boeing between 1992 and 2011. During that period, he had an opportunity to interact frequently with Alan Mulally who worked at Boeing until September 2006.

46. We gained insight into IBM's decision logic involved in selling the PC business to Lenovo and exiting the hard disk business from interviews we conducted with Bernie Meyerson, vice president, innovation and global university relations, IBM, on October 24, 2011, and Ted Hoff, global head of leadership development, IBM, on February 4, 2011.

47. "HP to Keep PC Division." *HP*, October 27, 2011. http://www .hp.com/hpinfo/newsroom/press/2011/111027xa.html

Chapter Six

1. Wendy Kopp, interview with Prasad Kaipa, June 4, 2012.

2. Wendy Kopp, Georgetown College commencement address, 2008.

3. Wendy Kopp, Dartmouth College Commencement address, June 12, 2012.

4. Ibid.

5. "Wendy Kopp and Teach for America." Harvard Business School Case Study 9–406–125. Boston: Harvard Business School, 2007.

6. "About Teach For America." http://www.teachforamerica.org /sites/default/files/2012–13_Press_Kit_Updated_08_28_12.pdf

7. Wendy Kopp, interview with Prasad Kaipa, June 4, 2012.

8. Kaipa, P. "Flip Side of Signature Strength." *SiliconIndia*, April 2007. http://www.siliconindia.com/magazine_articles/The_flip_side _of_signature_strength-PWVG638498597.html

9. Vance, A. "Ten Years After First Delay Intel's Itanium Is Still Late." *New York Times*, February 9, 2009. http://bits.blogs.nytimes .com/2009/02/09/ten-years-after-first-delay-intels-itanium-is-still -late/; Dvorak, J. "How Itanium Killed the Computer Industry." *PC Magazine* (January 2009). http://www.pcmag.com/article2 /0,2817,2339629,00.asp; McMillan, R. "HP Paid Intel $690 Million to Keep Itanium on Life Support." *Wired*, February 1, 2012. http:// www.wired.com/wiredenterprise/2012/02/hp-itanium/

10. Martin, S. "HP TouchPad Is a Casualty of iPad's Popularity." *USA Today*, August 19, 2011. http://www.usatoday.com/tech/news /story/2011/08/HP-TouchPad-is-a-casualty-of-iPads-popularity /50047542/1

11. Pattanaik, D. *Myth = Mithya: A Handbook of Hindu Mythology*. New Delhi: Penguin India, 2008.

12. "Oprah's Angel Network Fact Sheet." June 24, 2008. http://www .oprah.com/pressroom/About-Oprahs-Angel-Network

13. "Oprah's Angel Network and Other Charitable Work." About.com. http://oprah.about.com/od/philanthropy/p/anglenethistory .htm and http://www.huffingtonpost.com/2010/05/26/oprah -winfreys-angel-netw_n_590941.html

14. "Fresh Copy: How Ursula Burns Reinvented Xerox." *Fast Company*, November 19, 2011. http://www.fastcompany.com/magazine/161 /ursula-burns-xerox, Xerox now generates nearly half of its reve-nues from such services as business process management.

15. Baumeister, R., and J. Tierney. *Willpower: Rediscovering the Greatest Human Strength*. New York: Penguin Press, 2011; McGonigal, K. *The Willpower Instinct: How Self-Control Works, Why It Matters, and What You Can Do to Get More of It*. New York: Penguin, 2011.

16. Chrislip, D. D., and C. E. Larson. *Collaborative Leadership: How Citi-zens and Civic Leaders Can Make a Difference*. San Francisco: Jossey-Bass, 1994.

17. Sam Palmisano, e-mail interview with Prasad Kaipa and Navi Radjou, March 21, 2012.

18. Hemp, P., and T. A. Stewart. "Leading Change When Business Is Good." *Harvard Business Review* (December 2004): 60–71.

19. Palmisano, S. "Our Values at Work on Being an IBMer." *IBM*, http://www.ibm.com/ibm/values/us/

20. Ibid.

21. Pinker, S. "The Sugary Secret of Self-Control." *New York Times*, September 2, 2011.

22. Baumeister and Tierney. *Willpower.*

23. Schwartz, T., and C. McCarthy. "Manage Your Energy, Not Your Time." *Harvard Business Review* (October 2007): 63–73; Loehr, J., and T. Schwartz. *Power of Full Engagement.* New York: Free Press, 2004.

24. Hoffman, B. *American Icon: Alan Mulally and the Fight to Save Ford Motor Company.* New York: Crown Business, 2012.

25. "Xerox to Transfer Office Product Manufacturing Operations to Flextronics." *PR Newswire.* http://www.prnewswire.co.uk/news -releases/xerox-to-transfer-office-product-manufacturing -operations-to-flextronics-154594225.html

26. "Fresh Copy: How Ursula Burns Reinvented Xerox." *Fast Company*, November 19, 2011. http://www.fastcompany.com/1793533 /fresh-copy-how-ursula-burns-reinvented-xerox

27. Fred Luthans, interview with Prasad Kaipa, August 19, 2011; Youssef, C., and F. Luthans. "Psychological Capital: Meaning, Findings and Future Directions." http://centerforpos.org/conference2011 /wp-content/uploads/2011/02/POS-Hbk-Ch-02-Psychological -Capital-Youssef-Luthans.pdf

Chapter Seven

1. Foster, P., and P. Malhotra. "Ultimate Economy Drive: The £1,300 Car." *Telegraph*, January 10, 2008.

2. We built this case study on Ratan Tata and the Nano car based on our e-mail and face-to-face interactions with Ravi Kant, vice chair-man of Tata Motors, throughout 2011 and 2012.

3. *Ratan Tata: Radical Chieftain.* http://www.scribd.com/doc/77326029/Ratan-Tata-Book

4. "Ratan Tata: Exclusive Interview." Autocar. http://www.autocar.co.uk/car-news/industry/ratan-tata-exclusive-interview

5. "Tata Nano—The People's Car." Case No. 710–420. Boston: Harvard Business School, 2011.

6. de Tocqueville, A. *Democracy in America.* [http://xroads.virginia.edu/~HYPER/DETOC/; Ikerd, J. "Rethinking Economics of Self Interest." September 1999. http://web.missouri.edu/~ikerdj/papers/Rethinking.html; Griffith, M. R., and Lucas, J. R. *Ethical Economics.* London: Palgrave Macmillan, 1997, See chap. 13.

7. Canuto. O., and M. Giugale, eds. *The Day After Tomorrow.* Washington, DC: World Bank September 23, 2010. http://issuu.com/world.bank.publications/docs/9780821384985

8. Wood, C. "India Poised to Become World's Fourth Largest Auto Market by 2015." *AutoGuide.com*, February 7, 2011.

9. "Overview: A Rich Rubric of Ethics." *Tata Group*, http://www.tata.com/article.aspx?artid=PMMskByFUAc=

10. "Leadership with Trust." *Tata Group.*, http://www.tata.com/aboutus/sub_index.aspx?sectid=8hOk5Qq3EfQ=

11. "Leading Through Connections." *IBM.* http://www-935.ibm.com/services/us/en/c-suite/ceostudy2012/

12. "Pop Quiz: Can Indra Nooyi Revive PepsiCo?" *Knowledge@Wharton*, March 28, 2012.

13. Collins, J., and J. Porras. *Built to Last: Successful Habits of Visionary Companies.* New York: HarperBusiness.2002.

14. Collins, J. *Good to Great: In Social Sectors.* New York: HarperCollins, 2005.

15. Kiechel, W. "The Tempting of Rajat Gupta." *Harvard Business Review* (blog), March 24, 2011.

16. Suzanna, A. "How Gupta Came Undone." *Bloomberg BusinessWeek*, May 19, 2011. http://www.businessweek.com/magazine/content/11_22/b4230056624680.htm

17. "Followership." ChangingMinds.org. http://changingminds.org/disciplines/leadership/followership/followership.htm

18. Malone, R. "Remaking a Government-Owned Giant: An Interview with the Chairman of the State Bank of India." *McKinsey Quarterly* (April 2009). https://www.mckinseyquarterly.com/Remaking_a _government-owned_giant_An_interview_with_the_chairman_of _the_State_Bank_of_India_2249. We had more than twenty extended discussions with Om Prakash Bhatt between 2005 and 2012.

19. Chakraborti, R. *Grit, Guts and Gumption: Driving Change in a State-Owned Giant.* New York: Penguin Books, 2010.

20. Chakraborti, R., C. Dhanraj, and P. Kaipa. "State Bank of Indian and OP Bhatt: Transformational Leadership." Draft manuscript, March 2010.

21. Kaipa, P. "Fresh Perspective: A Conversation with Om Prakash Bhatt, Chairman of the Board State Bank of India." *Integral Leadership Review* (January 2010). http://integralleadershipreview .com/269-fresh-perspective

22. O. P. Bhatt, interview with Prasad Kaipa, March 29, 2011.

23. Schiller, B. "Patagonia Asks Its Customers to Buy Less." *Fast Company*, October 25, 2011. http://www.fastcompany.com/1790663 /patagonia-asks-its-customers-buy-less

24. Botsman, R. *What's Mine Is Yours: The Rise of Collaborative Consumption.* New York: HarperBusiness, 2010.

25. Stuart Crabb, director of learning at Facebook, interview with Prasad Kaipa, March 17, 2012.

26. Stobbe, M. "Facebook Organ Donor Initiative Prompts 100,000 Users to Select New Option." *Huffington Post*, May 2, 2012. http:// www.huffingtonpost.com/2012/05/02/facebook-organ-donor -users_n_1471821.html

27. Madhusudhan Reddy, vice president of human resources of the Gitanjali Group, interview with Prasad Kaipa and Meera Shenoy, April 3, 2012.

28. Kaipa, P., and M. Shenoy. "Workers with Disabilities Solved This Company's Talent Crisis." *Harvard Business Review* (blog), September 10, 2012. http://blogs.hbr.org/cs/2012/09/workers_with _disabilities_solv.html

29. "Smile Cards!" *HelpOthers.org,* http://www.helpothers.org/cards .php

30. Radjou, N., J. Prabhu, P. Kaipa, and S. Ahuja. "The New Arithmetic of Collaboration." *Harvard Business Review* (blog), November 4, 2010.

31. Prentice, R. A., and J. H. Langmore, "Beware of Vaporware: Product Hype and the Securities Fraud Liability of High-Tech Companies," *Harvard Journal of Law and Tehcnology* 8, no. 1 (1994): 1–74. http://jolt.law.harvard.edu/articles/pdf/v08/08HarvJLTech001.pdf

32. Williams, G. "GNU/Linux Desktop Survival Guide." N.d. http://www.togaware.com/linux/survivor/Fear_Uncertainty.html

33. Hiner, J. "The Ten Greatest Moments of Microsoft-Apple Collaboration." *ZDNet*, October 29, 2010. http://www.zdnet.com/blog/btl/the-10-greatest-moments-of-microsoft-apple-collaboration/41106

34. Radjou, N. *Innovation Networks: Global Progress Report 2006*. Cambridge, MA: Forrester Research report, June 14, 2006.

35. "Leading Through Connections: Insights from the 2012 Global IBM CEO Study." http://www-935.ibm.com/services/us/en/c-suite/ceostudy2012/

36. Shaich, R. "Corporations Must Become Socially Conscious Citizens." *Harvard Business Review* (blog), October 28, 2011.

37. "Household Food Security in the United States in 2011." Washington, DC: U.S. Department of Agriculture, Economic Research Service, September 2012. http://www.ers.usda.gov/media/884529/err-141-summary.pdf

38. Shaich, R. "Panera's Experiment in Human Nature: Let Customers Decide What to Pay." *Management Innovation Exchange*, October 17, 2012. http://www.managementexchange.com/story/panera's-experiment-human-nature-let-customers-decide-what-pay; Boodhoo, N. "Panera Sandwich Chain Explores 'Pay What You Want' Concept." *NPR*, September 7, 2012. http://www.npr.org/blogs/thesalt/2012/09/07/160685977/panera-sandwich-chain-explores-pay-what-you-want-concept

39. Ibid.

Chapter Eight

1. We found the following book and initiative to be excellent resources you can use to help create a field of leadership around you. Briskin,

A., S. Erickson, T. Callanan, and J. Ott. *The Power of Collective Wisdom: And the Trap of Collective Folly.* San Francisco: Berrett-Koehler, 2009. For the Collective Wisdom Initiative, go to http://www.collectivewisdominitiative.org/

2. Campbell, J. *The Hero with a Thousand Faces.* New York: New World, 2008.

3. Huspeni, A. "Meet Behind-the-Scenes Mentors of Fifteen Top Tech Executives." *Business Insider,* July 11, 2012. http://www.businessinsider.com/meet-the-mentors-behind-the-visionaries-of-tech-2012-7?op=1

4. The organizational evolution framework was developed by Prasad Kaipa, Chris Newham, and Russ Volckmann. We draw on the work of Ken Wilber, a leading thinker and author of over twenty books, who is known for his integral frameworks to create a unified approach to every field of discipline. In particular, we use the Wilber III framework set forth in his book *A Theory of Everything: An Integral Vision for Business, Politics, Science and Spirituality.* Boston: Shambhala, 2001.

5. Hanna, J. "Terror at the Taj." *Working Knowledge,* January 24, 2012. http://hbswk.hbs.edu/item/6602.html; Deshpande, R., and A. Raina. "Ordinary Heroes of the Taj." *Harvard Business Review* (December 2011): 119–123.

6. Karambir Singh Kang, interview with Prasad Kaipa, May 15, 2012.

7. Since November 2008, we have conducted several interviews with H. N. Shrinivas, senior vice president of human resources at Taj Hotels, and the Taj Hotels case study in this book was developed with his input.

8. For information about B Corporations, go to www.bcorporation.net. So far, 558 companies, including Patagonia and Method, have received B Corporation certification.

9. David Murphy, interview with Prasad Kaipa, June 4, 2012.

10. For the Tata Code of Conduct, go to http://www.tata.com/aboutus/articles/inside.aspx?artid=NyGNnLHkaAc=&sectid=1JjGM1BSf/c=

11. Kaipa, P., and M. Kriger. "The Inner Sides of Leadership and Lessons from the East: An Interview with Peter Senge." *Journal of Management Inquiry* 6 (2009): 183–193.

12. For information about Communities of the Future, go to http://communitiesofthefuture.org/

13. Block, P., and J. McKnight. *The Abundant Community: Awakening the Power of Families and Neighborhoods.* San Francisco: Berrett-Koehler, 2010.

14. Mastery foundation does seminars, workshops, and community building around the world. See http://www.masteryfoundation.org/ for general information.

15. "Peter Block and John McKnight with Wayne Hurlbert: Part One." *Abundant Community*, November 24, 2010. http://www.abundantcommunity.com/home/print_interviews/peter_block_and_john_mcknight_with_wayne_hurlbert_-_part_one.html; "A Conversation with Peter Block, Organizational Development Legend and Recipient of Linkage's Lifetime Achievement Award." January 12, 2011. http://mylinkage.com/blog/a-conversation-with-peter-block-organizational-development-legend-and-recipient-of-linkage's-lifetime-achievement-award/; Peter Block, interview with Prasad Kaipa, October 3, 2010.

16. Nipun Mehta, multiple conversations with Prasad Kaipa between 2006 and 2012.

17. For information on Karma Kitchen and ServiceSpace, see, respectively, http://www.karmakitchen.org/ and http://www.servicespace.org/

18. Raj Sisodia, interview with Prasad Kaipa, June 4, 2012.

19. "Can Technology Eliminate Poverty?" December 16, 2005. http://www.nextbillion.net/newsroom/2005/12/16/interview-with-mohammad-yunus

20. "What Is Conscious Capitalism?" *Conscious Capitalism Institute.* N.d. http://consciouscapitalism.org/learnmore/

21. Sisodia, R., Wolfe, D., and Sheth, J. *Firms of Endearment: How World-Class Companies Profit from Passion and Purpose.* Upper Saddle River, NJ: Pearson Prentice Hall, 2007.

22. "What Is Conscious Capitalism?" http://consciouscapitalism.org/

23. Ura, K., S. Alkire, T. Zangmo, and K. Wangdi. "A Short Guide to Gross National Happiness Index." Thimphu, Bhutan: Center for

Bhutan Studies, 2012. http://www.grossnationalhappiness.com
/wp-content/uploads/2012/04/Short-GNH-Index-final1.pdf

24. Ibid.

25. Kamenev, M. "Rating Countries for the Happiness Factor." *Bloomberg BusinessWeek*, October 11, 2006. http://www.businessweek.com/stories/2006-10-11/rating-countries-for-the-happiness-factorbusinessweek-business-news-stock-market-and-financial-advice

26. Herrera, S. "Healthy, Wealthy, and Wise?" *Technology Review* (August 2005).

27. Stiglitz, J. E., A. Sen, and J.-P. Fitoussi. "Report by the Commission on the Measurement of Economic Performance and Social Progress." 2010. http://www.stiglitz-sen-fitoussi.fr/documents/rapport_anglais.pdf

28. Ryback, T. W. "The U.N. Happiness Project." *New York Times*, March 28, 2012.

29. Bahadur, B. "Should My People Need Me." *Ms* (Winter 2012). http://www.msmagazine.com/winter2012/theladytakesoffice inburma.asp

30. Ibid.

31. "Full Text: Suu Kyi's Nobel Prize Speech." June 16, 2012. http://ibnlive.in.com/news/full-text-suu-kyis-nobel-prize-speech/266407-2.html

32. "IBM 2010 Global CEO Study: Creativity Selected as Most Crucial Factor for Future Success." *IBM*, May 18, 2010. http://www-03.ibm.com/press/us/en/pressrelease/31670.wss

33. "Charlene Li: Leading by Letting Go." *Management Innovation Exchange*. http://www.managementexchange.com/video/charlene-li-leading-letting-go.

34. Radjou, N., J. Prabhu, and S. Ahuja. *Jugaad Innovation: Think Frugal, Be Flexible, Generate Breakthrough Growth*. San Francisco: Jossey-Bass, 2012.

35. Radjou, N., J. Prabhu, and S. Ahuja. "More for Less for More: How to Disrupt in the Age of Scarcity." *Harvard Business Review* (blog), February 22, 2010.

36. Aristotle called practical wisdom *phronesis*—in contrast with *sophia,* which represents spiritual wisdom.

37. Nonaka, I., and H. Takeuchi. "The Big Idea: The Wise Leader." *Harvard Business Review* (May 2011): 59–67; McKenna, B., D. Rooney, and K. Boal. "Wisdom Principles as a Meta-Theoretical Basis for Evaluating Leadership. *Leadership Quarterly* 20 (2009): 177–190; Miller, W., and D. Miller. "Wisdom Leadership: Exploring Its Relation to Spirituality." Australia, 2005–2006. http://www .globaldharma.org/Files%20-%20Adobe%20Acrobat/Publications /SBL%20Wisdom%20Leadership%20and%20Spirituality%20 (Paper).pdf

38. The six wise leadership capabilities discussed in this book are independently identified in both wisdom traditions and empirical research. The Holy Gita Commentary by Swami Chinmayananda, Central Chinmaya Mission Trust, 10th Edition, 1996; Krishnamurthy, "Live Happily: The Gita Way," Readworthy Publications, 2008; Adams, J. "Building a Sustainable World: A Challenging OD Opportunity." In B. Jones and M. Brazzel, eds., *The NTL Handbook of Organization Development and Change.* San Francisco: Jossey-Bass/ Pfeiffer, 2006.

ACKNOWLEDGMENTS

First and foremost, we extend our profound gratitude to Professor V. Krishnamurthy. Seventeen years ago, he introduced Prasad to the six wise leadership principles enunciated in the Bhagavad Gita and encouraged him to explore whether those principles could be practiced and validated in today's management context. The discovery of those principles accelerated Prasad's journey into practical wisdom. Later, Ed Haskell and Nirmala Lavu graciously helped Prasad develop an assessment tool built around these six principles. Over the past twelve years, Prasad has used this tool to assess over eight hundred executives worldwide and develop their leadership perspective and capabilities. The very foundation of this book is built on those six principles, which we are positioning as the six wise leadership capabilities, and on our own experiences helping hundreds of leaders apply these principles in their daily life.

We could have written this book by churning out page after page of pedantic content based on our collective thirty years of experience studying the topic of wise leadership. Instead, we willingly unlearned our "expert" attitude and learned the magic of humility. We reached out to dozens of people in academia, business, and the social sector who, as experts or as practitioners, had great insights to offer us on how leaders can act and lead with wisdom. We couldn't have produced this book without their generous intellectual contribution.

In particular, we thank the following leaders whom we interviewed for this book: Prakash Apte, Nancy Badore, Subroto Bagchi, Anthony Carter, Doug Conant, Stuart Crabb, Desh Deshpande, Francis Garcia-Fritts, Kris Gopalakrishnan, Ted Hoff, Arun Jain, Gary Jusela, Nan Keohane, Uday Kotak, Tim Leberecht, Charlene Li, Fred Luthans, Steve Milovich, Mark Milani, Bernie Myerson, Subhanu Saxena, and Liz Wiseman. Our special thanks go to Carey Barbour and Laurie Friedman at IBM for arranging interviews with Ted Hoff and Bernie Myerson as well as IBM's chairman, Sam Palmisano. We also appreciate Raj Sisodia for introducing us to John Mackay, CEO of Whole Foods Market, and Kip Tindell, chairman and CEO of the Container Store; we had the pleasure of interviewing both of them for this book.

We are also grateful to M. T. Mohan Rao and Swami Bodhananda for clarifying our doubts in differentiating practical wisdom from spiritual wisdom. We are equally thankful to Art Kleiner for seeding the concept of wisdom logic in our mind and helping us reframe the book.

We are greatly indebted to the following generous souls who took time to read our manuscript and offer us constructive feedback: Paul Gleiberman, Ed Haskell, Satya Iluri, Ravi Kant, Juan Lopez, Pavi Mehta, Viral Mehta, Ram Nidumolu, Srinath Pendyala, Jaideep Prabhu, Somik Raha, Sudhakar Ram, Thulsi Ravilla, Arun Sawhney, Syed Shariq, Nirmal Sethia, Dinesh Subraveti, Partha Sundararajan, Bo Tep, Prasad Vemuri, and Al Viswanathan. We also owe much to Stephen H. Rhinesmith, who diligently read each chapter and provided us insightful comments.

This book wouldn't have materialized without Carolyn Monaco, who introduced us to Jossey-Bass in 2010. At Jossey-Bass, we were lucky to have found Genoveva Llosa, a caring and professional editor. Genoveva is a demanding editor—our manuscript went through a half-dozen iterations under her careful supervision—but her enthusiasm for high-quality work is contagious. In the end, she managed to bring the best out of us as authors by expanding our creative limits.

We are also very lucky to have worked with two highly competent editors: Ernest Beck and Clancy Drake. Ernest worked closely with us to fine-tune the content of our manuscript, and Clancy perfected it and got it to the finish line in great shape. Ahalya Samtaney provided us thoughtful editorial support while revising the earlier versions of our manuscript. In addition, Sarwath Khizrana provided the research assistance for this book project and provided timely and excellent support. We are also thankful to the larger Jossey-Bass team—John Maas, Carol Hartland, and Beverly Miller—for coordinating the whole editing process very smoothly. We also appreciate the timely help by Kathleen Davies at John Wiley in designing the wise leader assessment. We owe them all a great debt of gratitude.

This book is a true labor of love. It took us nearly two years to complete it. During that long period, we politely ignored our friends and even our family members, concentrated as we were on researching and writing this book. And yet rather than feeling rebuffed, our family and friends constantly reached out to us and offered us their full support. Without their caring attitude and continuous encouragement, we wouldn't have sustained the emotional stamina needed to complete a task as arduous as writing a book. Our deepest gratitude goes to Vinoda, Pravin, and Vidya (Prasad's family) and Ousha, Lada, Ravi, Guiry, Hari, and Pari (Navi's family).

Our research on wise leadership was partially supported by the Indian School of Business with generous funding from the SBI Cell for Public Leadership and the Biocon Cell for Innovation Management. We thank and appreciate the support of Dean Ajit Rangnekar, Dean Emeritus M. R. Rao, and Meena Saxena, and our colleagues at the Indian School of Business.

ABOUT THE AUTHORS

Photo by Edwin Haskell

Prasad Kaipa, PhD, a CEO coach and advisor since 1990, has worked with about 120 C-level executives in Global Fortune 500 companies in the areas of innovation and leadership development. He is a senior research fellow and founding executive director of the Centre for Leadership, Innovation, and Change at the Indian School of Business (ISB) and has taught executive education programs through ISB, INSEAD, the London Business School, and the Tuck School of Business. He was the Richardson Visiting Fellow at the Center for Creative Leadership between 2010 and 2011.

Prasad cofounded the TiE Institute in Silicon Valley in 2002 to assist entrepreneurs in developing effective management teams, communication skills, and leadership perspective. He has served on the boards of the International Leadership Association, Society for Organizational Learning, Marico Innovation Foundation, Samskrita Bharati, Integral Leadership Review, and Hindu University of North America.

Prasad's research on wise leadership started when he was asked to research how people learn (and unlearn), lead, think, communicate, and collaborate while he was a research fellow at Apple University in 1989. He published the book *Discontinuous Learning: Igniting Genius Within by Aligning Self, Work, and Family* in 2006, and his writings are available on prasadkaipa.com and kaipagroup.com. He blogs regularly on HBR.org and has been featured in or written for *Business Week, Economic Times, New York Times, Financial Times, CFO Magazine, San Jose Mercury News, Washington Post,* among others.

• • •

Navi Radjou is an innovation and leadership consultant based in Palo Alto, California. He is also a Fellow at Judge Business School, University of Cambridge, and a World Economic Forum (WEF) faculty member. He is a member of WEF's Global Agenda Council on Design Innovation and a columnist on HBR.org.

Navi coauthored the acclaimed *Jugaad Innovation: Think Frugal, Be Flexible, Generate Breakthrough Growth,* which the *Economist* calls "the most comprehensive book yet to appear on the subject" of frugal innovation.

Photo by Ben Watkins

Most recently, he served as executive director of the Centre for India & Global Business at Judge Business School. Previously he was a long-time vice president and analyst at Forrester Research in Boston and San Francisco, advising senior executives worldwide on breakthrough growth strategies. Navi has consulted with Global Fortune 1000 companies, including Ernst & Young, General Motors, IBM, Microsoft, Procter & Gamble, SAP, and Tata Consultancy Services, on innovation and leadership strategies.

Featured in the *New York Times,* the *Wall Street Journal,* the *Economist,* and the *Financial Times,* he has authored articles for *MIT Sloan Management Review, Bloomberg Businessweek,* and CNN. com. He has spoken at the World Economic Forum, Council on Foreign Relations, the Conference Board, Asia Society, and more.

An Indian-born French national, Navi earned a postgraduate degree from Ecole Centrale Paris and attended the Yale School of Management. Navi is a lifelong student of Eastern spiritual practices such as yoga, Ayurveda, and Buddhist meditation. Learn more about him at NaviRadjou.com.

INDEX

Page reference followed by *fig* indicates an illustrated figure.